zen pencils

CARTOON QUOTES FROM INSPIRATIONAL FOLKS

zen pencils

CARTOON QUOTES FROM INSPIRATIONAL FOLKS

GAVIN AUNG THAN

Andrews McMeel
Publishing®

a division of Andrews McMeel Universal

CONTENTS

IT'LL SPREAD INTO YOUR WORK.
88, 89, 90...
203, 204...

ACKNOWLEDGMENTS

Neil deGrasse Tyson quote taken from *Time Magazine*'s "10 Questions for Neil deGrasse Tyson."

Neil Gaiman quote: Excerpt from *Make Good Art* by Neil Gaiman, copyright © 2013 by Neil Gaiman. Published by William Morrow, an imprint of HarperCollins Publishers. Used courtesy of HarperCollins Publishers.

Stephen Fry quote taken from 2007 BBC program *Mark Lawson Talks To... Stephen Fry.*

Winston Churchill quote reproduced with permission from Curtis Brown, London on behalf of the Estate of Sir Winston S. Churchill. Copyright © Winston S. Churchill.

Excerpt from *The Four Loves* by C.S. Lewis. Used by permission of Houghton Mifflin Harcourt Publishing Company in the United States, the Philippines, and the Open Market, copyright © 1960 by C.S. Lewis, copyright © renewed 1988 by Arthur Owen Barfield, all rights reserved; and by permission of The C.S. Lewis Company Ltd. throughout the world excluding the United States © copyright CS Lewis Pte Ltd 1960.

Ithaka by C.P. Cavafy: KEELEY, EDMUND; C.P. CAVAFY SELECTED POEMS. © 1992 by Edmund Keeley and Philip Sherrard. Reprinted by permission of Princeton University Press.

BRUCE LEE® and the Bruce Lee signature are registered trademarks of Bruce Lee Enterprises, LLC. The Bruce Lee name, image, likeness, and all related indicia are intellectual property of Bruce Lee Enterprises, LLC. All rights reserved. www.brucelee.com

J. Krishnamurti quote taken from the books *Talks and Dialogues Saanen 1967* and *Freedom From the Known*, copyright © 1967, 1969 Krishnamurti Foundation Trust, Ltd. For more information about J. Krishnamurti, please visit www.jkrishnamurti.org.

Roger Ebert quote taken from the blog *Roger Ebert's Journal*, May 2, 2009. Used with permission of The Ebert Co., Ltd.

INTRODUCTION

Bruce Lee. Mark Twain. Albert Einstein. Vincent van Gogh. What did all of these people have in common? Nothing. Except that their life stories and quotes would often keep me company during downtime at my old cubicle job. While my boss wasn't looking, I would read interesting biographies on Wikipedia, desperately waiting for the clock to hit knock-off time. I was unhappy at my uninspiring graphic design job and was trying to think of an idea to start a new webcomic site.

Even though I had been working as a graphic designer for eight years, I had always been in love with cartooning and dreamt of one day being able to do it as a full-time profession. My dream was kept alive over the years by taking the odd freelance cartooning gig and having a few comics published, but it eventually dawned on me that something drastic had to be done if I wanted that dream to become a reality.

Then it struck me. What if I took those quotes that had inspired me while killing time at work and somehow combined them with my passion for cartooning? And with that, Zen Pencils was born.

Normally a risk-adverse type of guy, in the span of four months I had quit my job, sold my house and in February 2012, launched Zen Pencils—a website that adapted inspirational quotes and poems into comic strips.

This book collects the best quotes and comics from the first two years of the website's archives. You'll notice a gradual progression in the length and complexity of the comics as I became more confident with my storytelling ability, and kind of figured out what I was trying to do each week.

After a nervous start, the website managed to build an audience and much to my delight, eventually grew successful enough to become a full-time job. Zen Pencils was initially an excuse to draw whatever I wanted and adapt quotes that I had always liked, but it's grown into a destination where people from all around the world visit for inspiration, motivation, and joy. The positive effect the comics have on readers continues to amaze and humble me.

It's easy to get tired of all the "anything is possible" and "follow your passion" mantras that saturate today's social media world, but Zen Pencils is proof that it worked for me, and if it only does one thing, I hope that this book shows that it can work for you too.

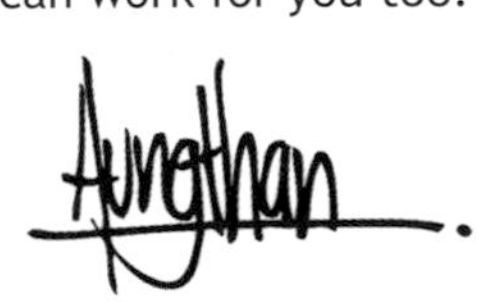

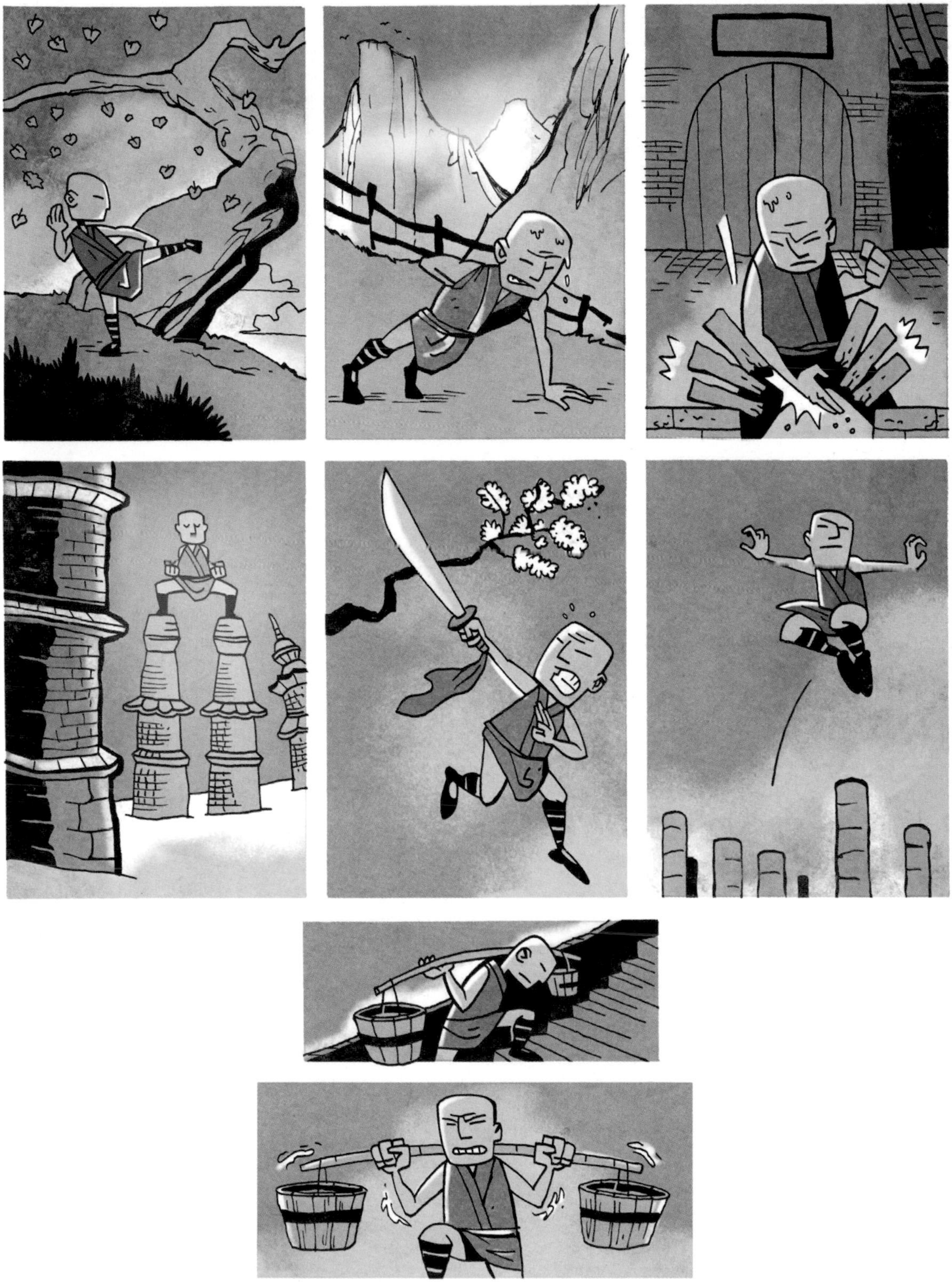

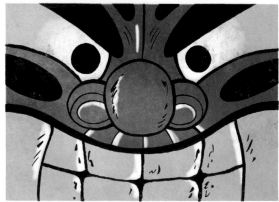

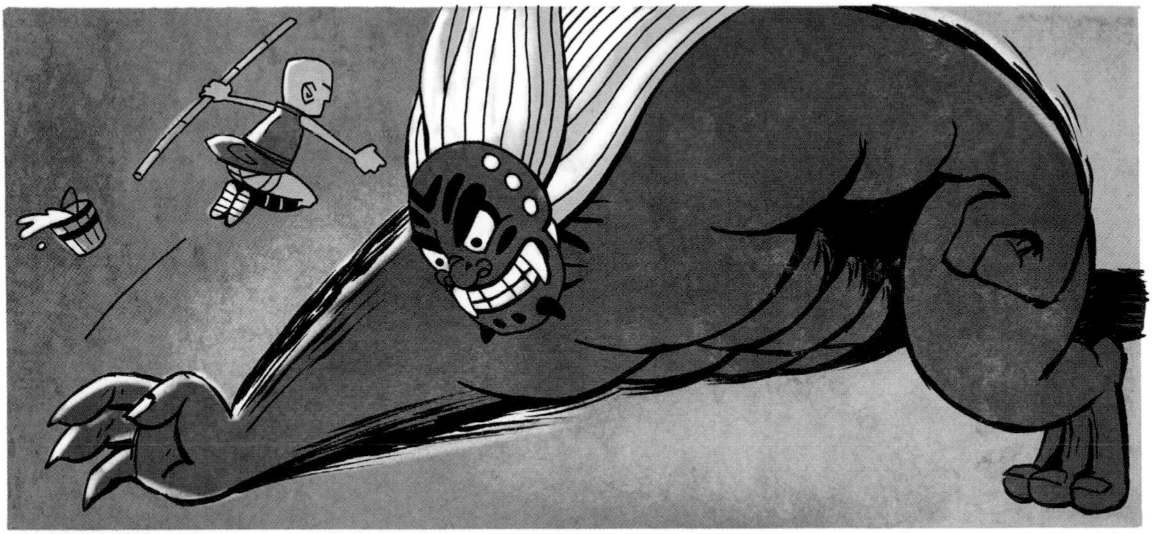

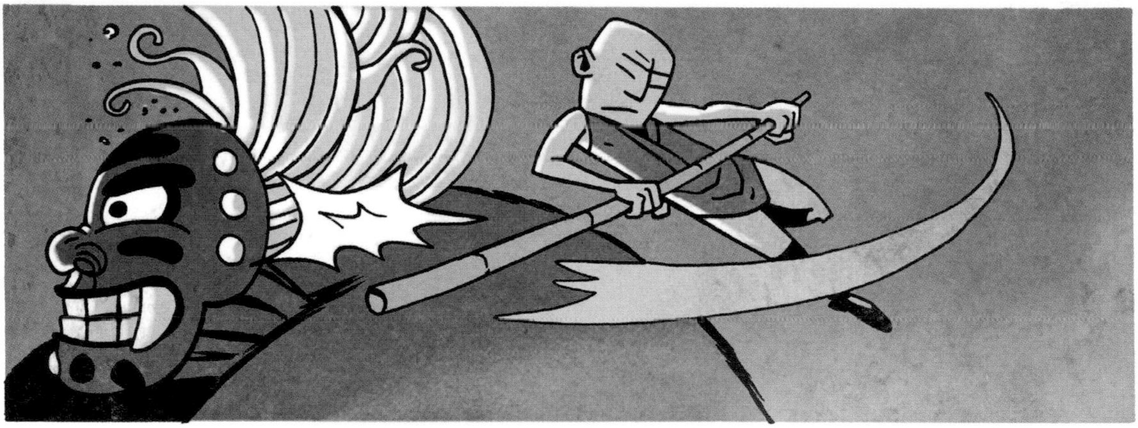

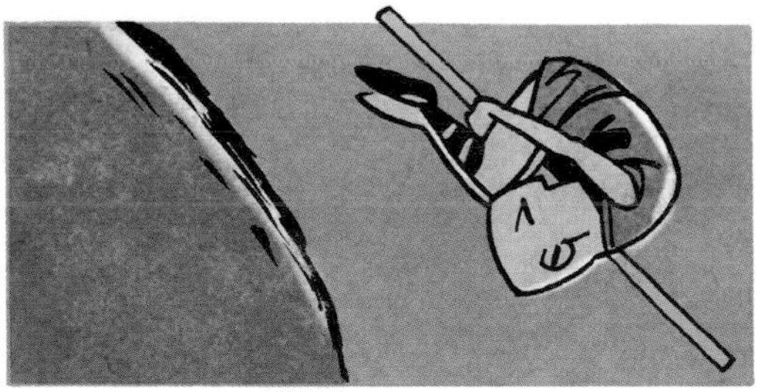

The more
you sweat
in training,
the less
you bleed
in battle.

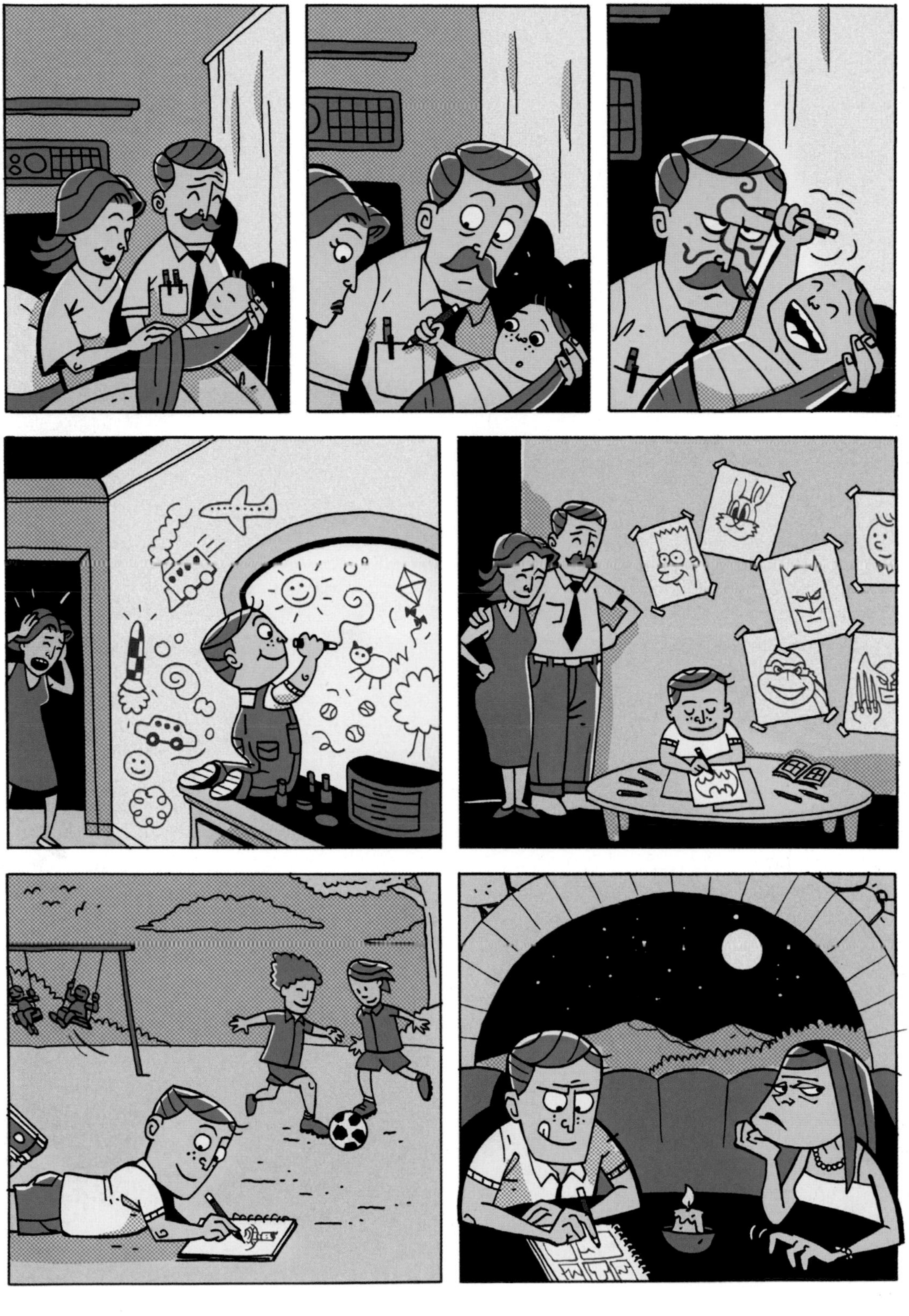

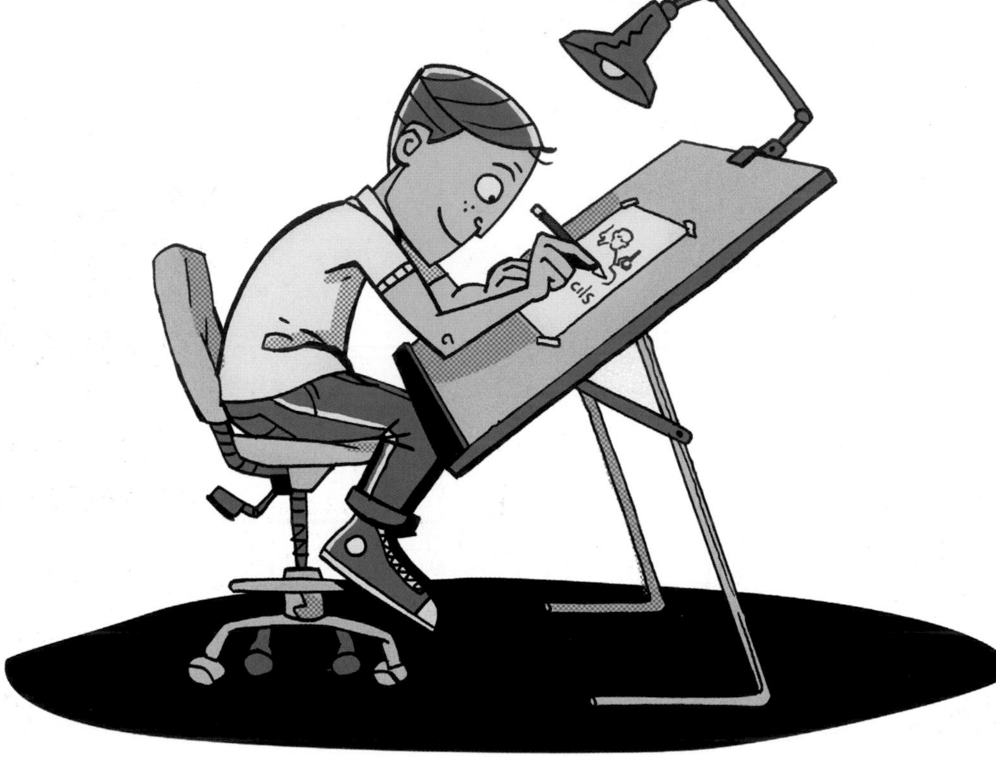
cils

CHOOSE A JOB YOU LOVE,
AND YOU WILL NEVER HAVE
TO WORK A DAY IN YOUR LIFE.

-CONFUCIUS

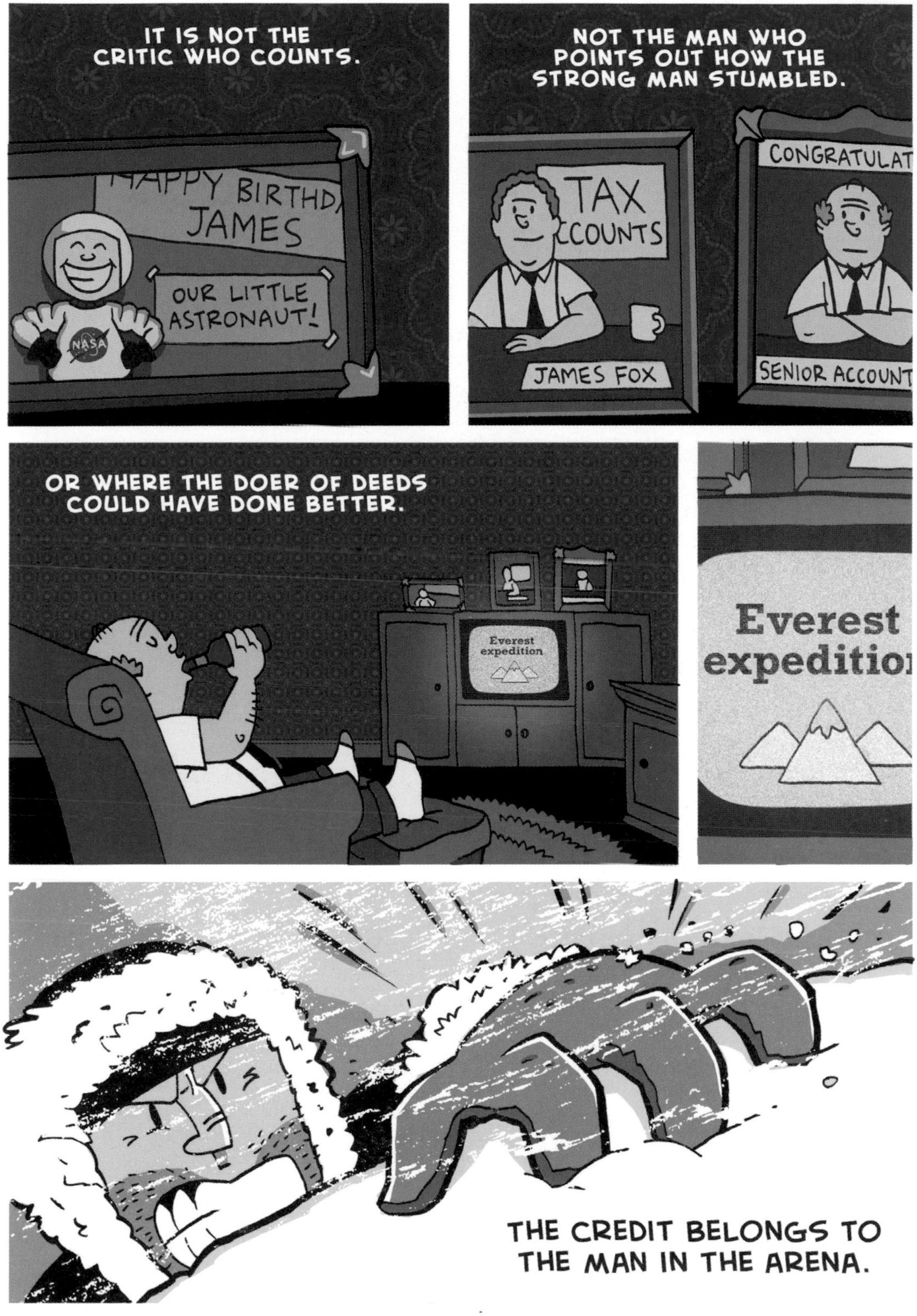
IT IS NOT THE CRITIC WHO COUNTS.
HAPPY BIRTHD JAMES
OUR LITTLE ASTRONAUT!
NASA
NOT THE MAN WHO POINTS OUT HOW THE STRONG MAN STUMBLED.
TAX CCOUNTS
JAMES FOX
CONGRATULAT
SENIOR ACCOUNT
OR WHERE THE DOER OF DEEDS COULD HAVE DONE BETTER.
Everest expedition
Everest expeditio
THE CREDIT BELONGS TO THE MAN IN THE ARENA.

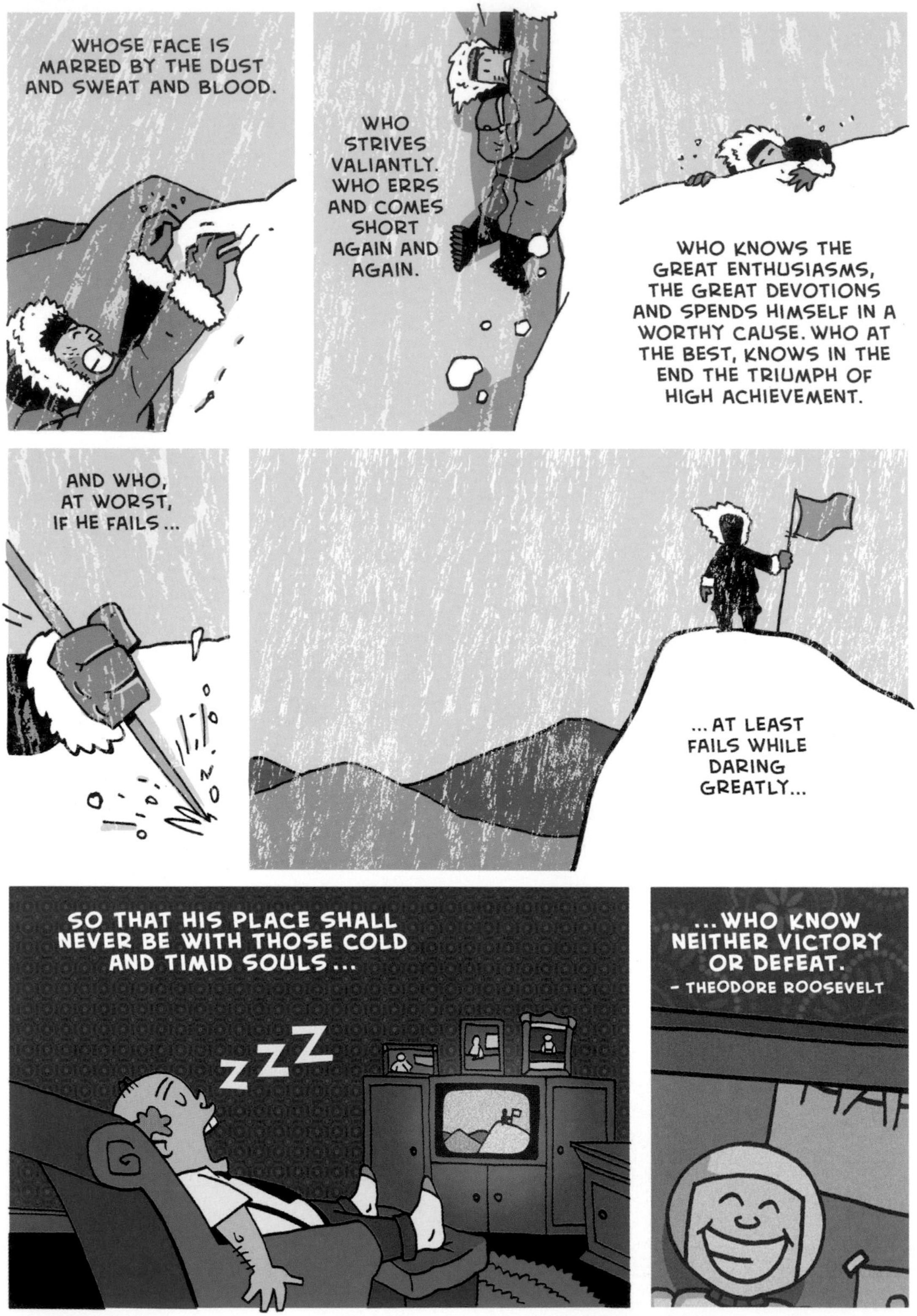
WHOSE FACE IS MARRED BY THE DUST AND SWEAT AND BLOOD.
WHO STRIVES VALIANTLY. WHO ERRS AND COMES SHORT AGAIN AND AGAIN.
WHO KNOWS THE GREAT ENTHUSIASMS, THE GREAT DEVOTIONS AND SPENDS HIMSELF IN A WORTHY CAUSE. WHO AT THE BEST, KNOWS IN THE END THE TRIUMPH OF HIGH ACHIEVEMENT.
AND WHO, AT WORST, IF HE FAILS...
...AT LEAST FAILS WHILE DARING GREATLY...
SO THAT HIS PLACE SHALL NEVER BE WITH THOSE COLD AND TIMID SOULS...
ZZZ
...WHO KNOW NEITHER VICTORY OR DEFEAT.
- THEODORE ROOSEVELT

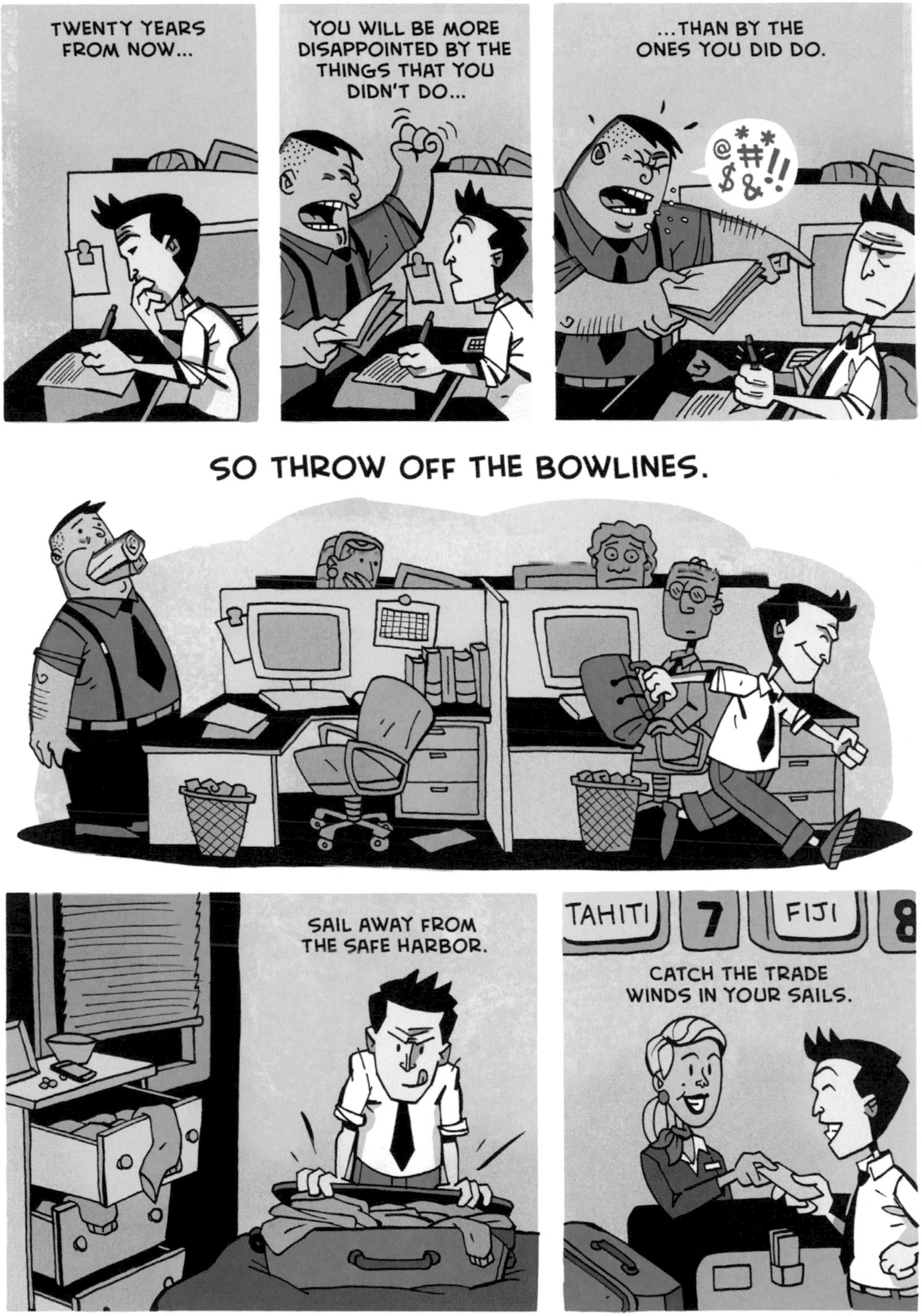
TWENTY YEARS FROM NOW...
YOU WILL BE MORE DISAPPOINTED BY THE THINGS THAT YOU DIDN'T DO...
...THAN BY THE ONES YOU DID DO.
@*#*!!$&!!
SO THROW OFF THE BOWLINES.
SAIL AWAY FROM THE SAFE HARBOR.
TAHITI
7
FIJI
8
CATCH THE TRADE WINDS IN YOUR SAILS.

EXPLORE
DREAM
DISCOVER

– H. JACKSON BROWN JR

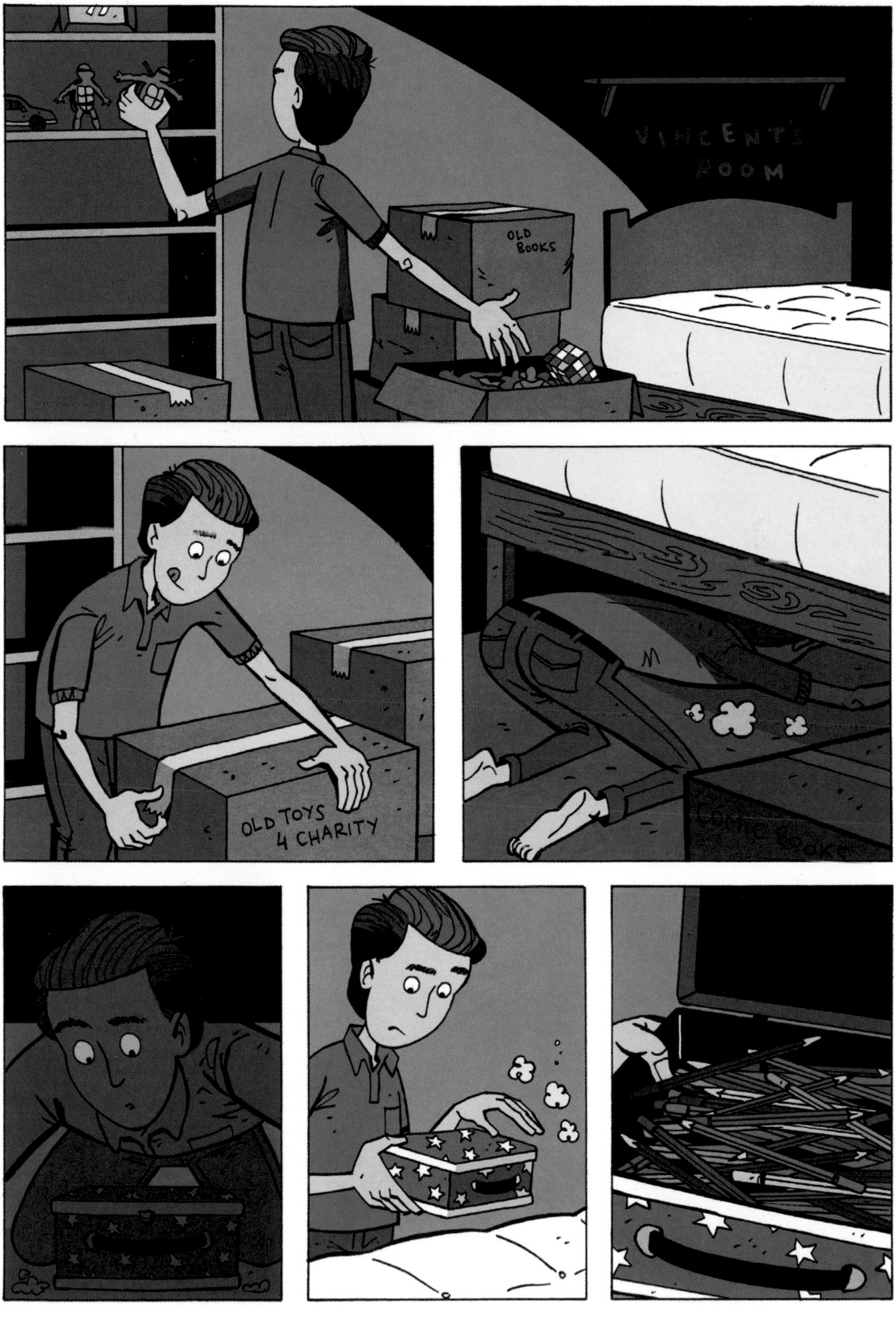
VINCENT'S ROOM
OLD BOOKS
OLD TOYS 4 CHARITY
COMIC BOOKS

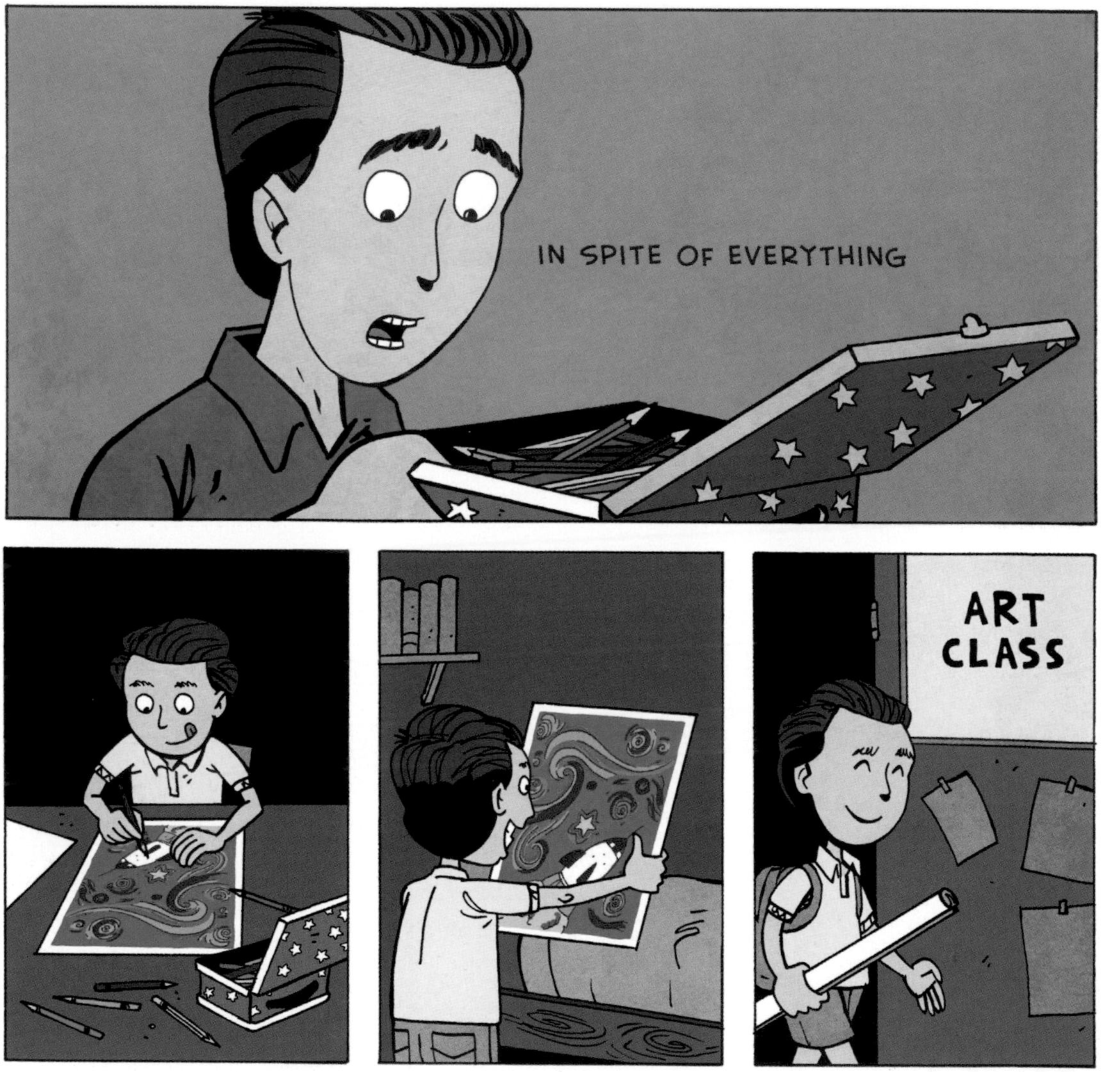
IN SPITE OF EVERYTHING
ART
CLASS

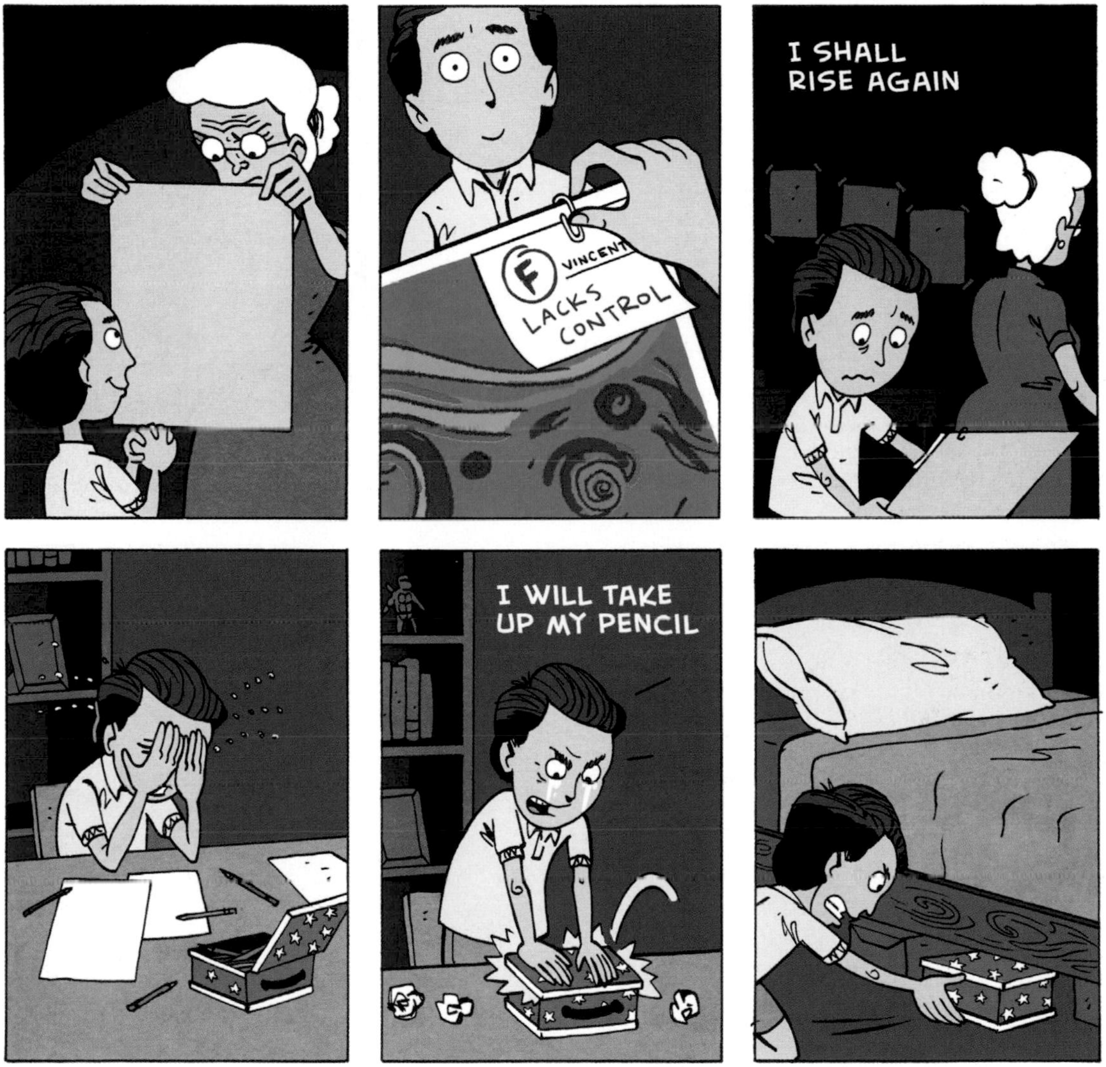
VINCENT
F
LACKS CONTROL
I SHALL RISE AGAIN
I WILL TAKE UP MY PENCIL

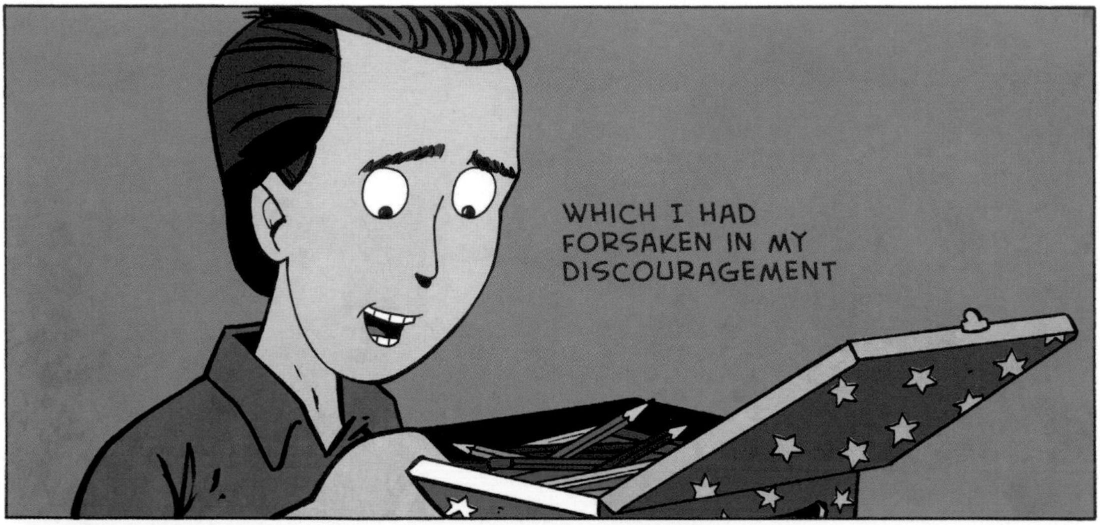
WHICH I HAD FORSAKEN IN MY DISCOURAGEMENT

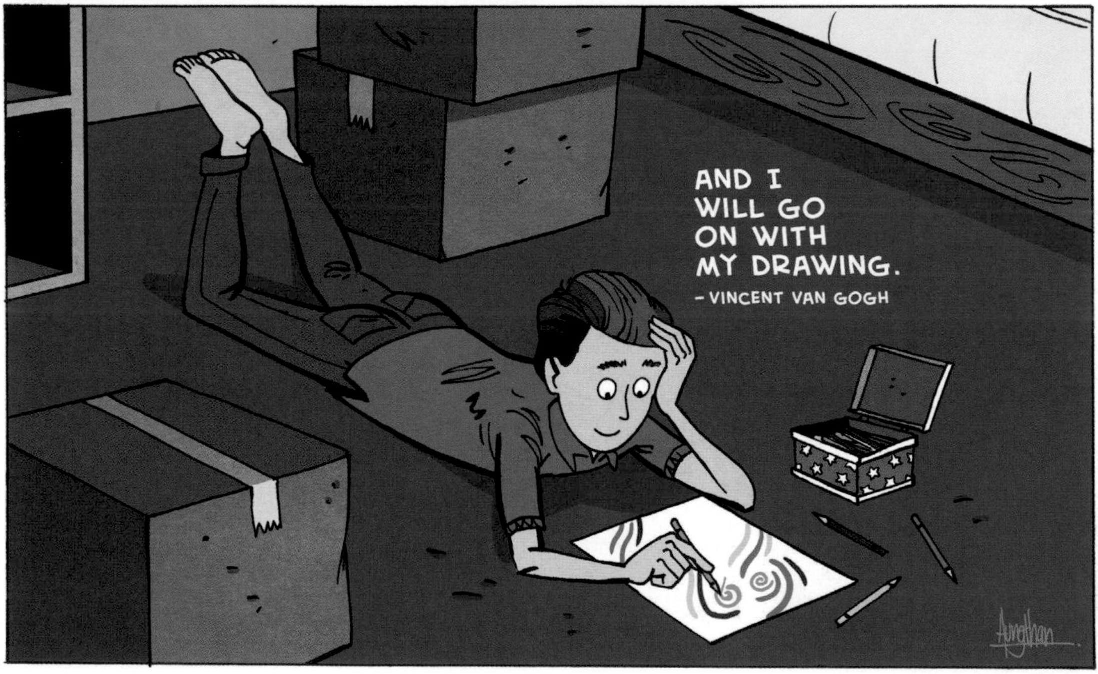
AND I WILL GO ON WITH MY DRAWING.
- VINCENT VAN GOGH

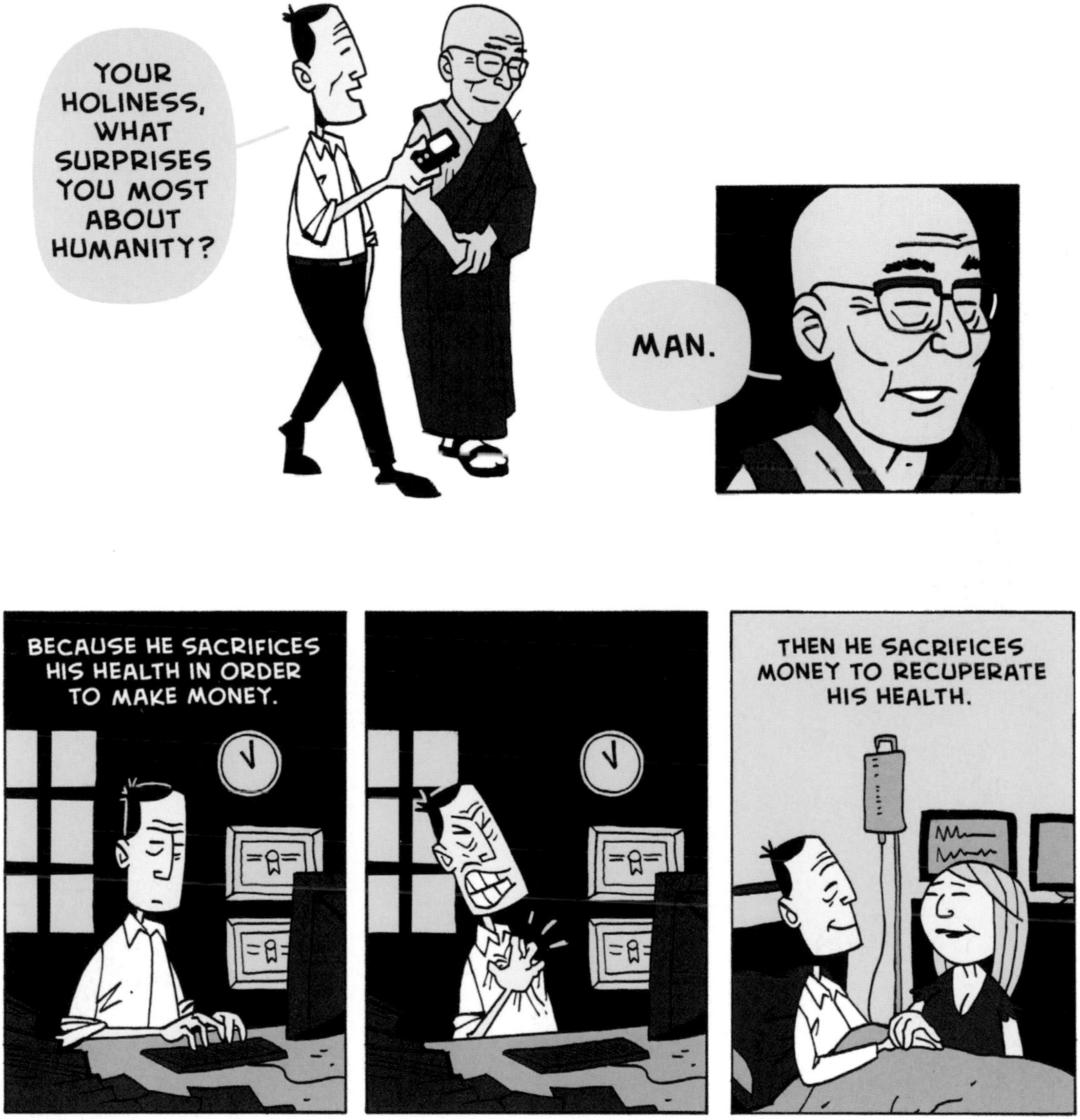
YOUR HOLINESS, WHAT SURPRISES YOU MOST ABOUT HUMANITY?
MAN.
BECAUSE HE SACRIFICES HIS HEALTH IN ORDER TO MAKE MONEY.
THEN HE SACRIFICES MONEY TO RECUPERATE HIS HEALTH.

AND THEN HE IS SO ANXIOUS ABOUT THE FUTURE ...

...THAT HE DOES NOT ENJOY THE PRESENT.

THE RESULT BEING THAT HE DOES NOT LIVE IN THE PRESENT OR THE FUTURE.

EDITOR-IN-CHIEF

ENTRAL TIBETAN ADMINISTRATION

DALAI LAMA PRESS JUNKET

INDIA AIRLINE

HE LIVES AS IF HE IS NEVER GOING TO DIE.

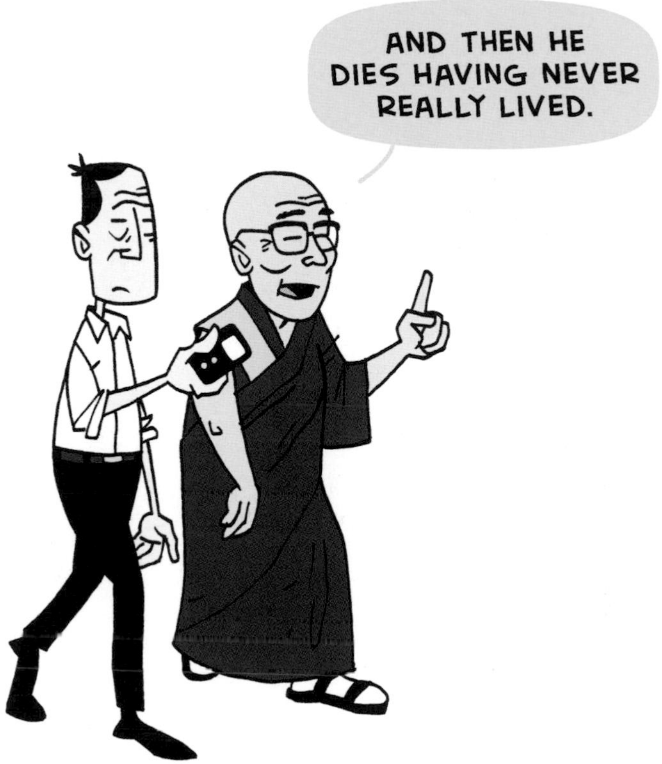
AND THEN HE DIES HAVING NEVER REALLY LIVED.

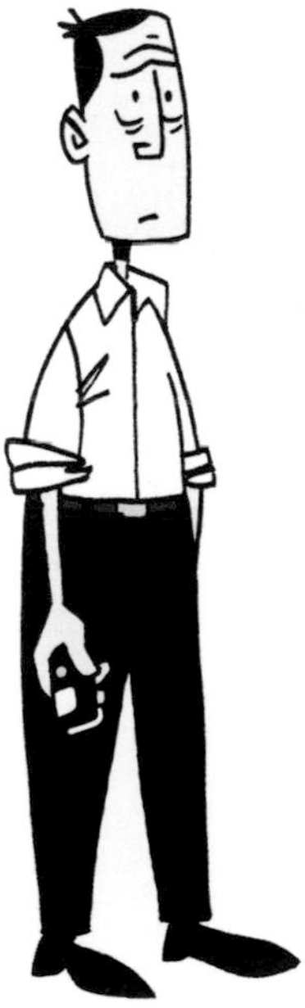

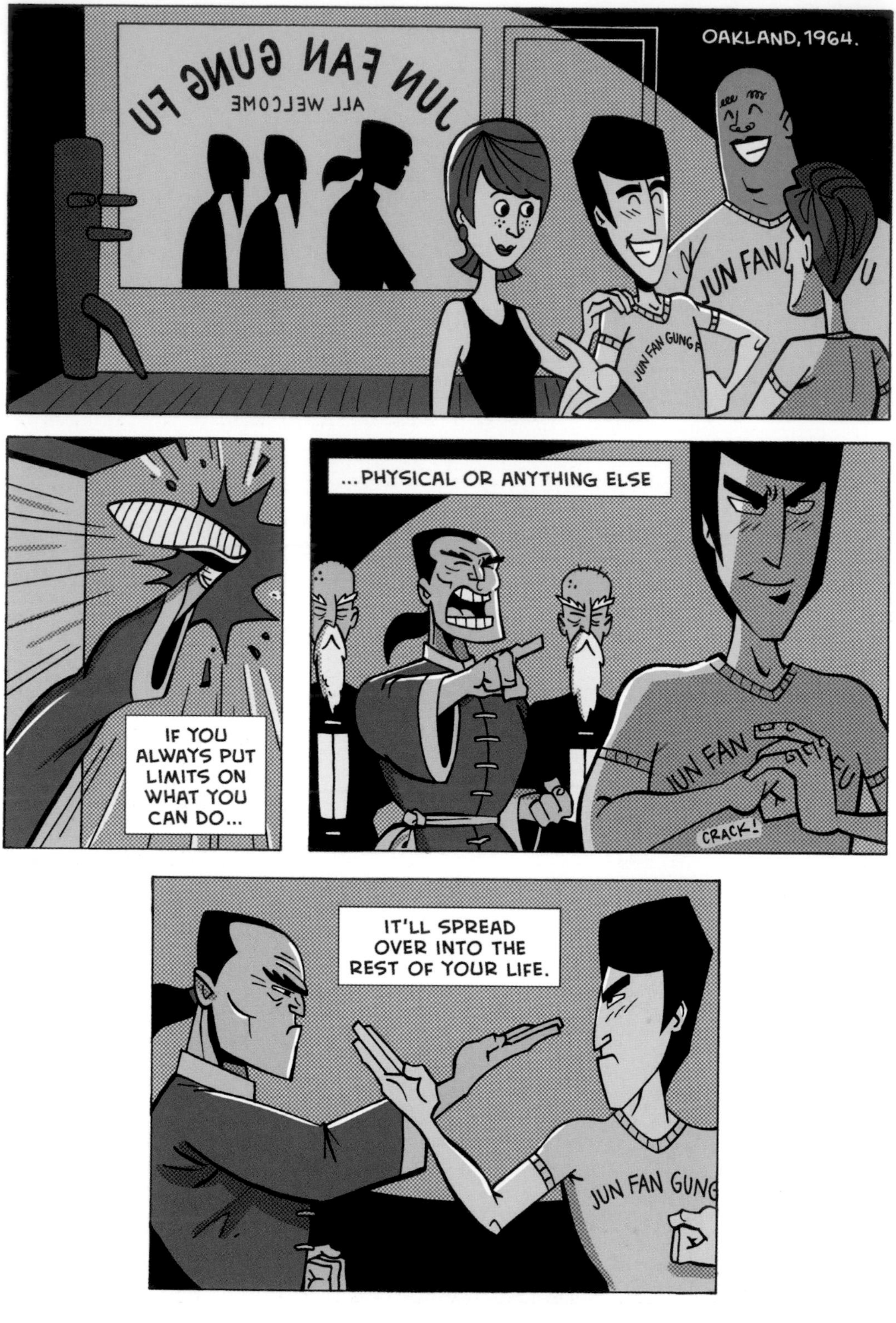
OAKLAND, 1964.
JUN FAN GUNG FU
ALL WELCOME
IF YOU ALWAYS PUT LIMITS ON WHAT YOU CAN DO...
...PHYSICAL OR ANYTHING ELSE
CRACK!
IT'LL SPREAD OVER INTO THE REST OF YOUR LIFE.

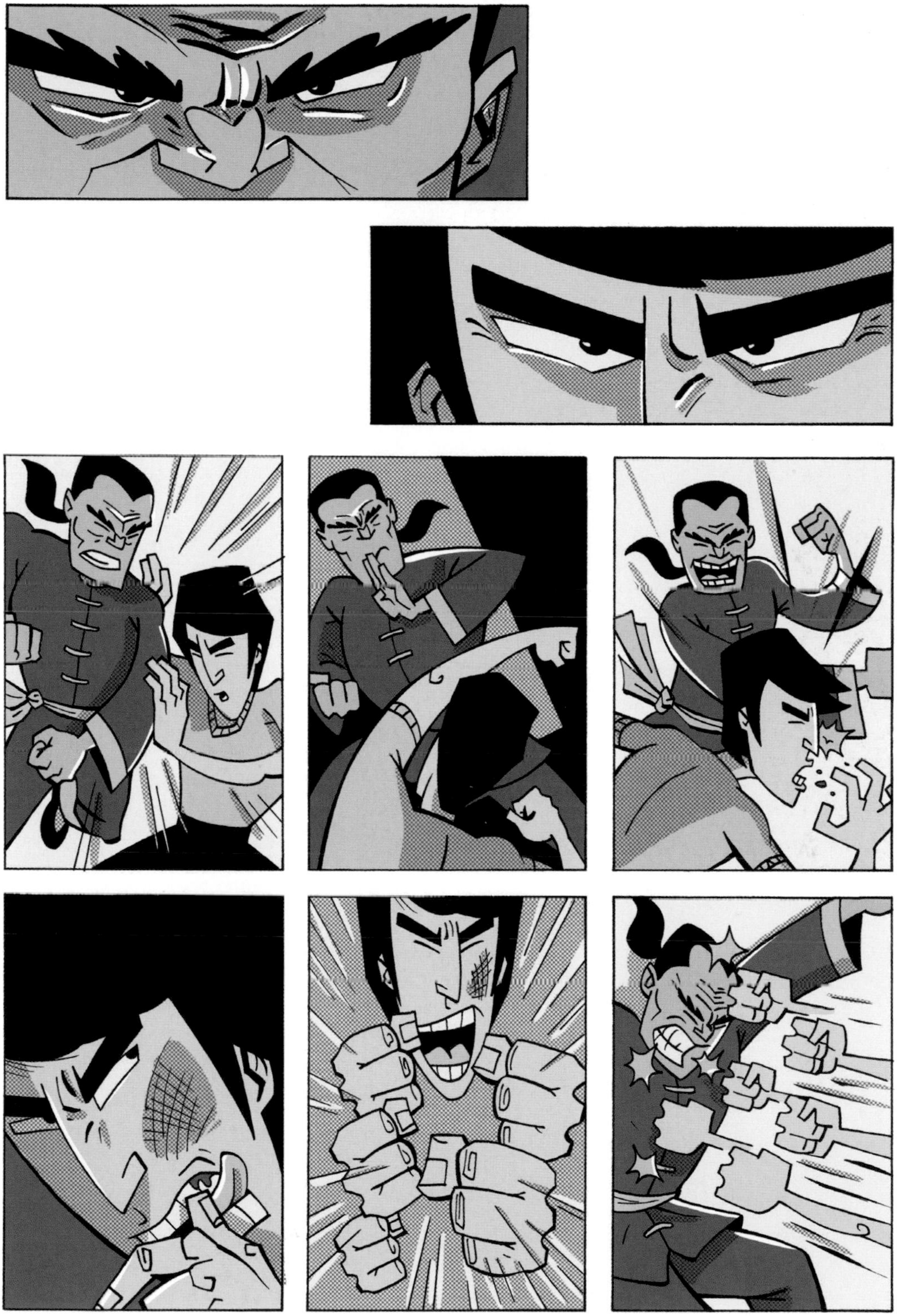

TAP
JUN FAN G
IT'LL SPREAD INTO YOUR WORK.
JUN FAN GU
INTO YOUR MORALITY.
JUN FAN GUNG FU
JUN FAN GUNG FU
INTO YOUR ENTIRE BEING.
THERE ARE NO LIMITS.
THERE ARE PLATEAUS.
54, 55, 56...
BUT YOU MUST NOT STAY THERE.
88, 89, 90...

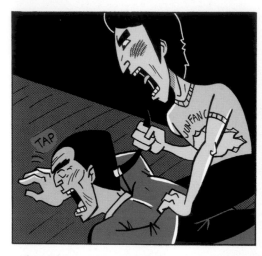

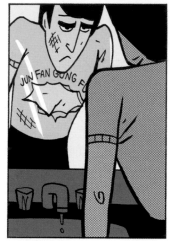

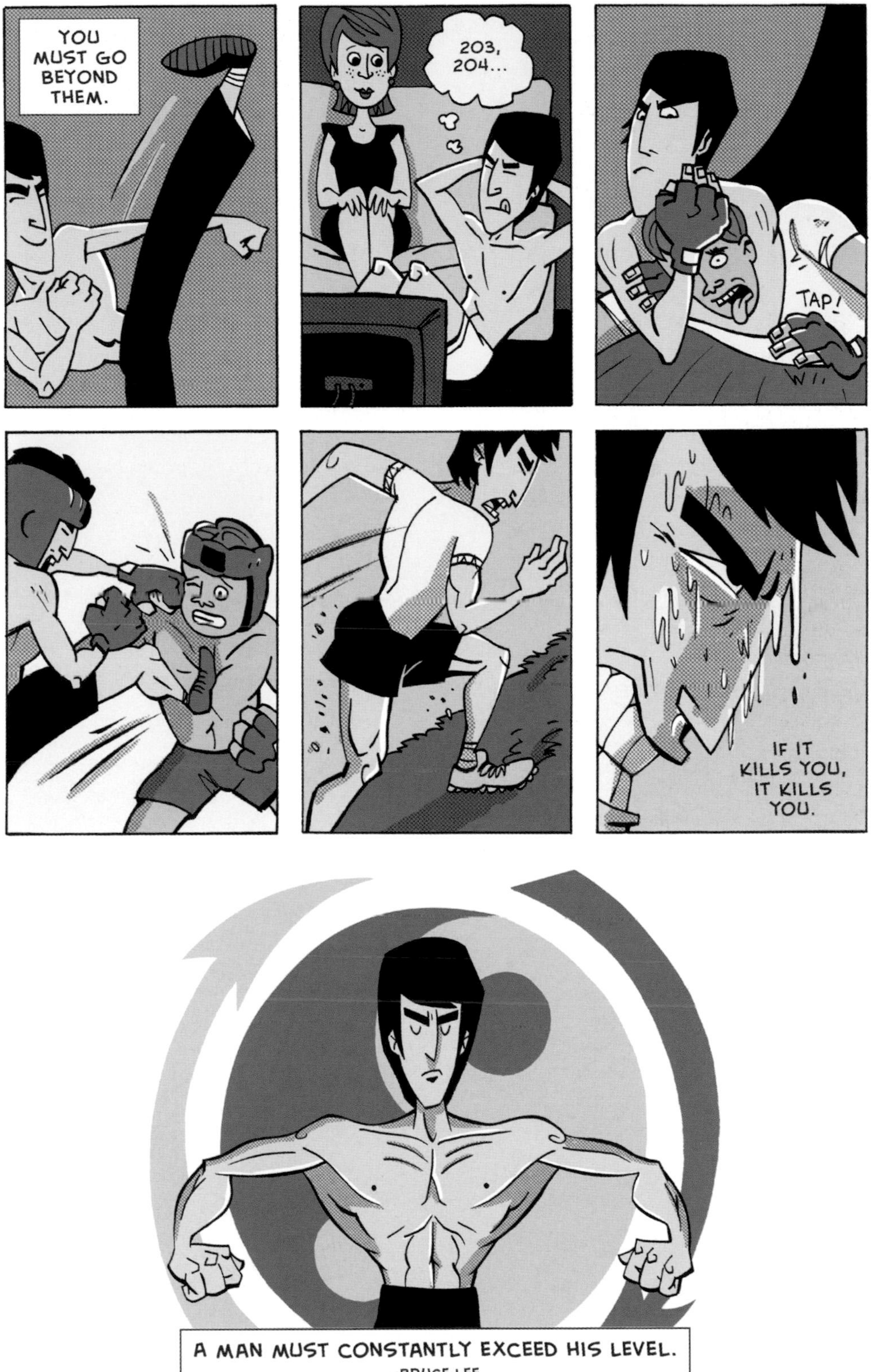

YOU MUST GO BEYOND THEM.
203, 204...
TAP!
IF IT KILLS YOU, IT KILLS YOU.
A MAN MUST CONSTANTLY EXCEED HIS LEVEL.
-BRUCE LEE

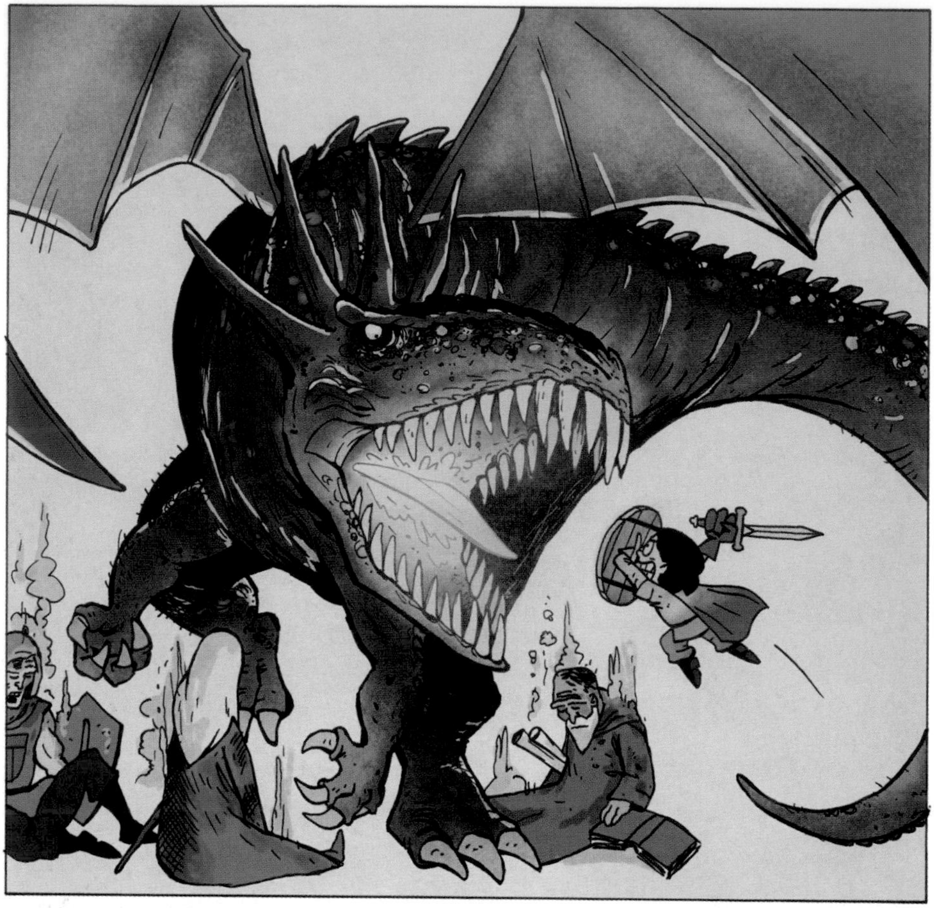

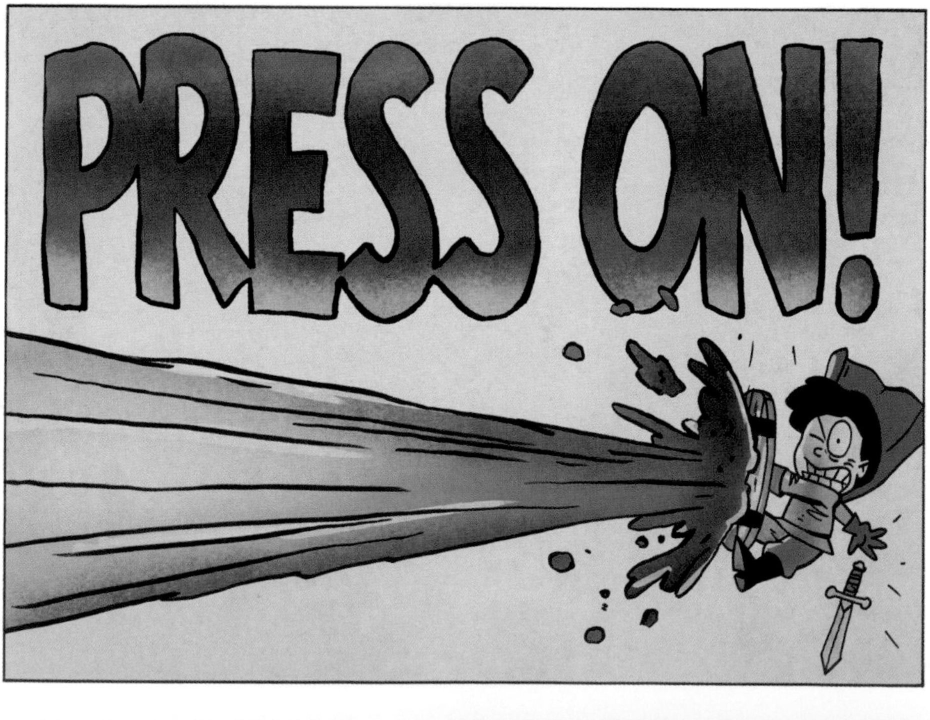
PRESS ON!

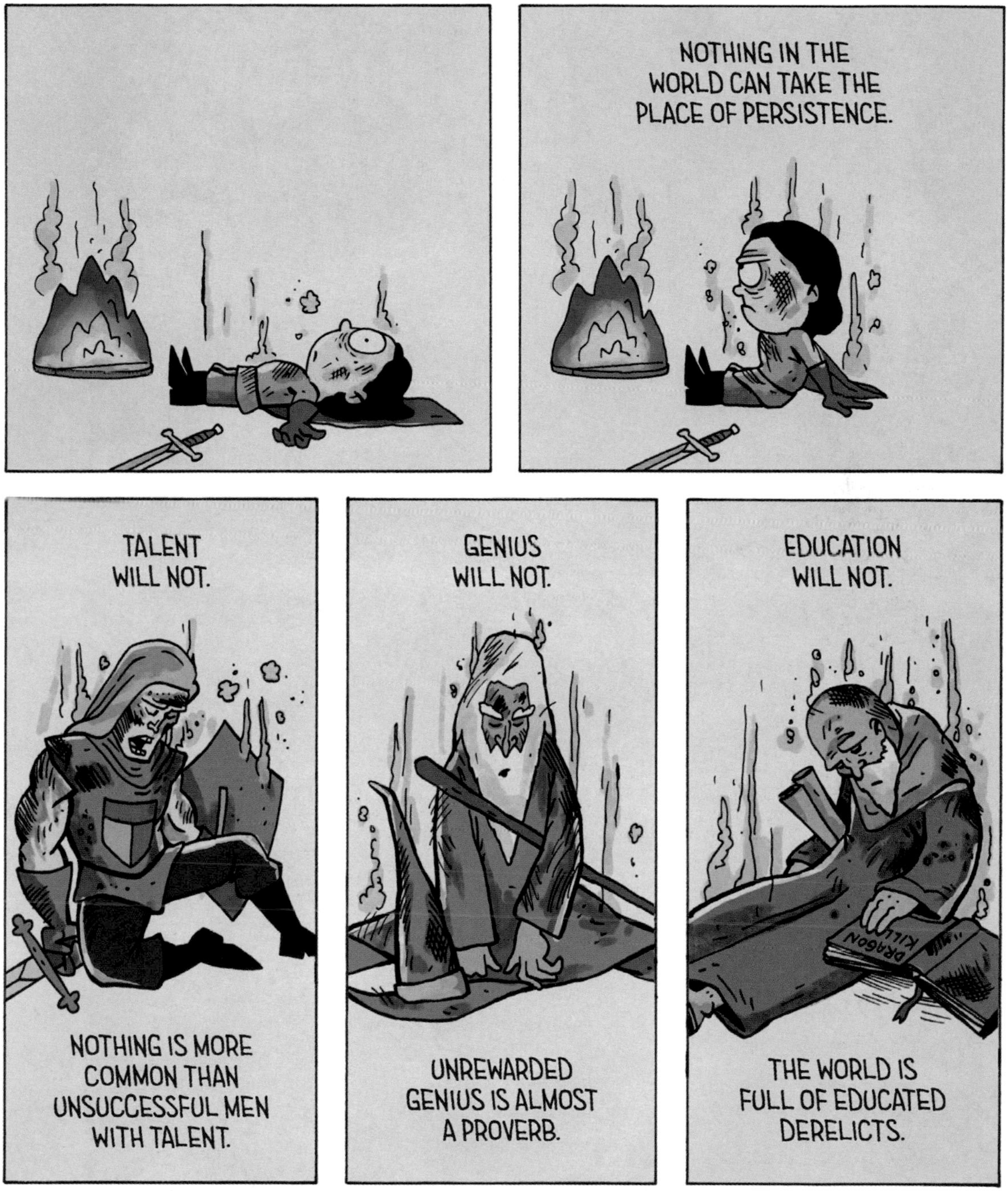
NOTHING IN THE WORLD CAN TAKE THE PLACE OF PERSISTENCE.
TALENT WILL NOT.
NOTHING IS MORE COMMON THAN UNSUCCESSFUL MEN WITH TALENT.
GENIUS WILL NOT.
UNREWARDED GENIUS IS ALMOST A PROVERB.
EDUCATION WILL NOT.
THE WORLD IS FULL OF EDUCATED DERELICTS.

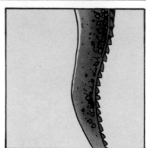

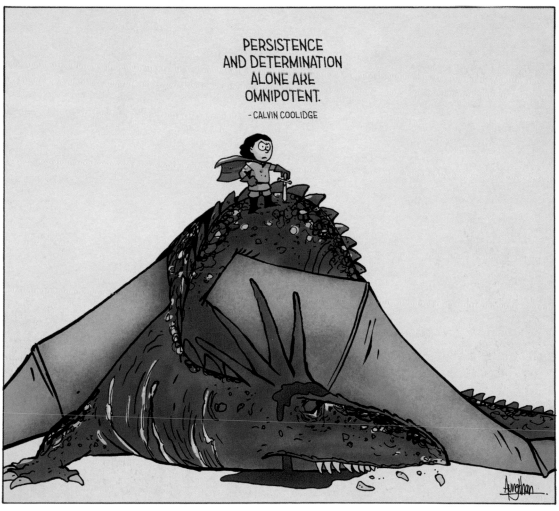

PERSISTENCE
AND DETERMINATION
ALONE ARE
OMNIPOTENT.

– CALVIN COOLIDGE

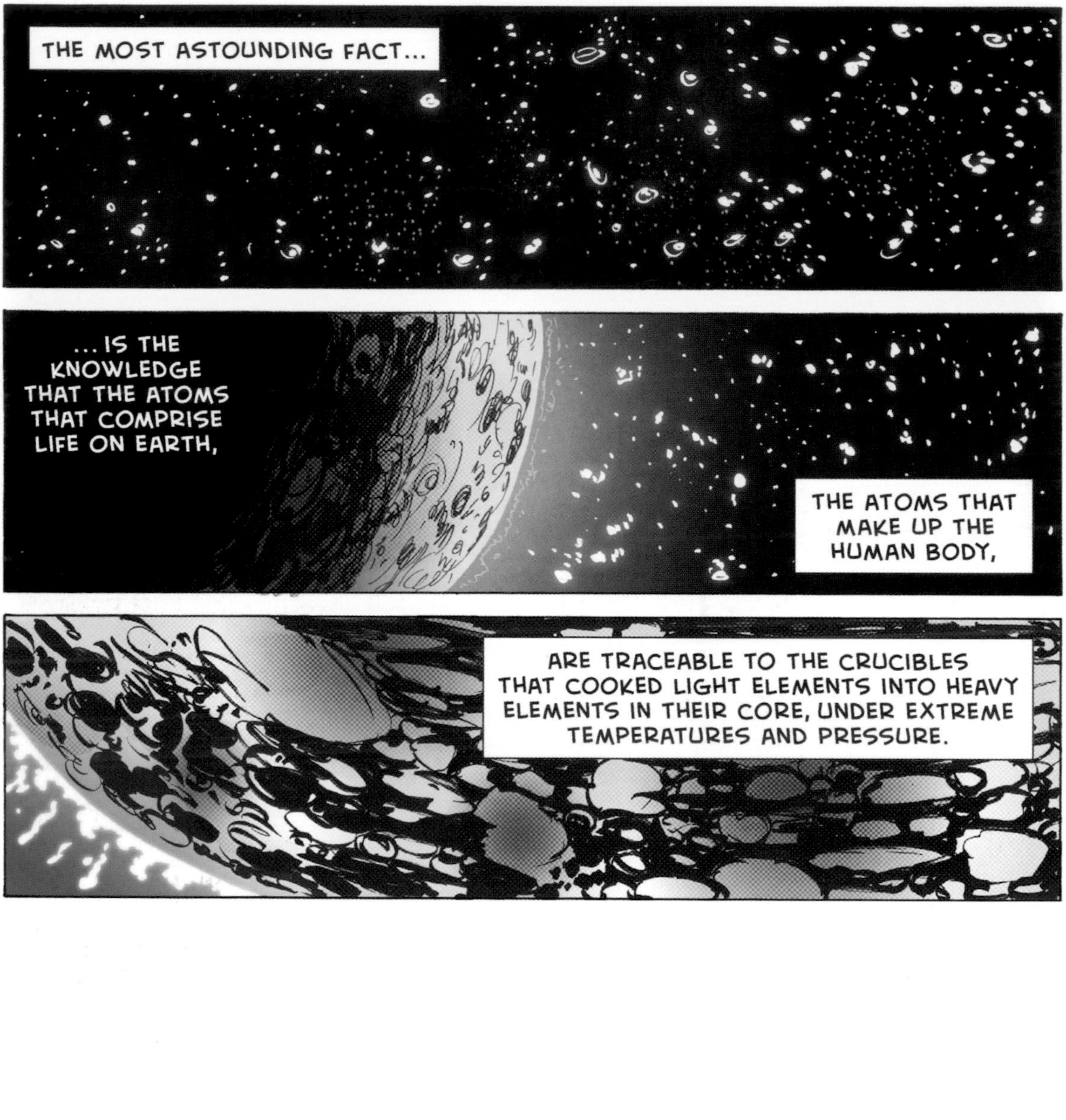
THE MOST ASTOUNDING FACT...
...IS THE KNOWLEDGE THAT THE ATOMS THAT COMPRISE LIFE ON EARTH,
THE ATOMS THAT MAKE UP THE HUMAN BODY,
ARE TRACEABLE TO THE CRUCIBLES THAT COOKED LIGHT ELEMENTS INTO HEAVY ELEMENTS IN THEIR CORE, UNDER EXTREME TEMPERATURES AND PRESSURE.

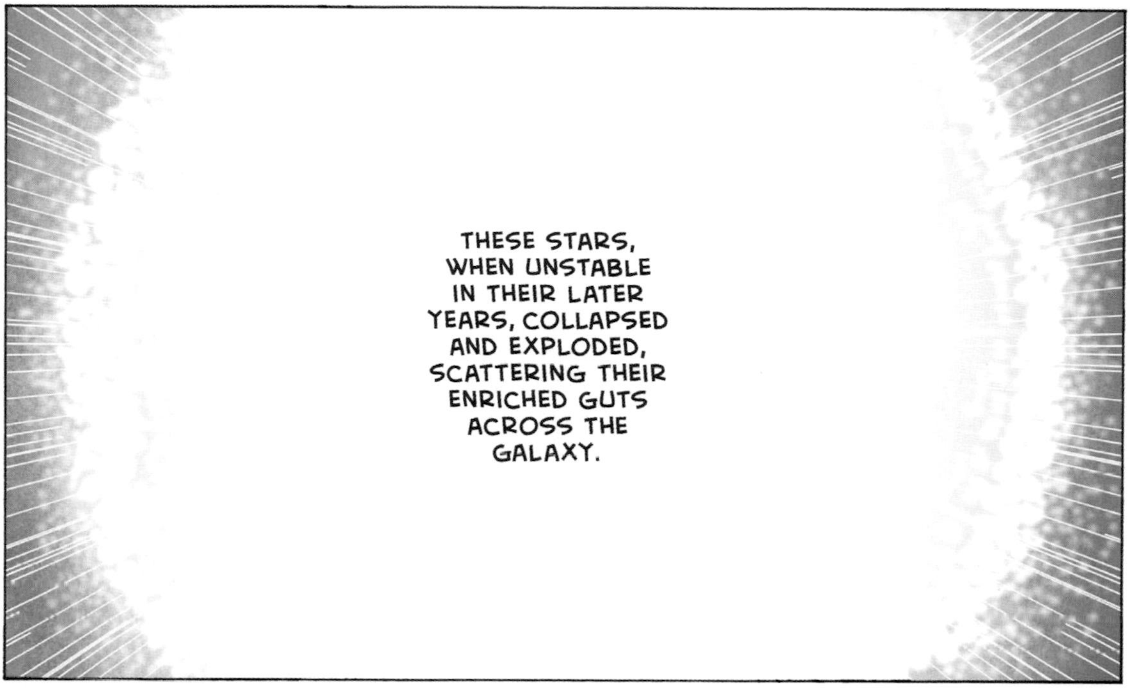
THESE STARS, WHEN UNSTABLE IN THEIR LATER YEARS, COLLAPSED AND EXPLODED, SCATTERING THEIR ENRICHED GUTS ACROSS THE GALAXY.

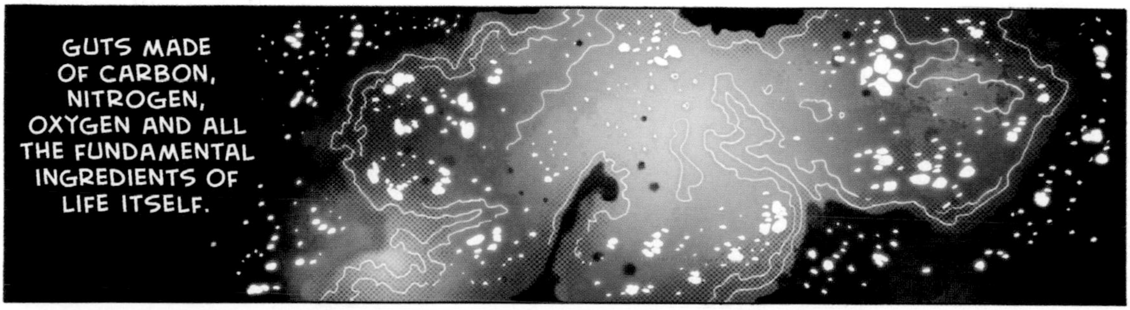
GUTS MADE OF CARBON, NITROGEN, OXYGEN AND ALL THE FUNDAMENTAL INGREDIENTS OF LIFE ITSELF.

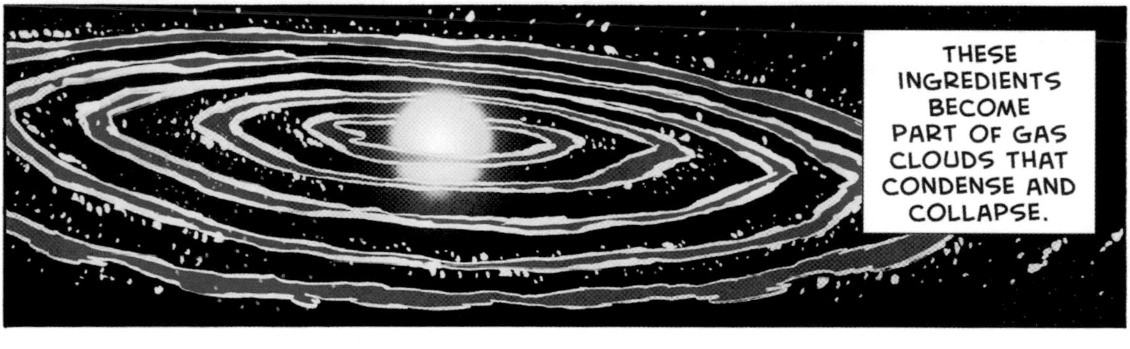
THESE INGREDIENTS BECOME PART OF GAS CLOUDS THAT CONDENSE AND COLLAPSE.

FORMING THE NEXT GENERATION OF SOLAR SYSTEMS – STARS WITH ORBITING PLANETS.

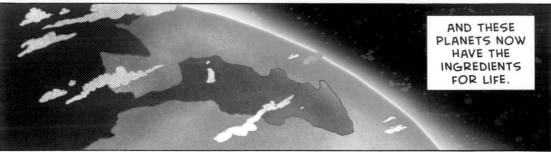

AND THESE PLANETS NOW HAVE THE INGREDIENTS FOR LIFE.

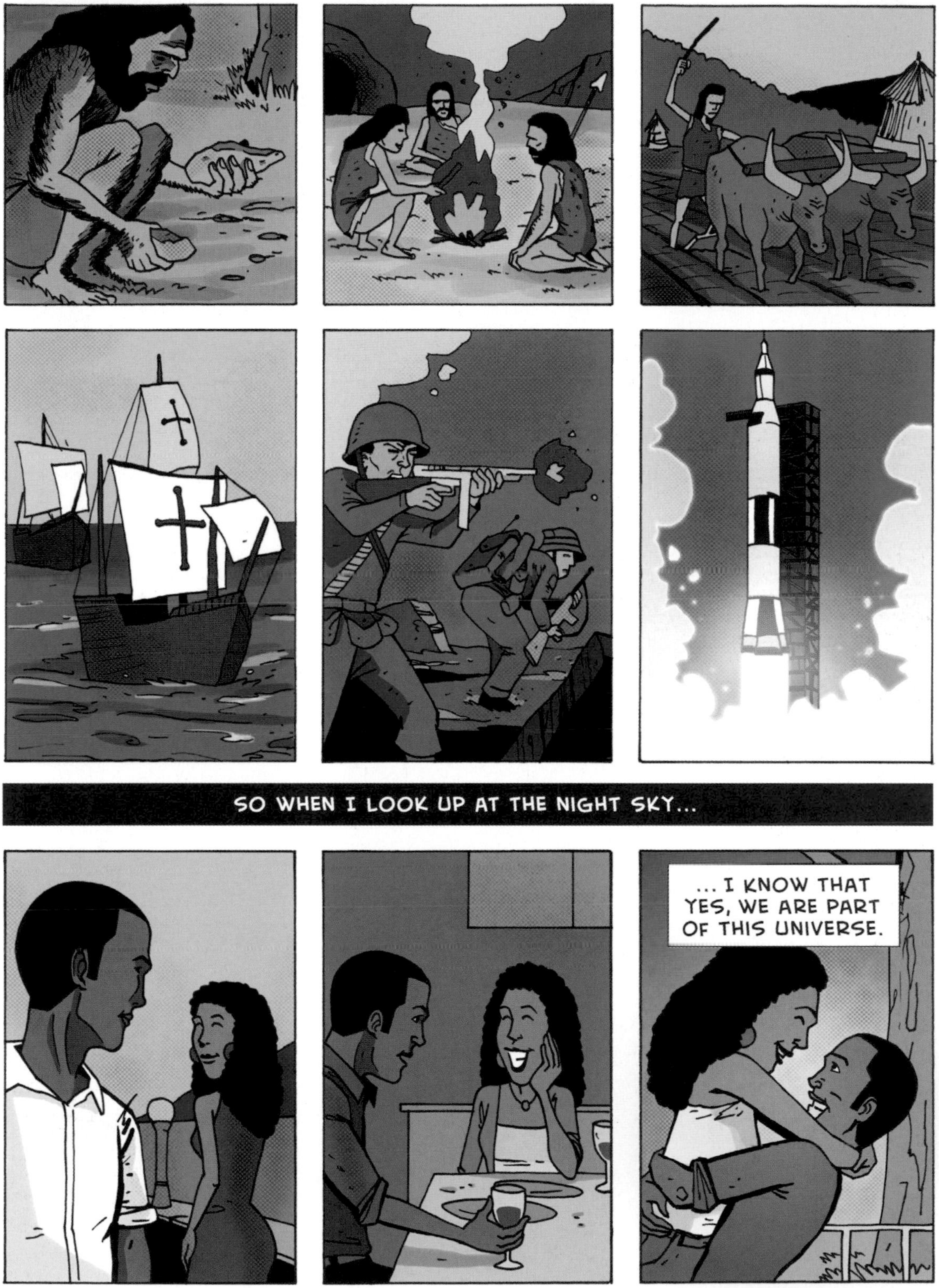
SO WHEN I LOOK UP AT THE NIGHT SKY...
... I KNOW THAT YES, WE ARE PART OF THIS UNIVERSE.

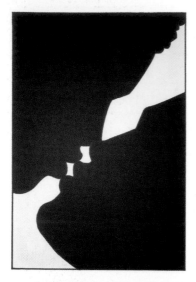

WE ARE IN
THIS UNIVERSE.

BUT PERHAPS MORE IMPORTANT
THAN BOTH OF THOSE FACTS...

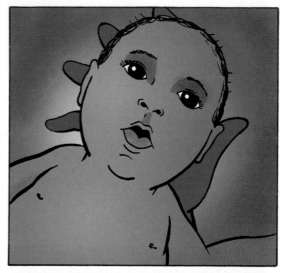

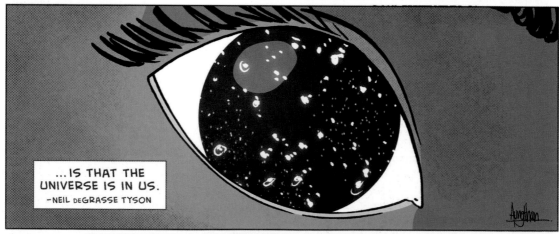

...IS THAT THE
UNIVERSE IS IN US.
—NEIL deGRASSE TYSON

THE INTERPRETATION OF THIS QUOTE IS MINE AND IS NOT NECESSARILY WHAT NEIL deGRASSE TYSON HAD IN MIND WHEN HE USED THESE WORDS. – GAV

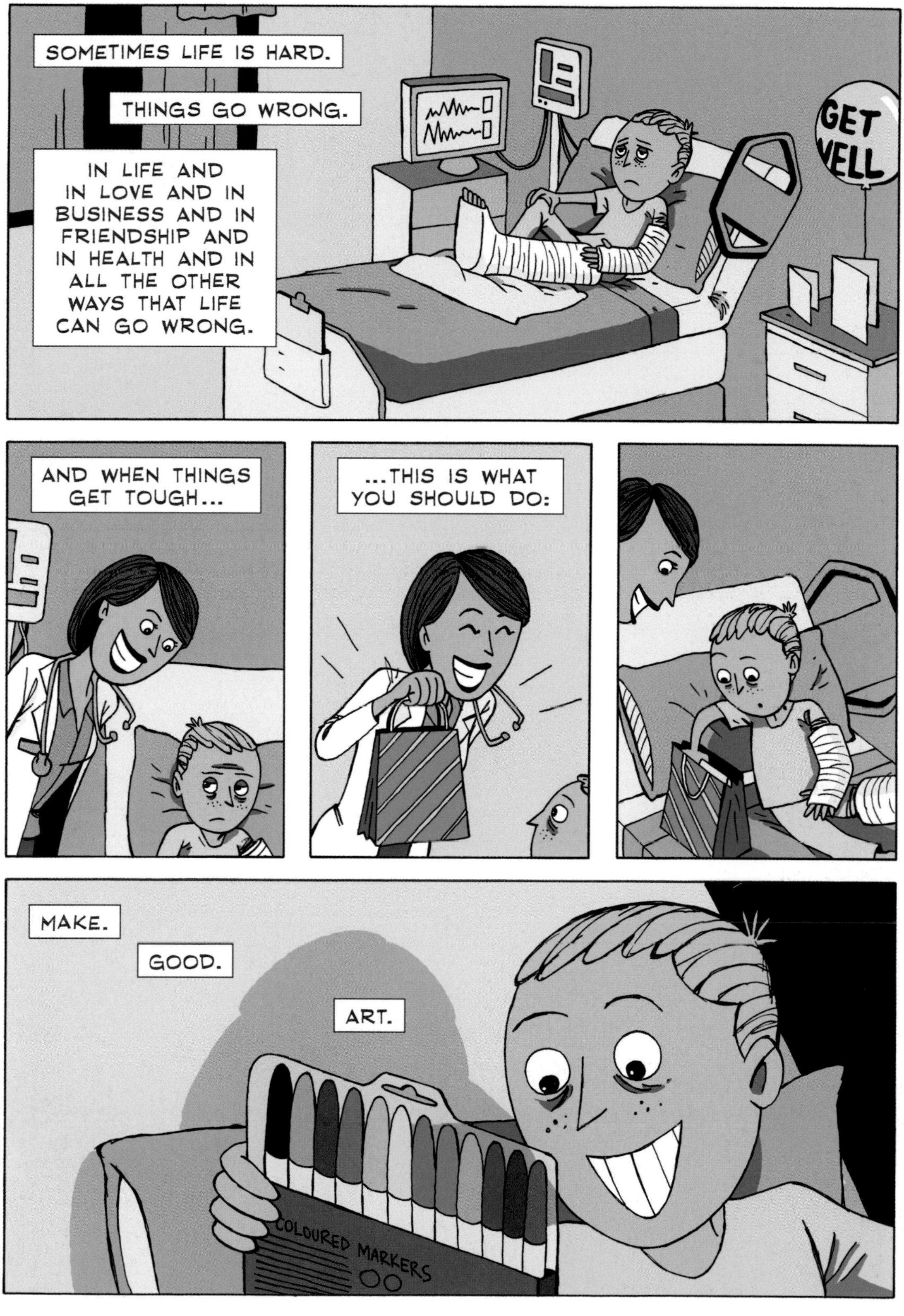
SOMETIMES LIFE IS HARD.
THINGS GO WRONG.
IN LIFE AND IN LOVE AND IN BUSINESS AND IN FRIENDSHIP AND IN HEALTH AND IN ALL THE OTHER WAYS THAT LIFE CAN GO WRONG.
GET WELL
AND WHEN THINGS GET TOUGH...
...THIS IS WHAT YOU SHOULD DO:
MAKE.
GOOD.
ART.
COLOURED MARKERS

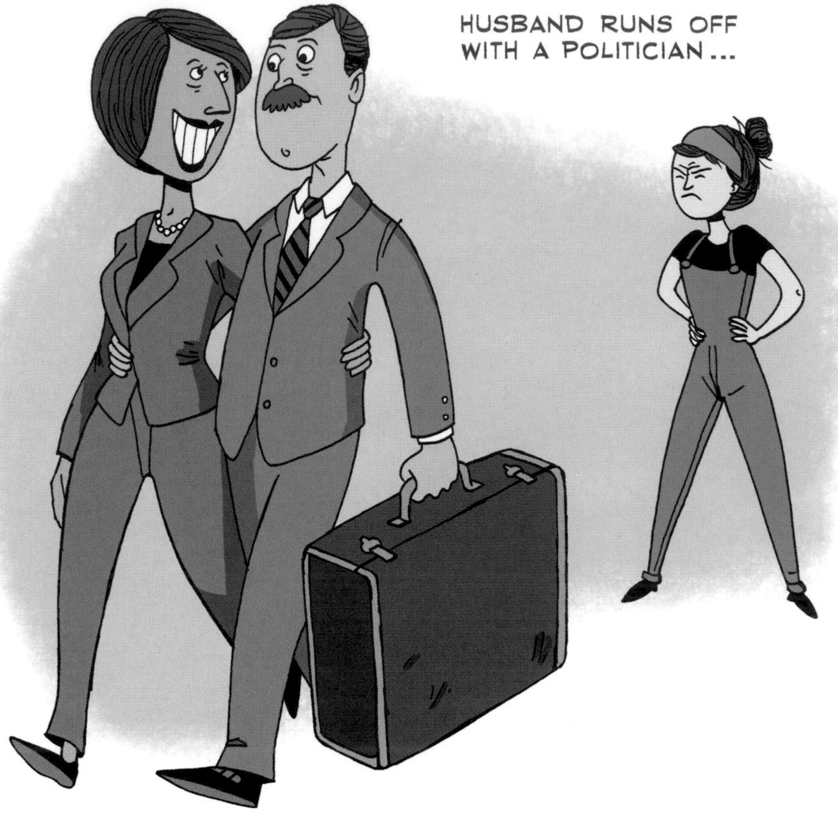
HUSBAND RUNS OFF WITH A POLITICIAN...

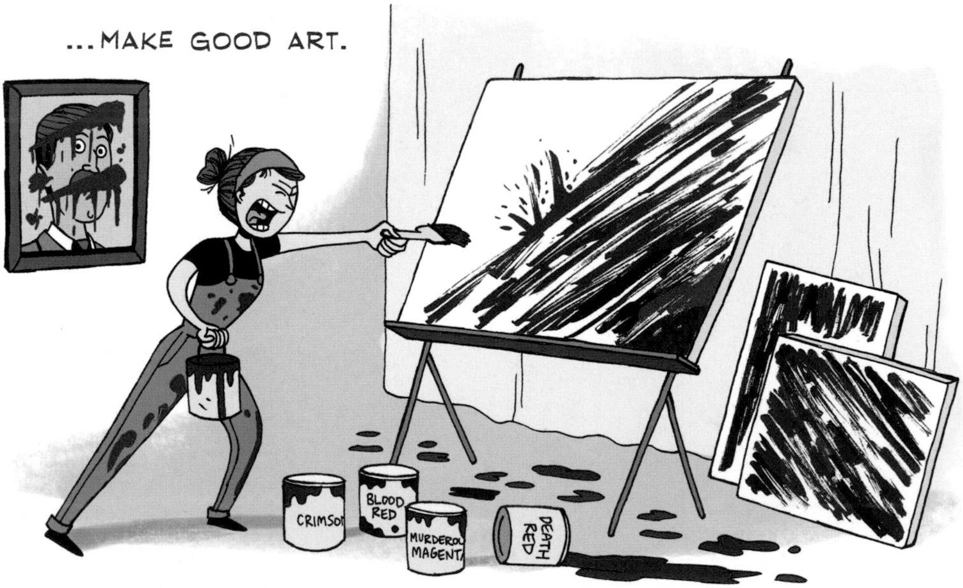
...MAKE GOOD ART.
CRIMSO
BLOOD RED
MURDERO
MAGENT
DEATH RED

LEG CRUSHED AND THEN EATEN
BY A MUTATED BOA CONSTRICTOR...

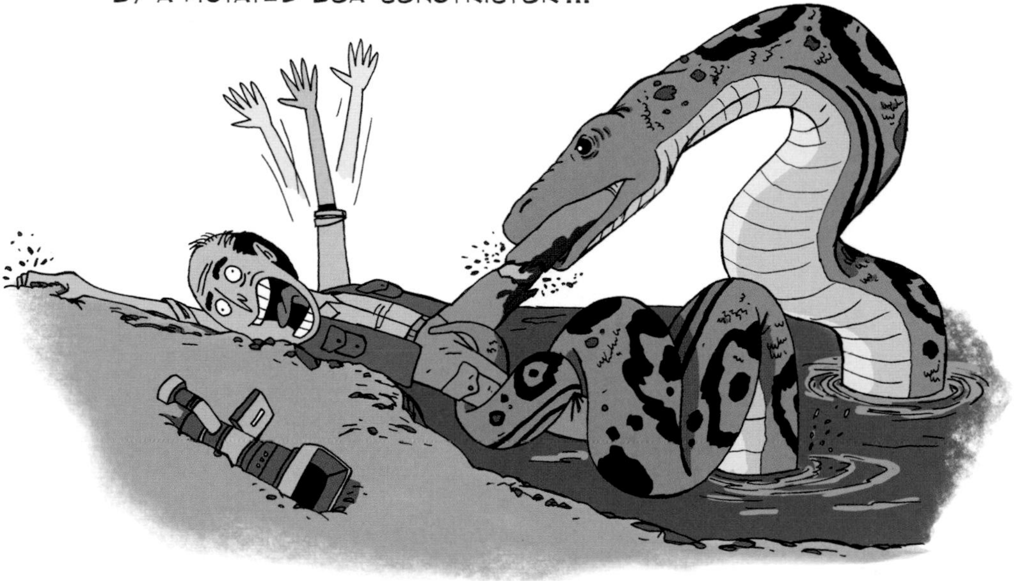

...MAKE
GOOD ART.

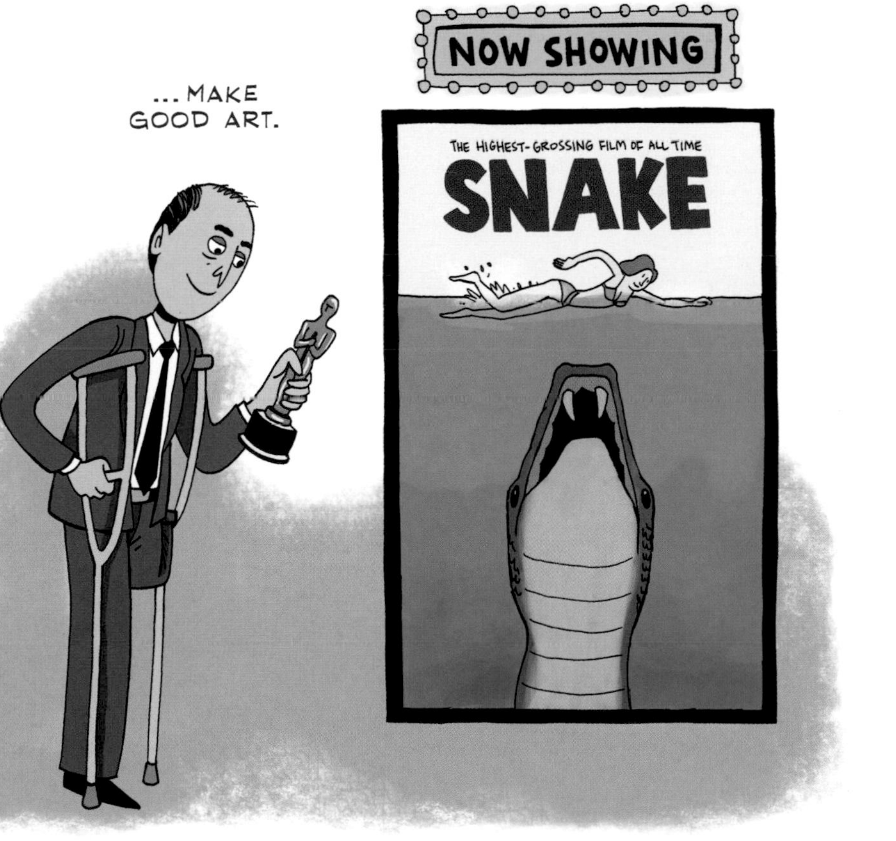
NOW SHOWING
THE HIGHEST-GROSSING FILM OF ALL TIME
SNAKE

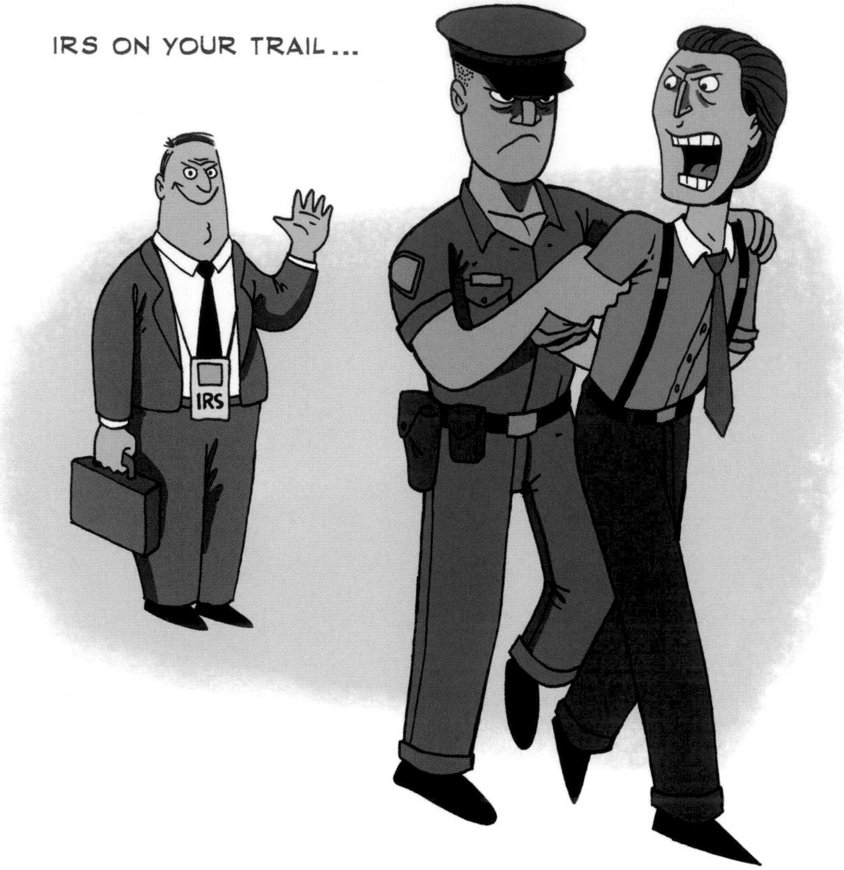
IRS ON YOUR TRAIL...
IRS

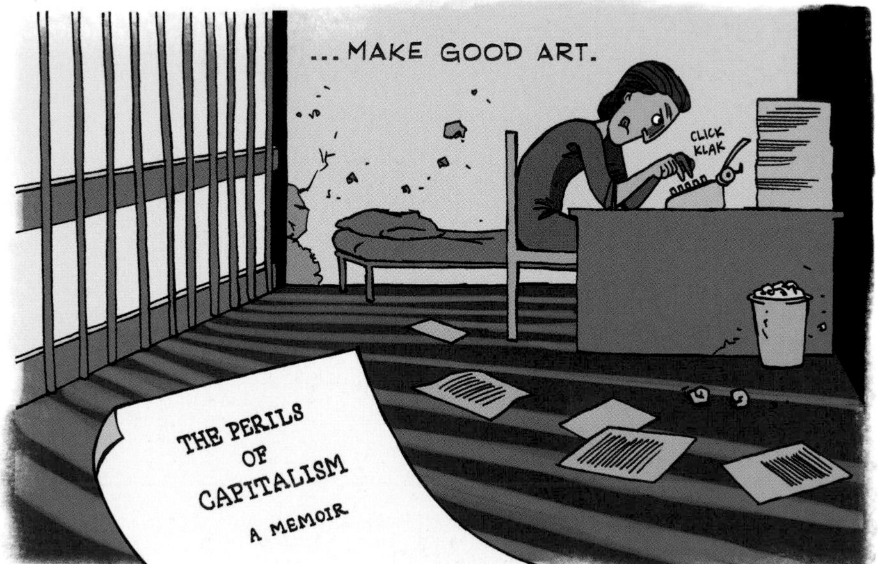
...MAKE GOOD ART.
CLICK KLAK
THE PERILS OF CAPITALISM
A MEMOIR

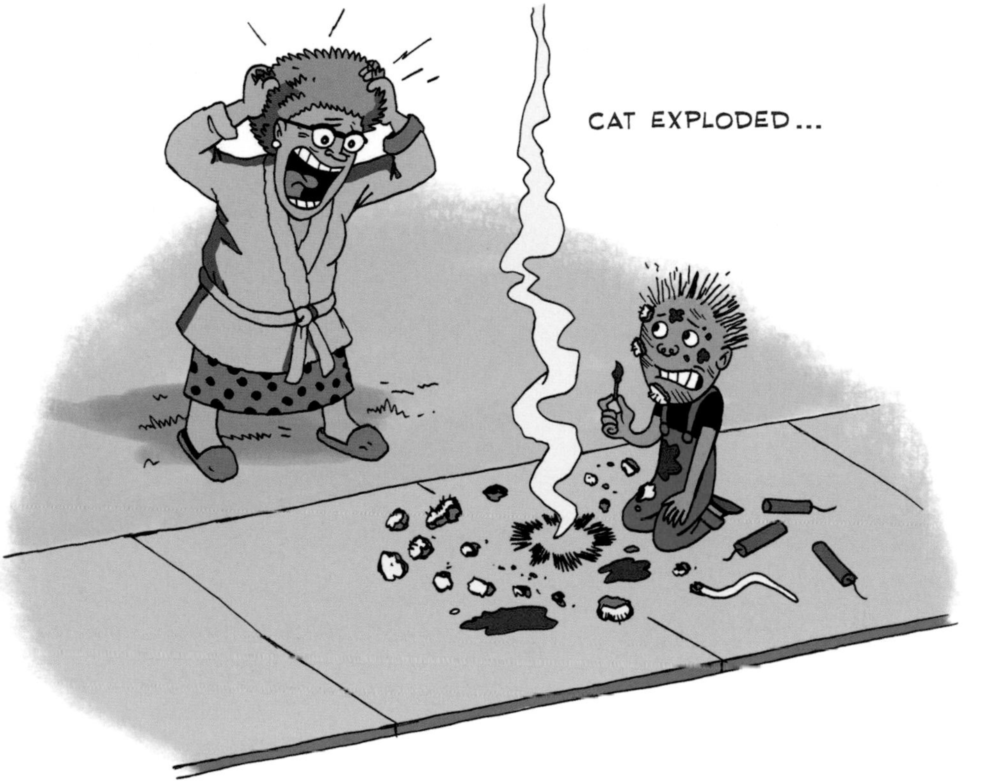
CAT EXPLODED...

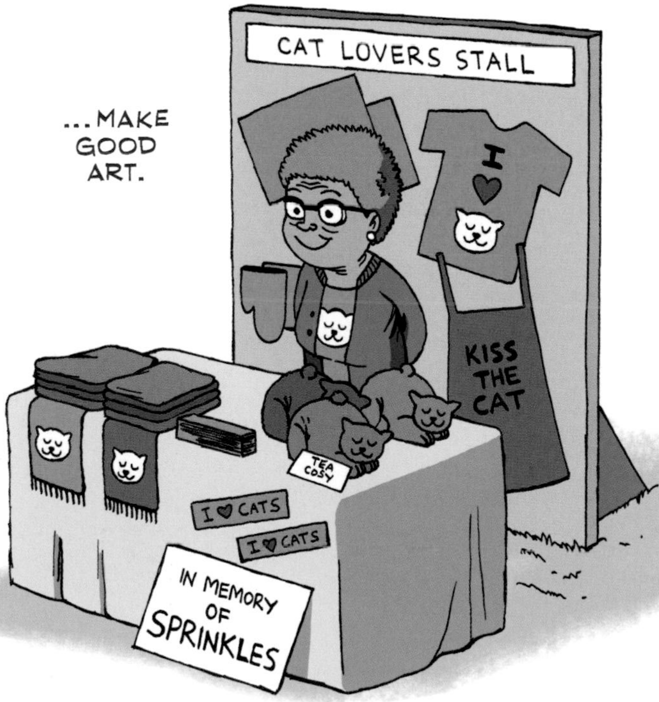
...MAKE GOOD ART.
CAT LOVERS STALL
I ♥
KISS THE CAT
TEA COSY
I ♥ CATS
I ♥ CATS
IN MEMORY OF SPRINKLES

SOMEONE ON THE INTERNET THINKS WHAT YOU'RE DOING IS STUPID OR EVIL OR IT'S ALL BEEN DONE BEFORE...

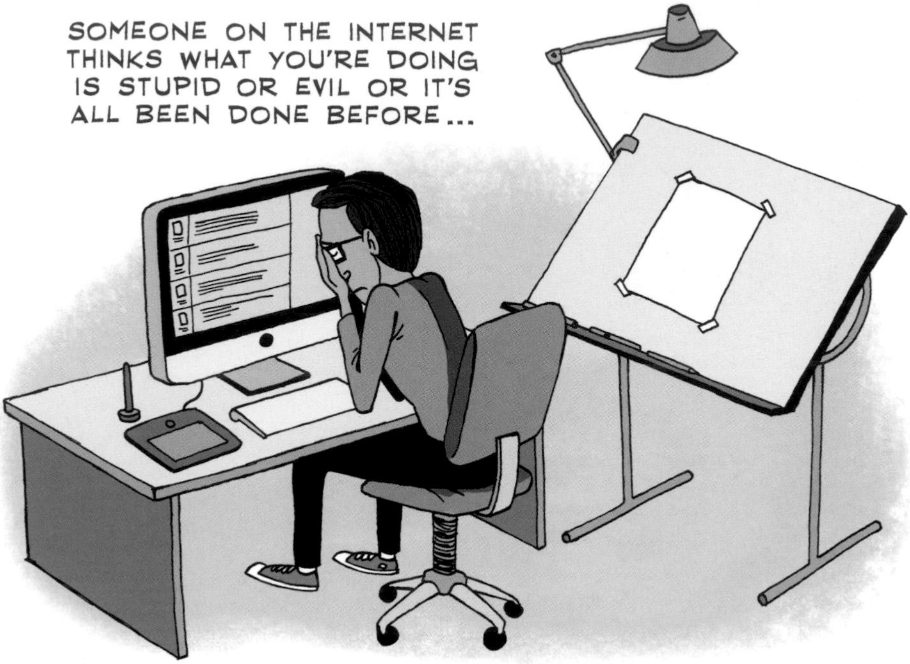

...MAKE GOOD ART.

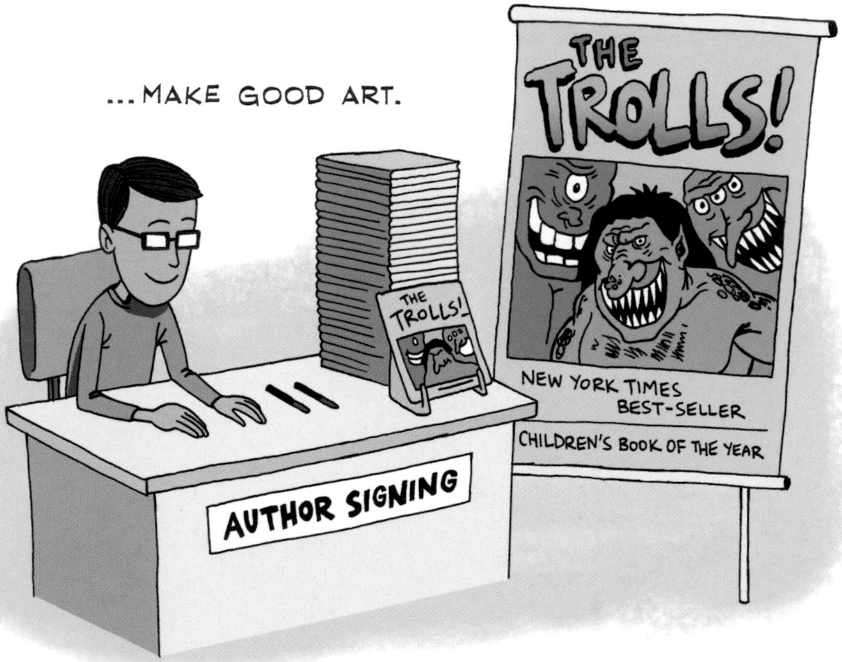
THE TROLLS!
NEW YORK TIMES BEST-SELLER
CHILDREN'S BOOK OF THE YEAR
THE TROLLS!
AUTHOR SIGNING

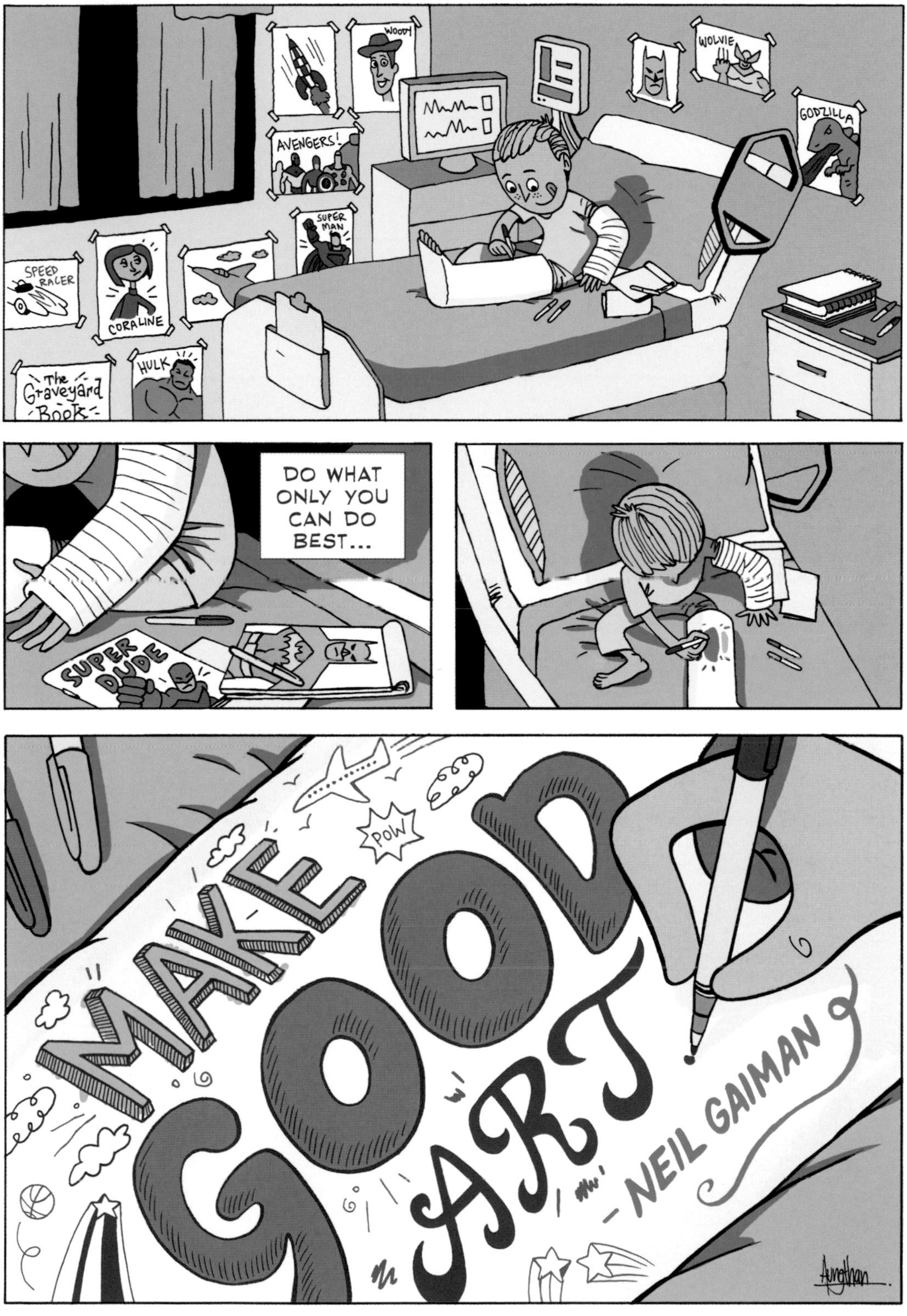
WOODY
WOLVIE
GODZILLA
AVENGERS!
SUPER MAN
SPEED RACER
CORALINE
HULK
The Graveyard Book
DO WHAT ONLY YOU CAN DO BEST...
SUPER DUDE
POW
MAKE GOOD ART.
- NEIL GAIMAN

I KNOW A PLACE WHERE THE SUN NEVER SHINES.

IT'S AT THE BOTTOM OF THE OCEAN.

A CRACK IN THE CRUST THERE EXUDES CHEMICALS AND HEATS THE WATER TO BOILING POINT.

THIS WOULD KILL A HUMAN INSTANTLY.

BUT THERE ARE CREATURES THERE, BACTERIA, THAT THRIVE. THEY EAT THE SULFUR FROM THE VENT, AND EXCRETE SULFURIC ACID.

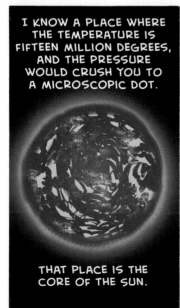

I KNOW A PLACE WHERE THE TEMPERATURE IS FIFTEEN MILLION DEGREES, AND THE PRESSURE WOULD CRUSH YOU TO A MICROSCOPIC DOT.

THAT PLACE IS THE CORE OF THE SUN.

I KNOW A PLACE WHERE THE MAGNETIC FIELDS WOULD RIP YOU APART, ATOM BY ATOM.

THE SURFACE OF A NEUTRON STAR, A MAGNETAR.

I KNOW A PLACE WHERE LIFE BEGAN, BILLIONS OF YEARS AGO.

THAT PLACE IS HERE, THE EARTH.

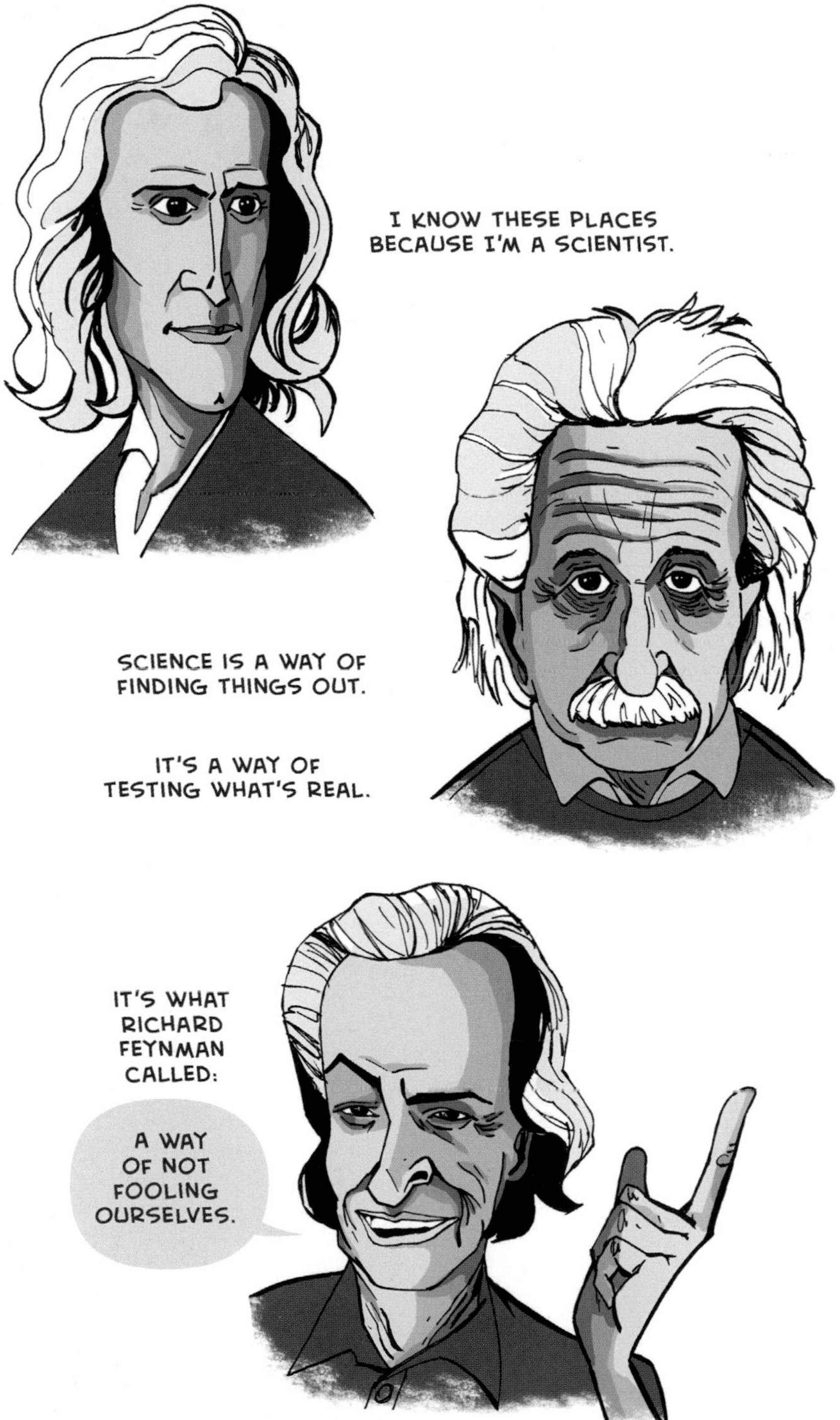
I KNOW THESE PLACES BECAUSE I'M A SCIENTIST.
SCIENCE IS A WAY OF FINDING THINGS OUT.
IT'S A WAY OF TESTING WHAT'S REAL.
IT'S WHAT RICHARD FEYNMAN CALLED:
A WAY OF NOT FOOLING OURSELVES.

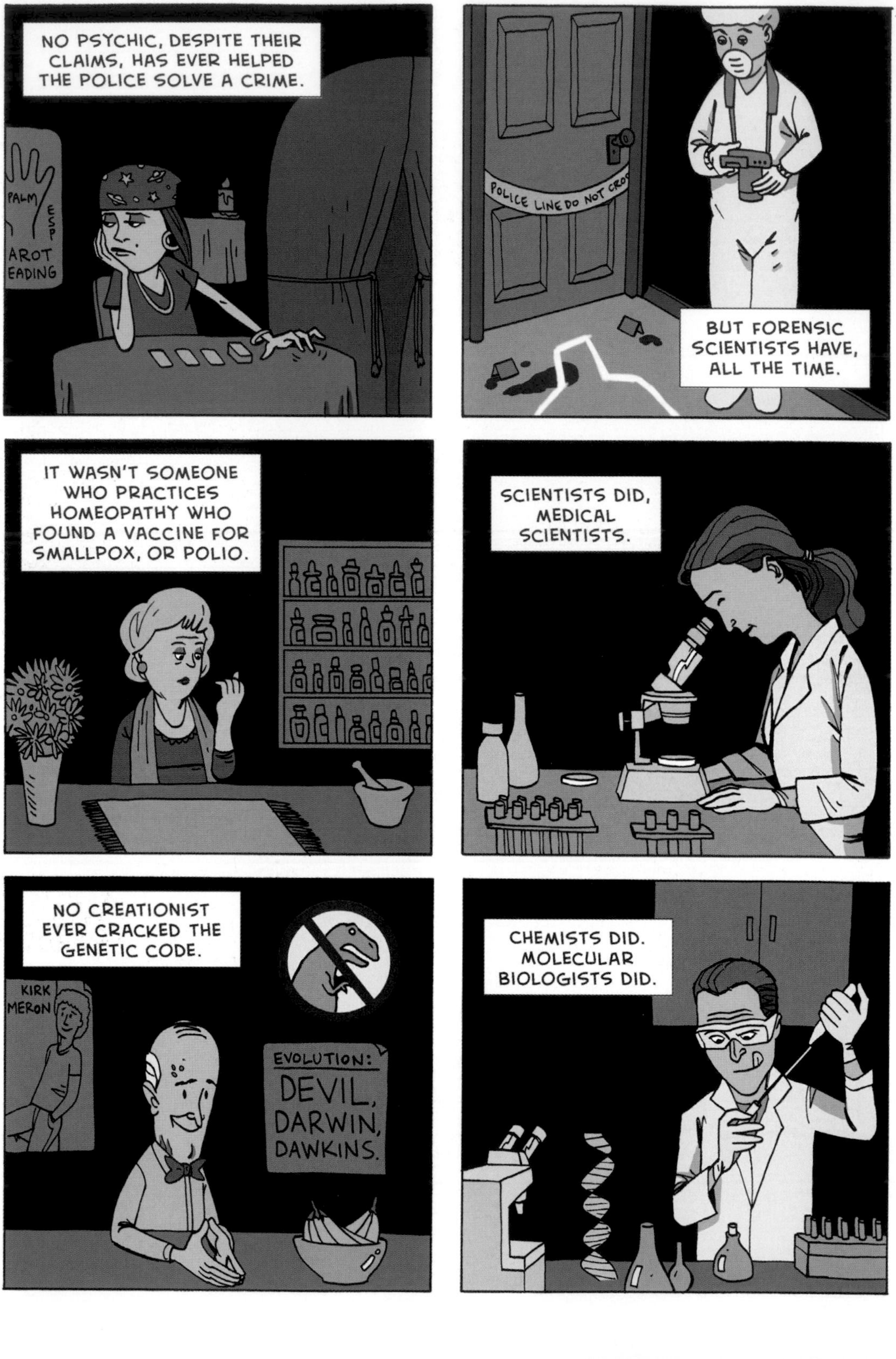
NO PSYCHIC, DESPITE THEIR CLAIMS, HAS EVER HELPED THE POLICE SOLVE A CRIME.
PALM
ESP
AROT EADING
POLICE LINE DO NOT CRO
BUT FORENSIC SCIENTISTS HAVE, ALL THE TIME.
IT WASN'T SOMEONE WHO PRACTICES HOMEOPATHY WHO FOUND A VACCINE FOR SMALLPOX, OR POLIO.
SCIENTISTS DID, MEDICAL SCIENTISTS.
NO CREATIONIST EVER CRACKED THE GENETIC CODE.
KIRK MERON
EVOLUTION: DEVIL, DARWIN, DAWKINS.
CHEMISTS DID. MOLECULAR BIOLOGISTS DID.

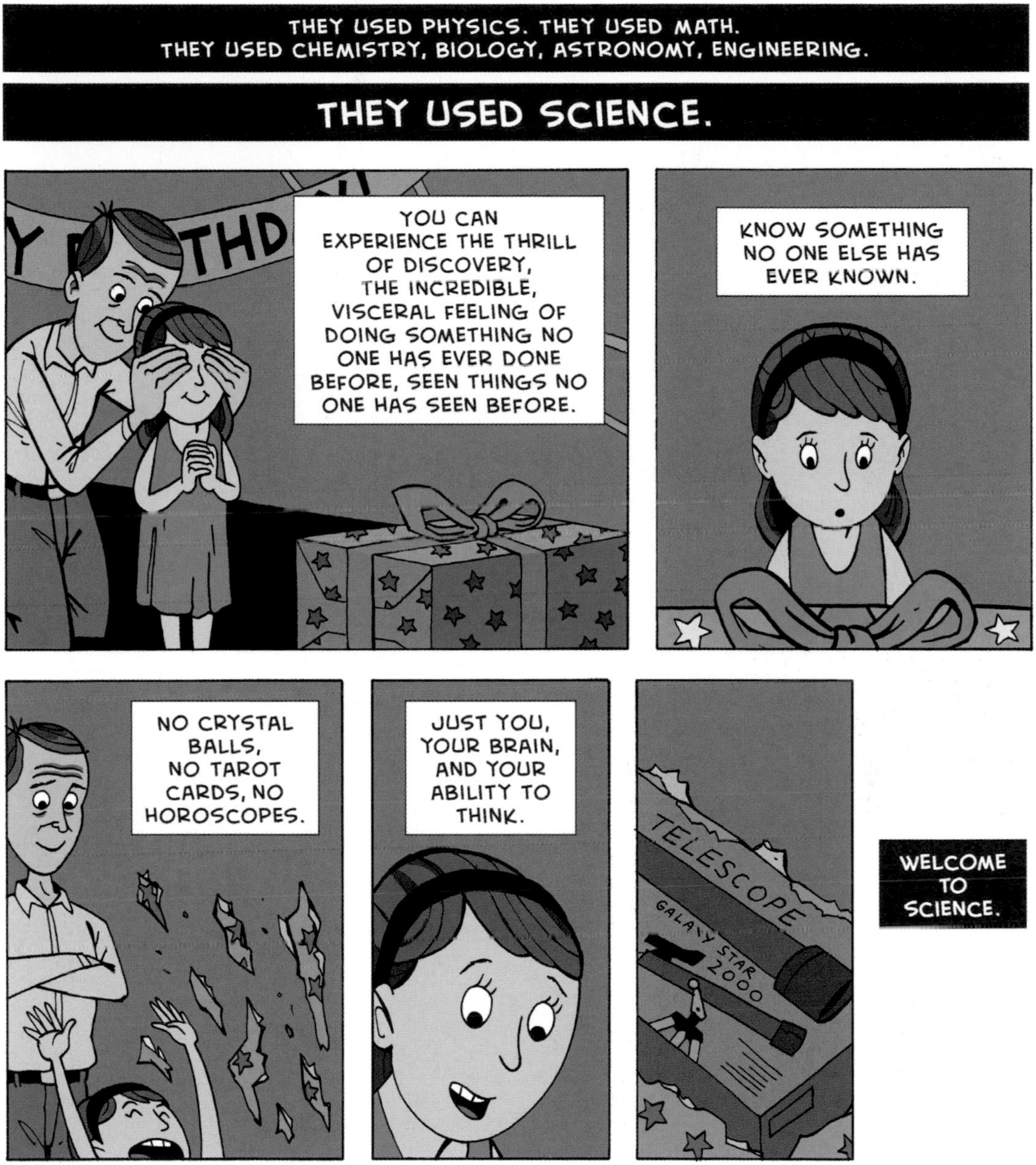
THEY USED PHYSICS. THEY USED MATH.
THEY USED CHEMISTRY, BIOLOGY, ASTRONOMY, ENGINEERING.
THEY USED SCIENCE.
YOU CAN EXPERIENCE THE THRILL OF DISCOVERY, THE INCREDIBLE, VISCERAL FEELING OF DOING SOMETHING NO ONE HAS EVER DONE BEFORE, SEEN THINGS NO ONE HAS SEEN BEFORE.
KNOW SOMETHING NO ONE ELSE HAS EVER KNOWN.
NO CRYSTAL BALLS, NO TAROT CARDS, NO HOROSCOPES.
JUST YOU, YOUR BRAIN, AND YOUR ABILITY TO THINK.
TELESCOPE
GALAXY STAR 2000
WELCOME TO SCIENCE.

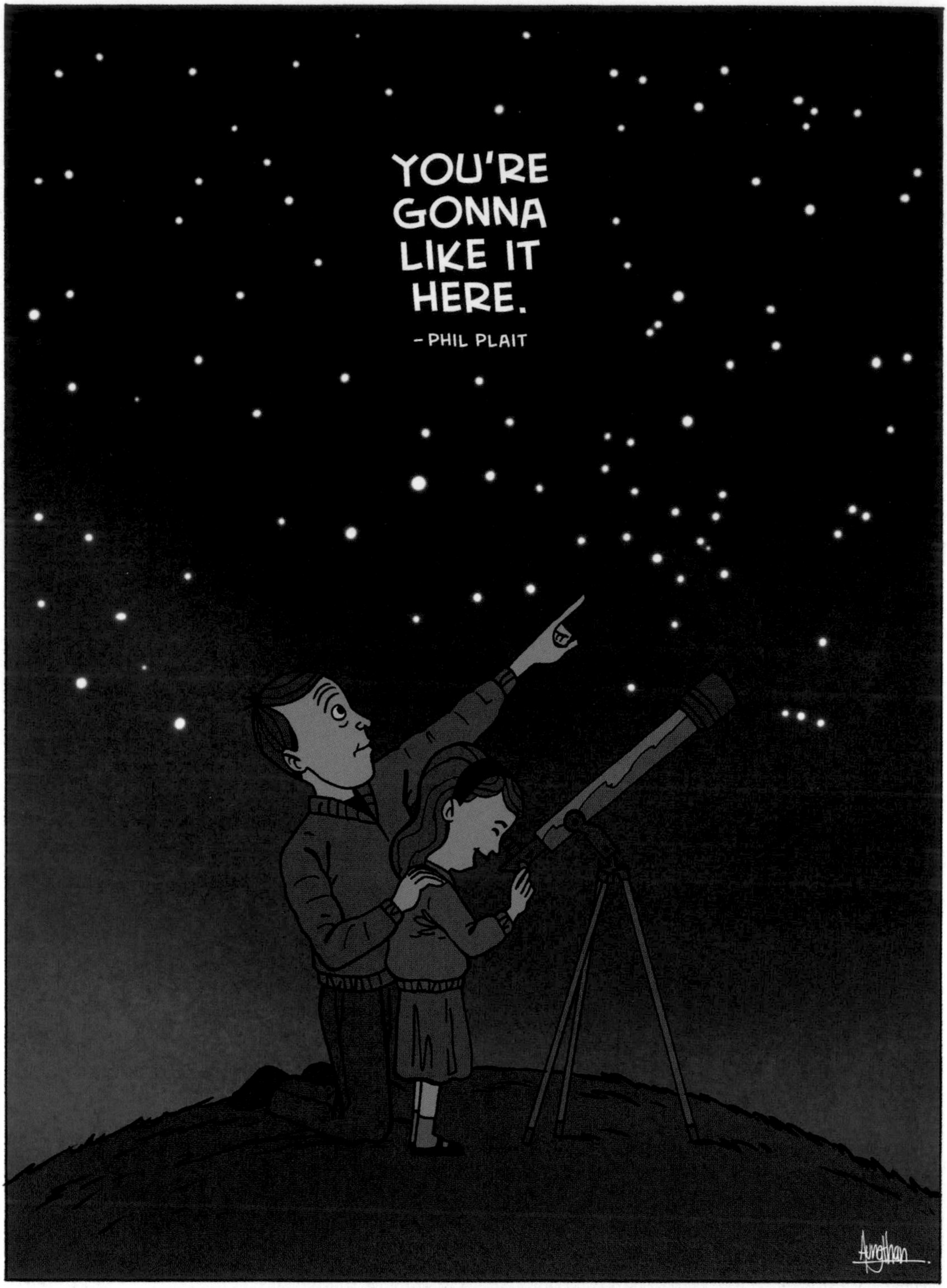
YOU'RE GONNA LIKE IT HERE.
- PHIL PLAIT

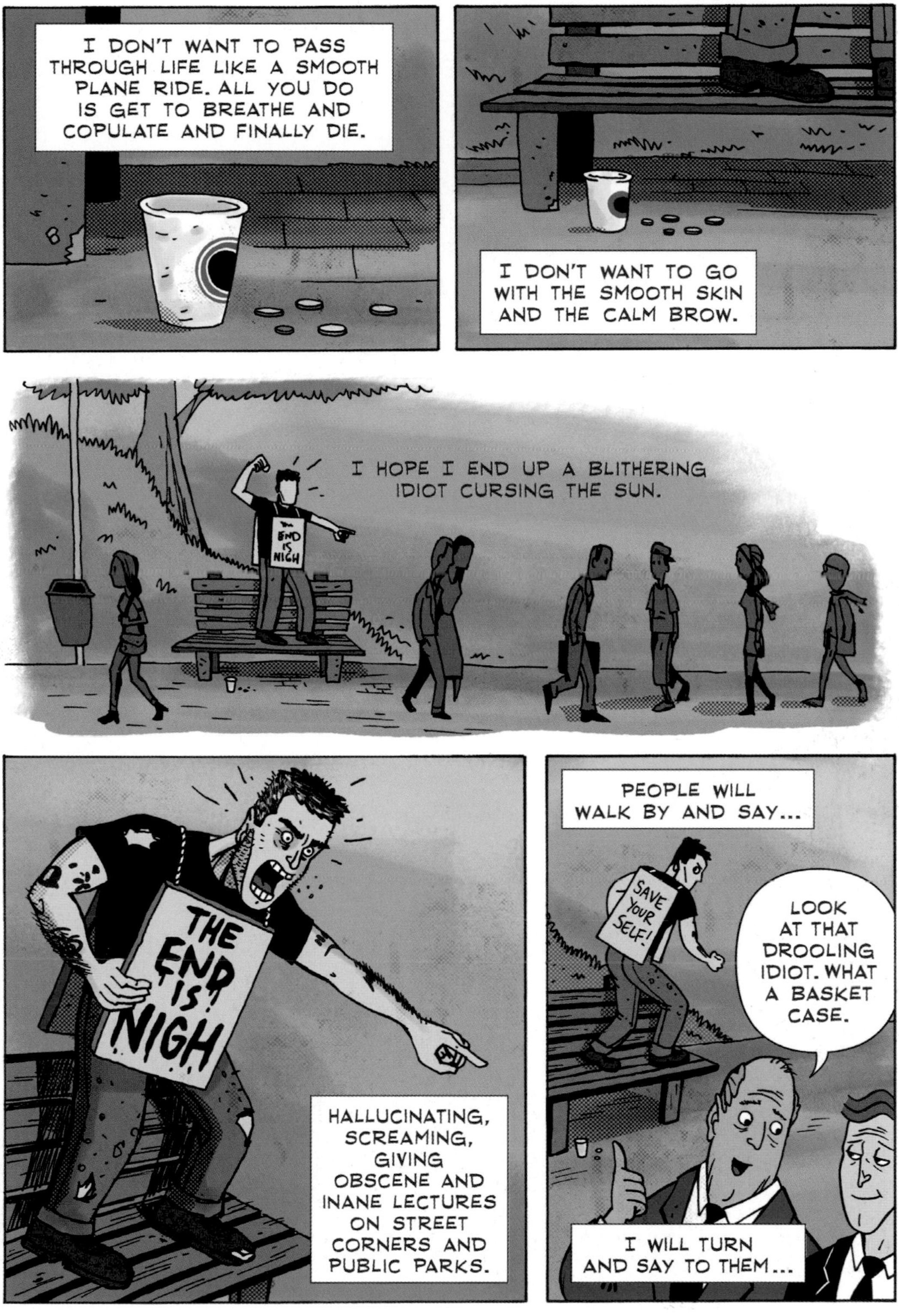
I DON'T WANT TO PASS THROUGH LIFE LIKE A SMOOTH PLANE RIDE. ALL YOU DO IS GET TO BREATHE AND COPULATE AND FINALLY DIE.
I DON'T WANT TO GO WITH THE SMOOTH SKIN AND THE CALM BROW.
I HOPE I END UP A BLITHERING IDIOT CURSING THE SUN.
THE END IS NIGH
THE END IS NIGH
HALLUCINATING, SCREAMING, GIVING OBSCENE AND INANE LECTURES ON STREET CORNERS AND PUBLIC PARKS.
PEOPLE WILL WALK BY AND SAY...
SAVE YOUR SELF!
LOOK AT THAT DROOLING IDIOT. WHAT A BASKET CASE.
I WILL TURN AND SAY TO THEM...

IT IS YOU WHO ARE THE **BASKET CASE!**

FOR EVERY MOMENT YOU HATED YOUR JOB, CURSED YOUR WIFE AND SOLD YOURSELF TO A DREAM THAT YOU DIDN'T EVEN CONCEIVE!

FOR THE TIMES YOUR SOUL SCREAMED YES AND YOU SAID **NO!**

FOR ALL OF THAT. FOR YOUR SELF-TORTURE...

I SEE THE GLOWING EYES OF THE SUN! **THE AIR TALKS TO ME!**

I **AM** AT ALL TIMES!

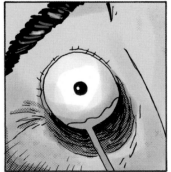

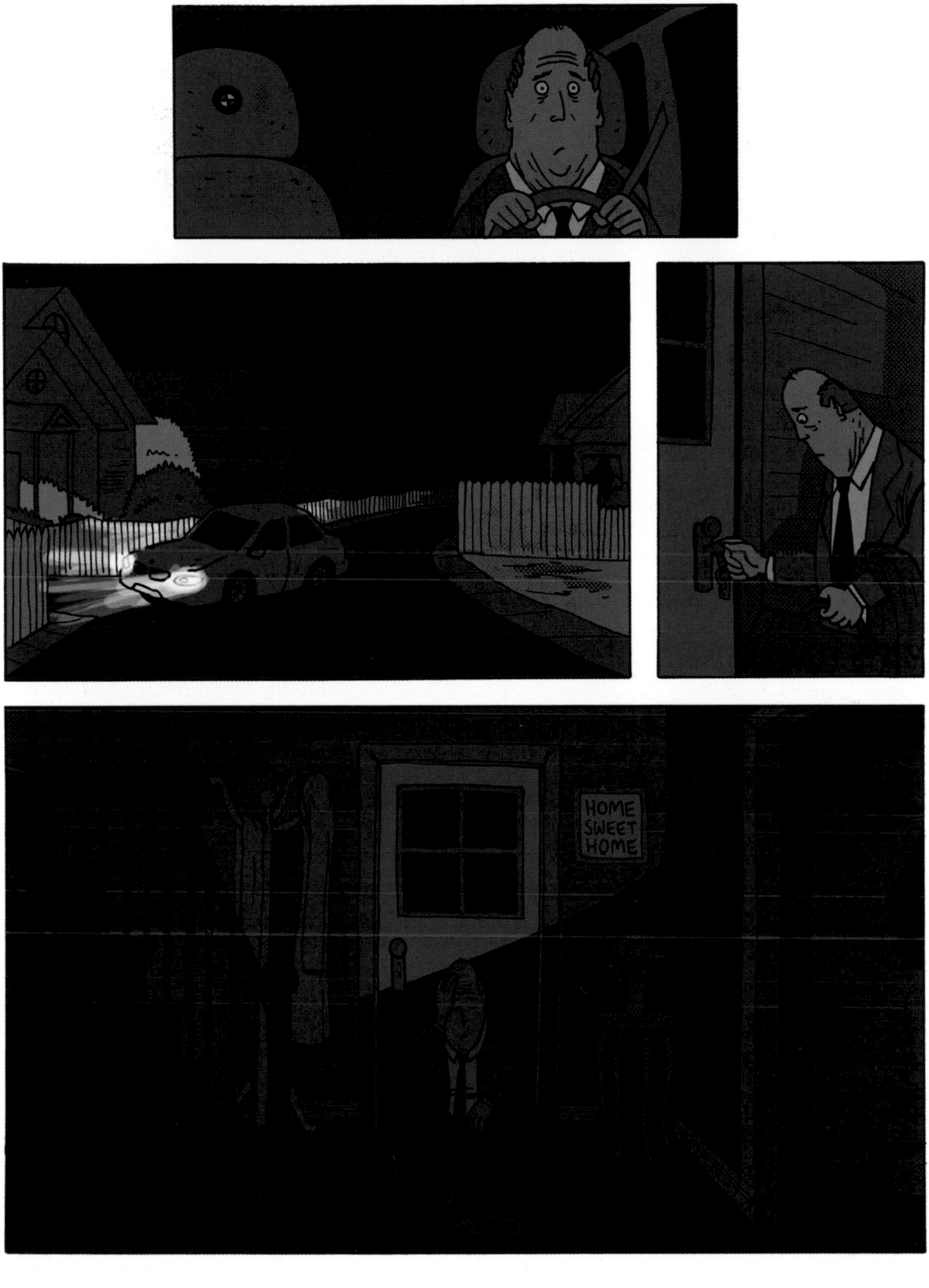
HOME
SWEET
HOME

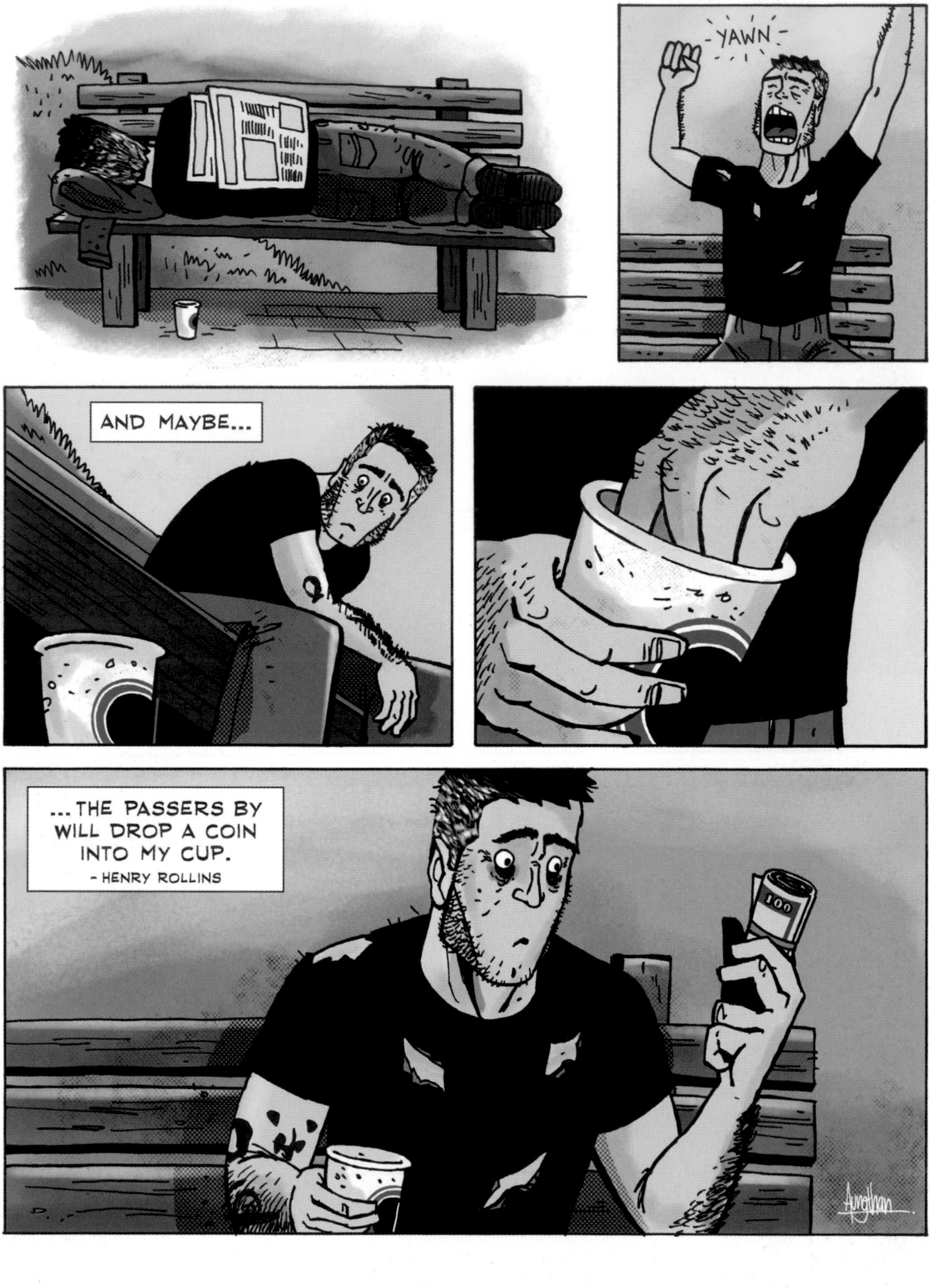
YAWN
AND MAYBE...
...THE PASSERS BY WILL DROP A COIN INTO MY CUP.
- HENRY ROLLINS
100

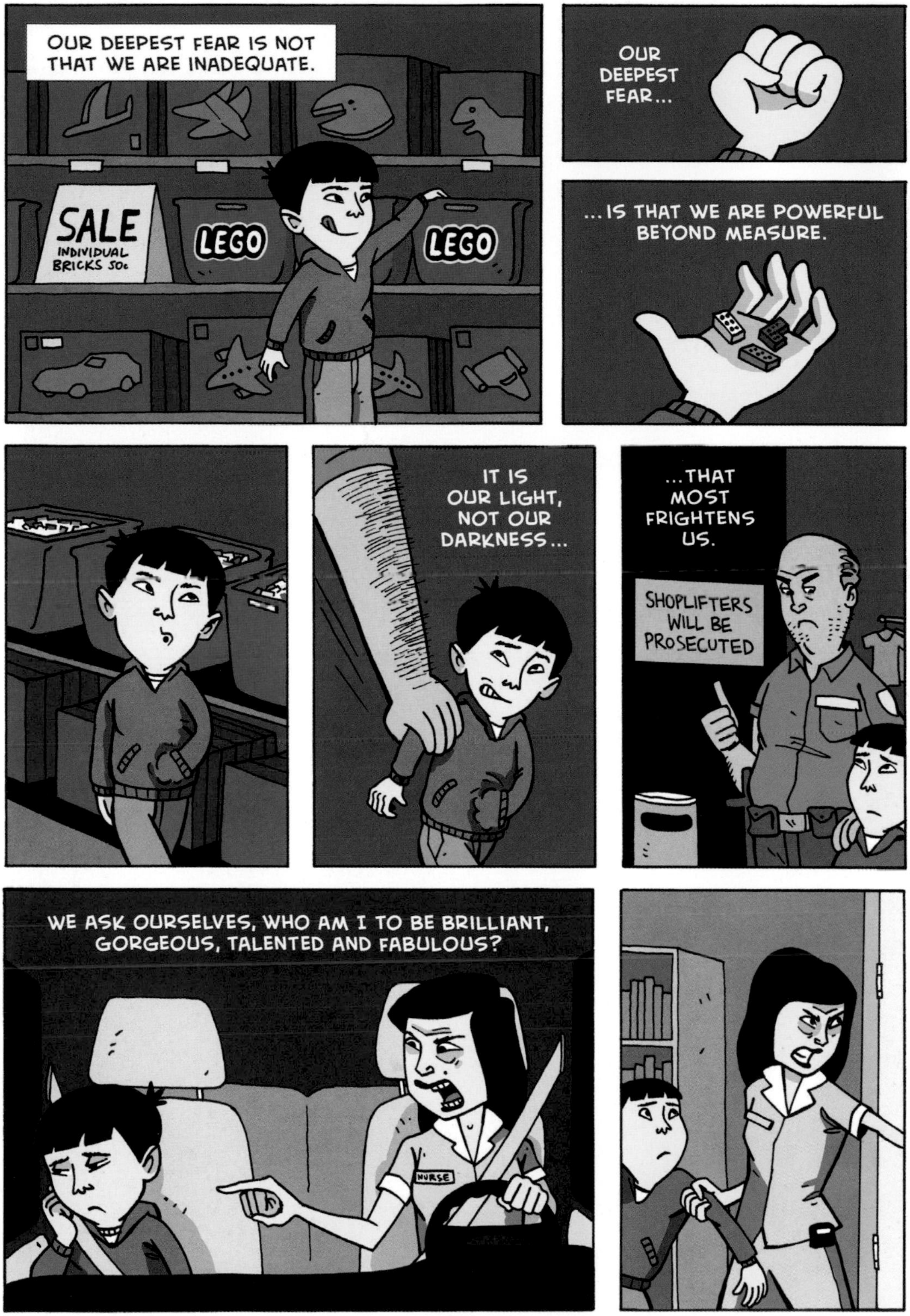
OUR DEEPEST FEAR IS NOT THAT WE ARE INADEQUATE.
SALE
INDIVIDUAL BRICKS 50¢
LEGO
LEGO
OUR DEEPEST FEAR...
...IS THAT WE ARE POWERFUL BEYOND MEASURE.
IT IS OUR LIGHT, NOT OUR DARKNESS...
...THAT MOST FRIGHTENS US.
SHOPLIFTERS WILL BE PROSECUTED
WE ASK OURSELVES, WHO AM I TO BE BRILLIANT, GORGEOUS, TALENTED AND FABULOUS?
NURSE

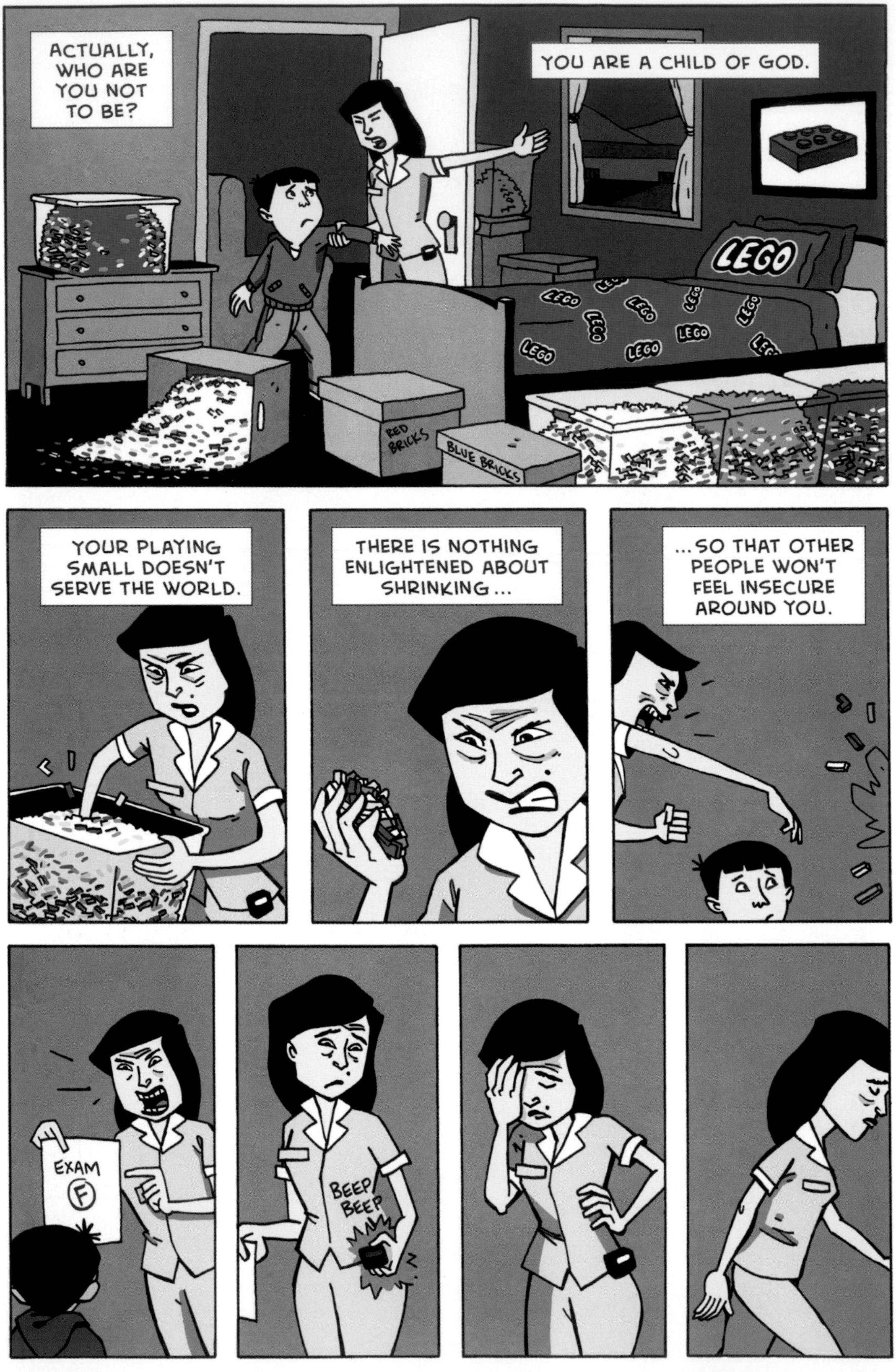
ACTUALLY, WHO ARE YOU NOT TO BE?
YOU ARE A CHILD OF GOD.
LEGO
RED BRICKS
BLUE BRICKS
YOUR PLAYING SMALL DOESN'T SERVE THE WORLD.
THERE IS NOTHING ENLIGHTENED ABOUT SHRINKING ...
... SO THAT OTHER PEOPLE WON'T FEEL INSECURE AROUND YOU.
EXAM
F
BEEP BEEP

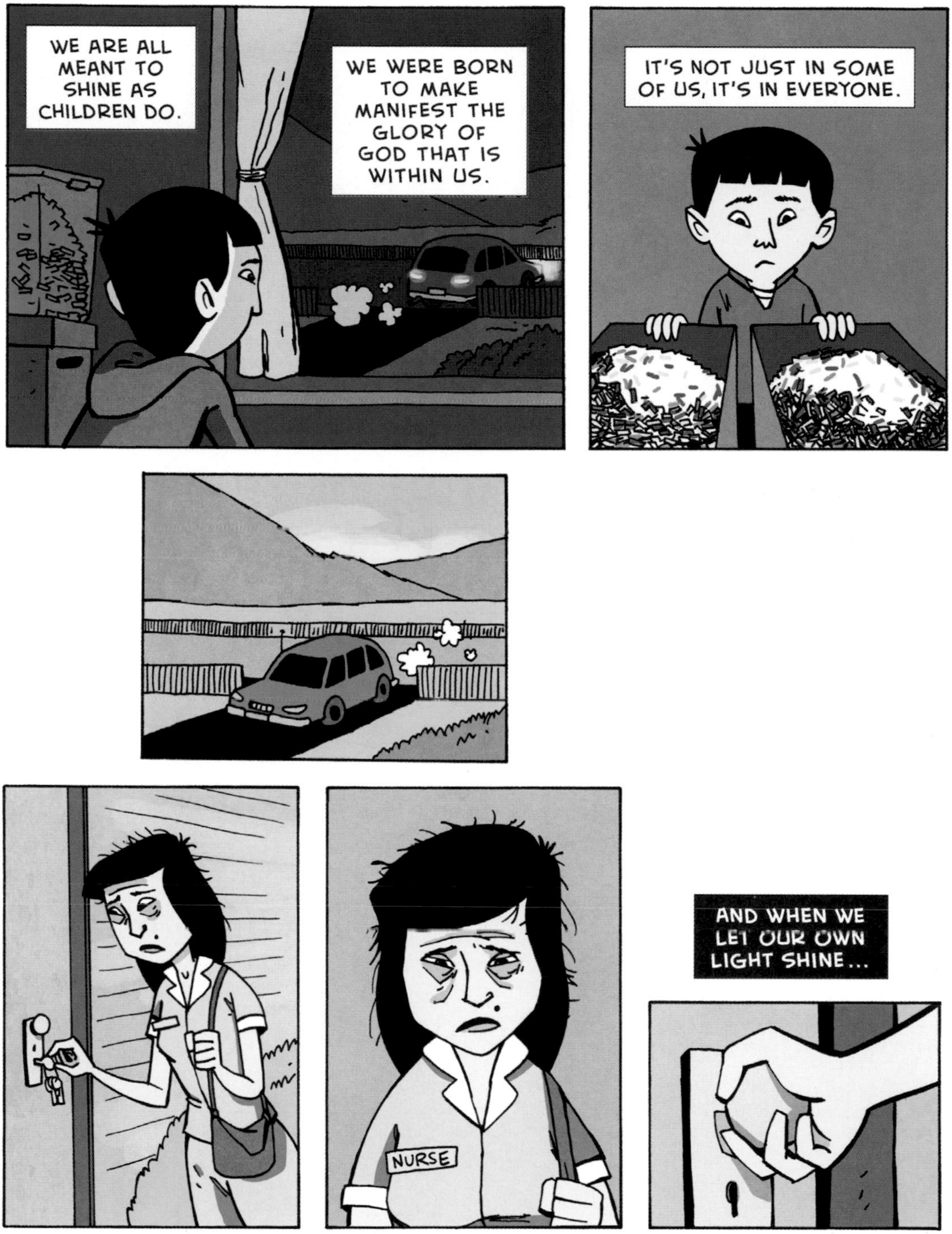
WE ARE ALL MEANT TO SHINE AS CHILDREN DO.
WE WERE BORN TO MAKE MANIFEST THE GLORY OF GOD THAT IS WITHIN US.
IT'S NOT JUST IN SOME OF US, IT'S IN EVERYONE.
NURSE
AND WHEN WE LET OUR OWN LIGHT SHINE...

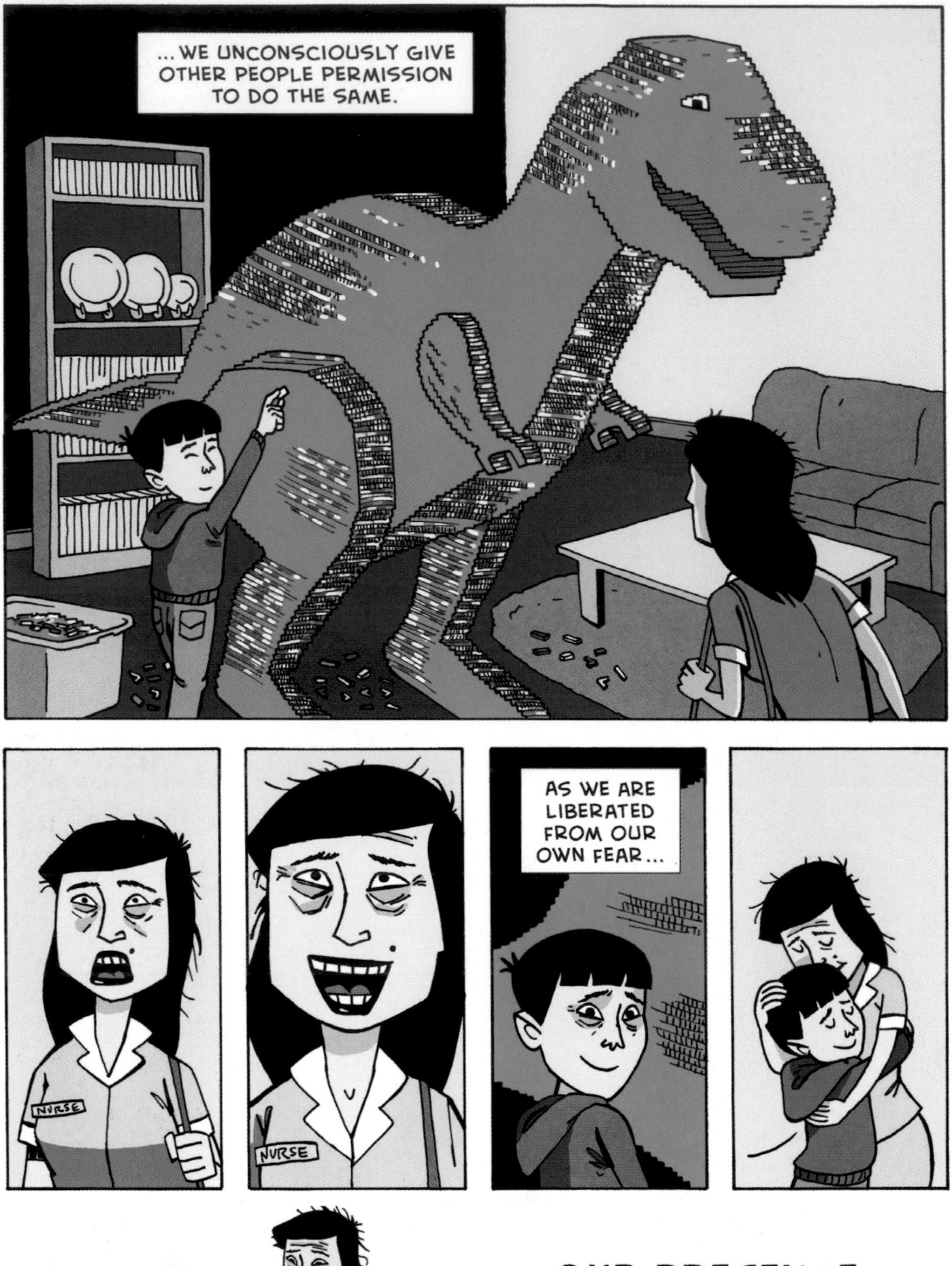
...WE UNCONSCIOUSLY GIVE OTHER PEOPLE PERMISSION TO DO THE SAME.
AS WE ARE LIBERATED FROM OUR OWN FEAR...
NURSE
NURSE

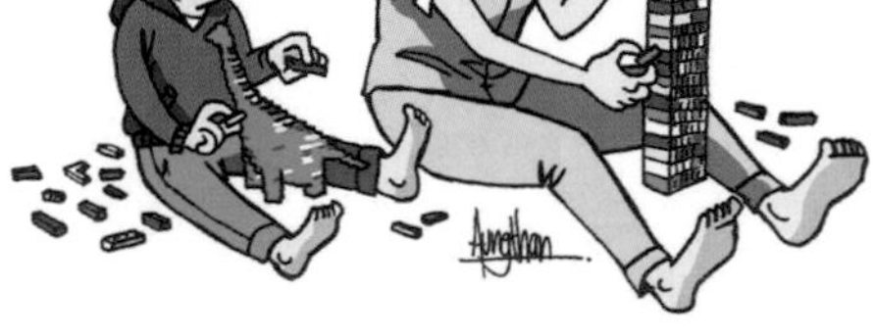

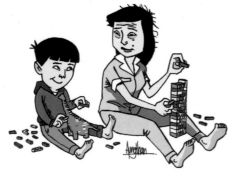

...OUR PRESENCE AUTOMATICALLY LIBERATES OTHERS.

- MARIANNE WILLIAMSON

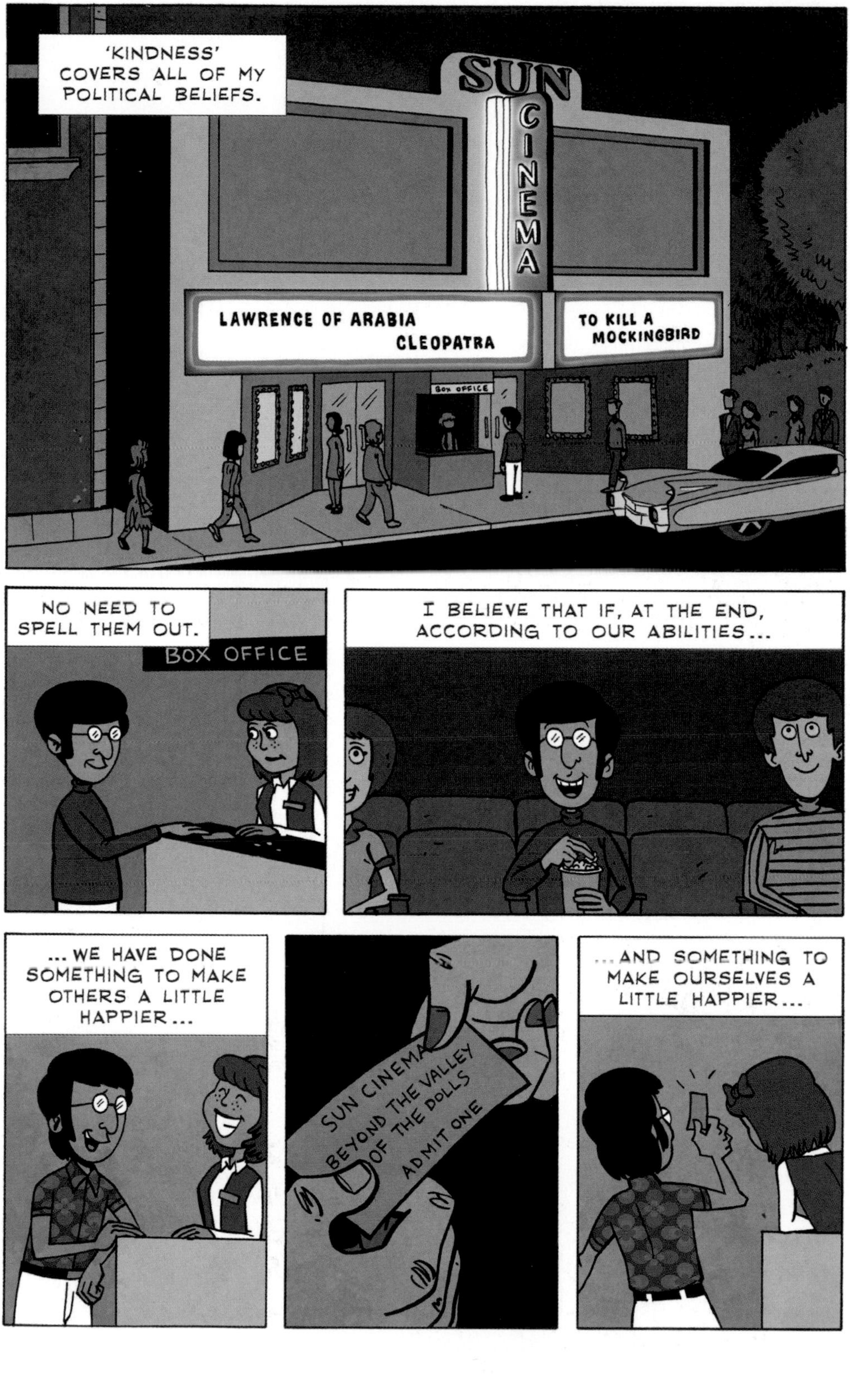
'KINDNESS' COVERS ALL OF MY POLITICAL BELIEFS.
SUN
CINEMA
LAWRENCE OF ARABIA
CLEOPATRA
TO KILL A MOCKINGBIRD
BOX OFFICE
NO NEED TO SPELL THEM OUT.
BOX OFFICE
I BELIEVE THAT IF, AT THE END, ACCORDING TO OUR ABILITIES...
...WE HAVE DONE SOMETHING TO MAKE OTHERS A LITTLE HAPPIER...
SUN CINEMA
BEYOND THE VALLEY OF THE DOLLS
ADMIT ONE
...AND SOMETHING TO MAKE OURSELVES A LITTLE HAPPIER...

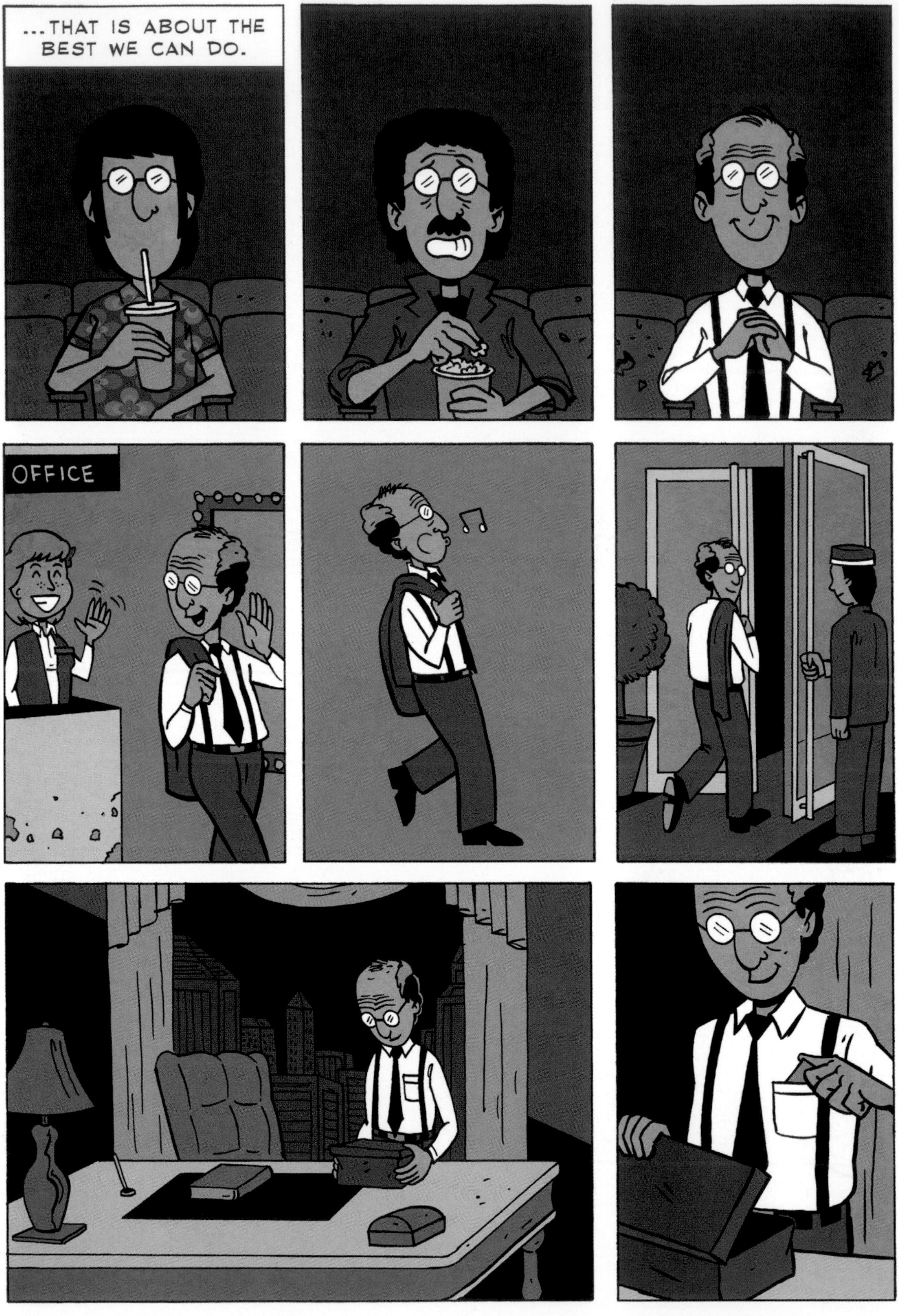
...THAT IS ABOUT THE BEST WE CAN DO.
OFFICE

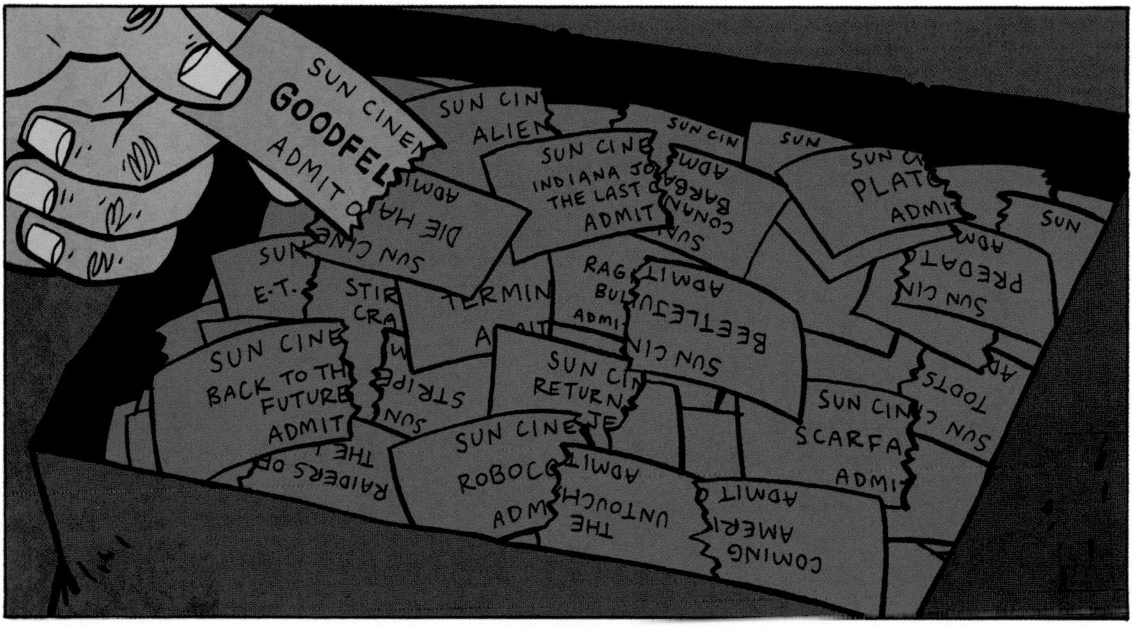
SUN CINE
GOODFEL
ADMIT O
SUN CIN
ALIEN
SUN CINE
INDIANA JO
THE LAST C
ADMIT
DIE HA
ADMI
SUN CINE
BARBA
CONAN
ADM
PLAT
ADMI
SUN
E.T.
STIR
CRA
TERMIN
RAG
BU
ADMI
BEETLEJU
ADMIT
SUN CI
PREDAT
ADM
SUN CINE
BACK TO TH
FUTURE
ADMIT
STRIPE
SUN CI
RETURN
SUN CIN
SCARFA
ADMI
TOOTS
SUN CINE
ROBOC
ADM
THE
UNTOUCH
ADMIT
RAIDERS OF
COMING
AMERI
ADMIT

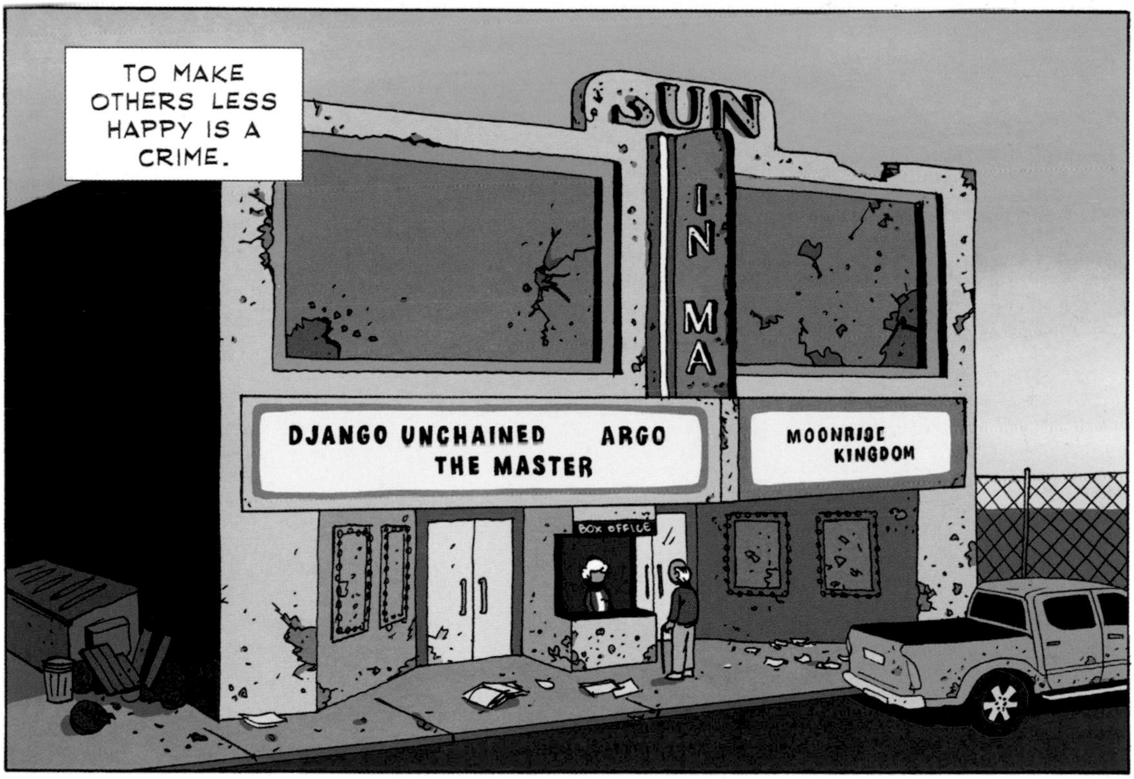
TO MAKE OTHERS LESS HAPPY IS A CRIME.
SUN
IN MA
DJANGO UNCHAINED ARGO
THE MASTER
MOONRISE KINGDOM
BOX OFFICE

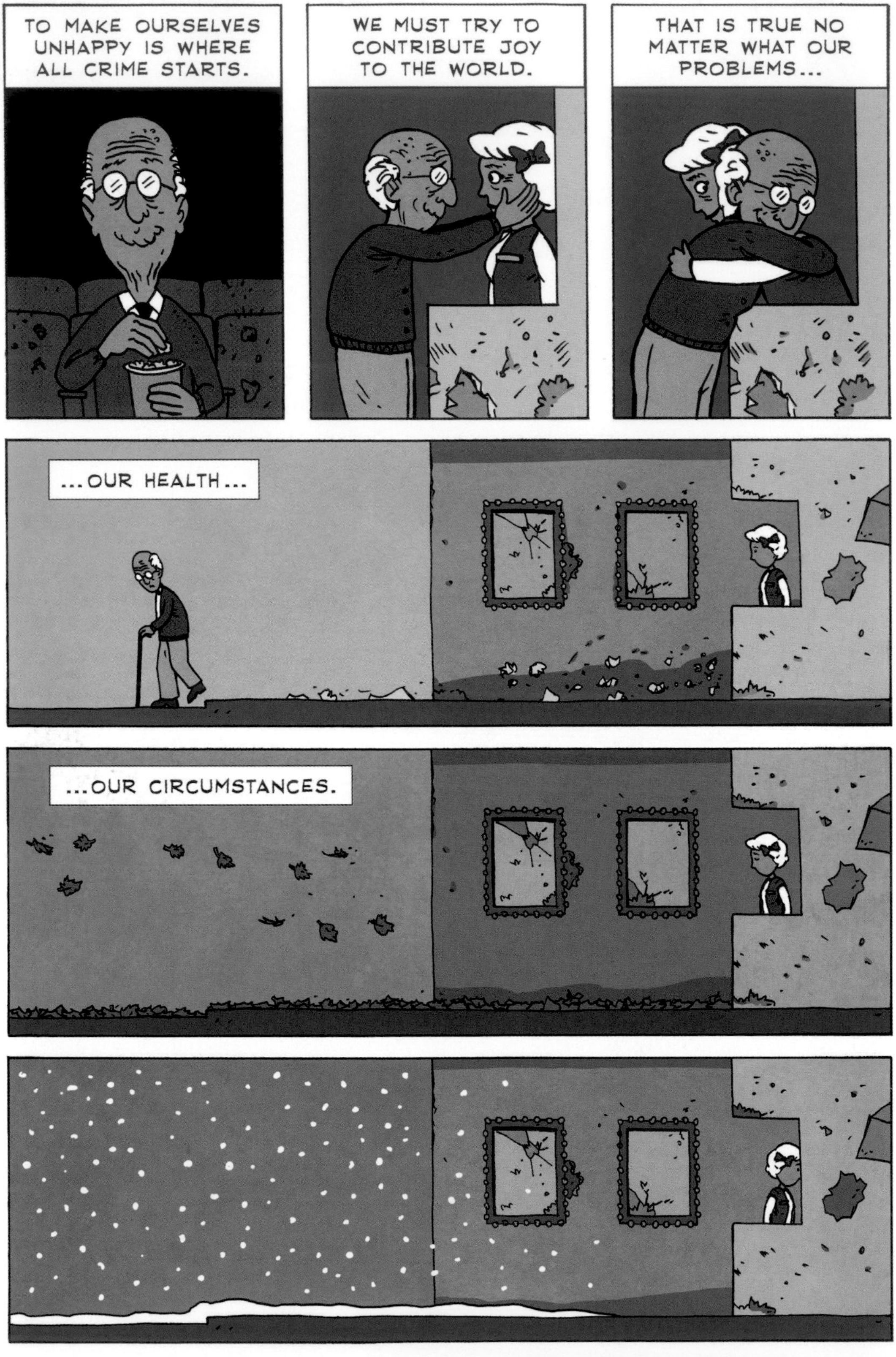
TO MAKE OURSELVES UNHAPPY IS WHERE ALL CRIME STARTS.
WE MUST TRY TO CONTRIBUTE JOY TO THE WORLD.
THAT IS TRUE NO MATTER WHAT OUR PROBLEMS...
...OUR HEALTH...
...OUR CIRCUMSTANCES.

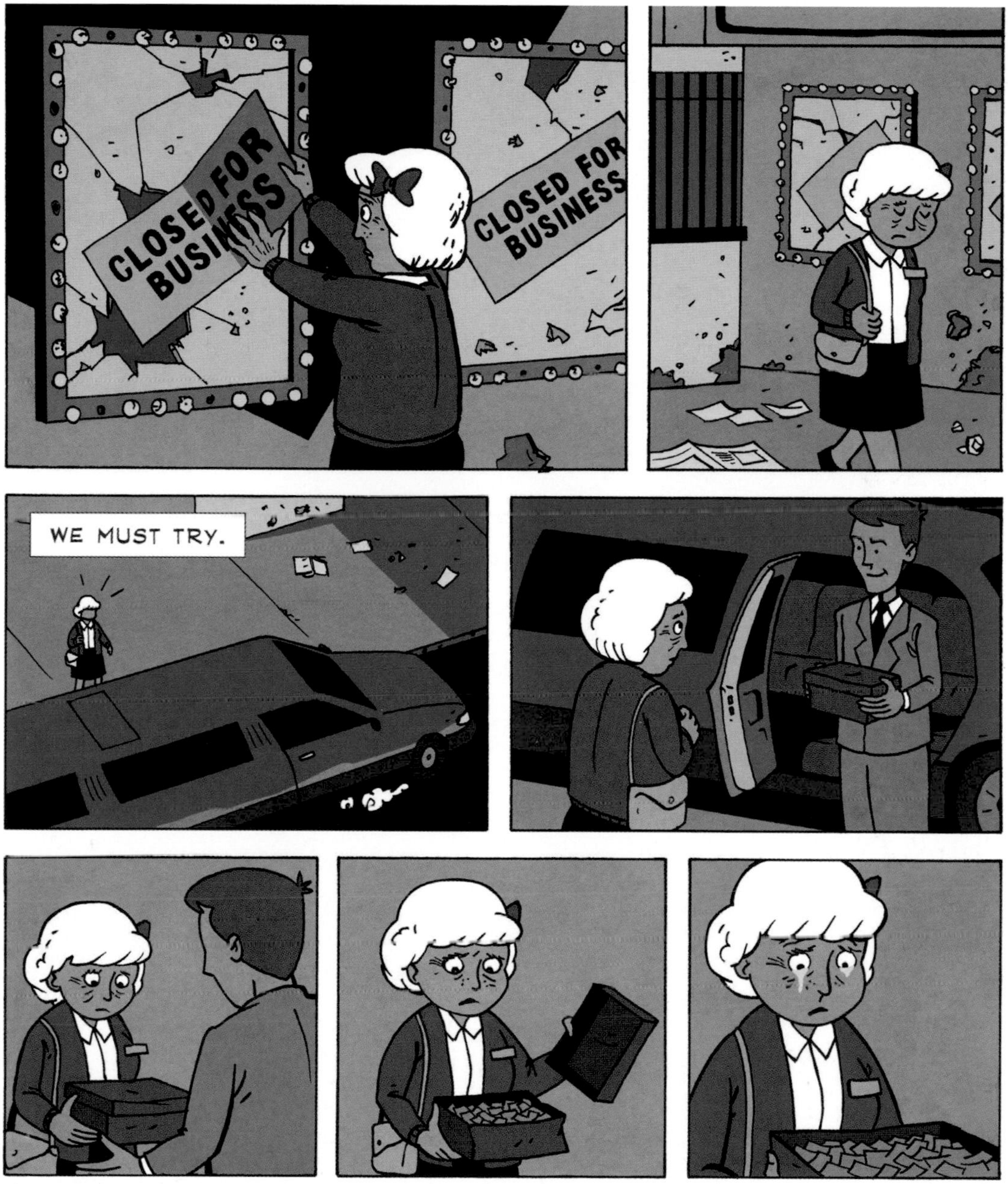

CLOSED FOR BUSINESS
CLOSED FOR BUSINESS
WE MUST TRY.

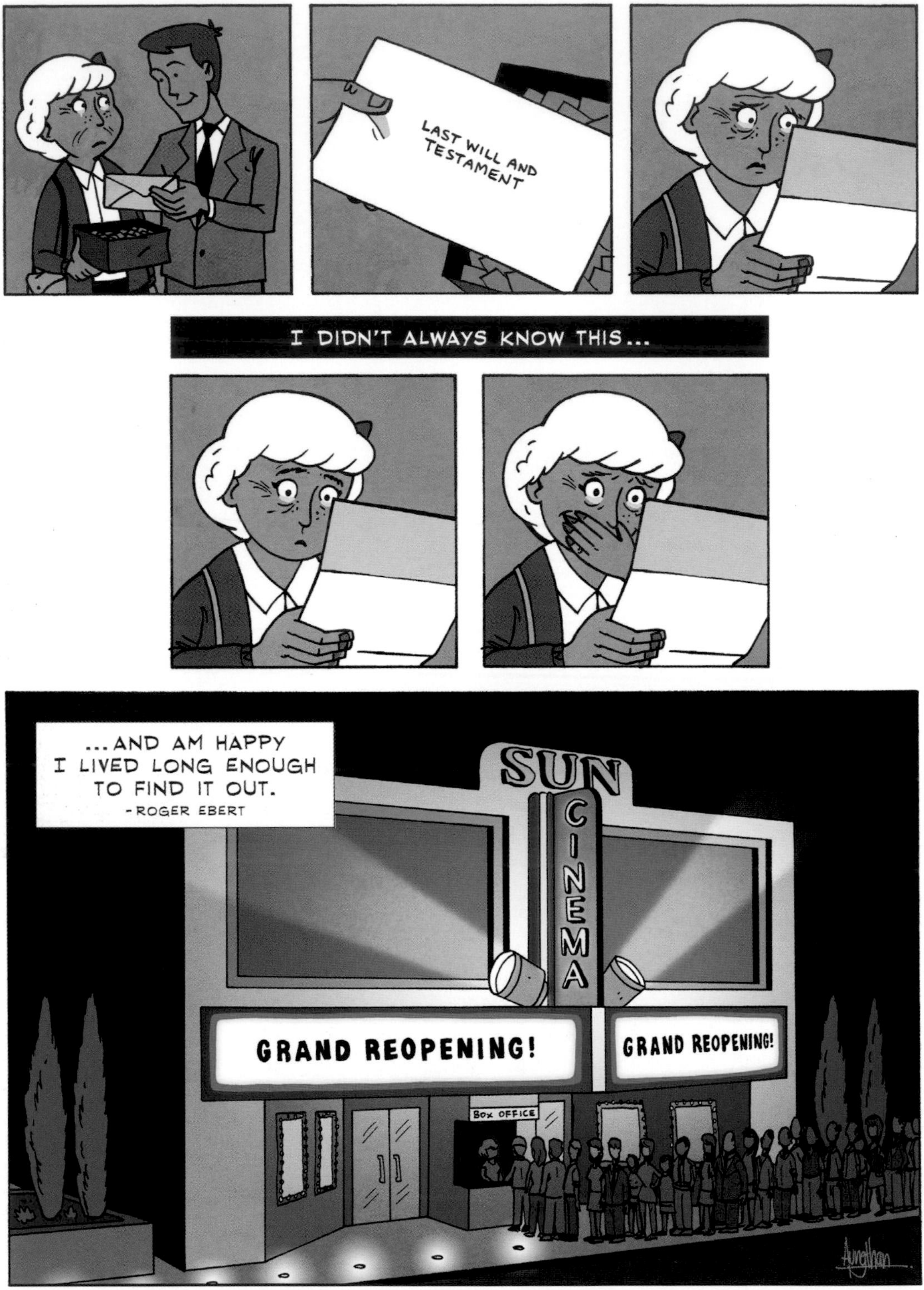
LAST WILL AND TESTAMENT
I DIDN'T ALWAYS KNOW THIS...
...AND AM HAPPY I LIVED LONG ENOUGH TO FIND IT OUT.
-ROGER EBERT
SUN
CINEMA
GRAND REOPENING!
GRAND REOPENING!
BOX OFFICE

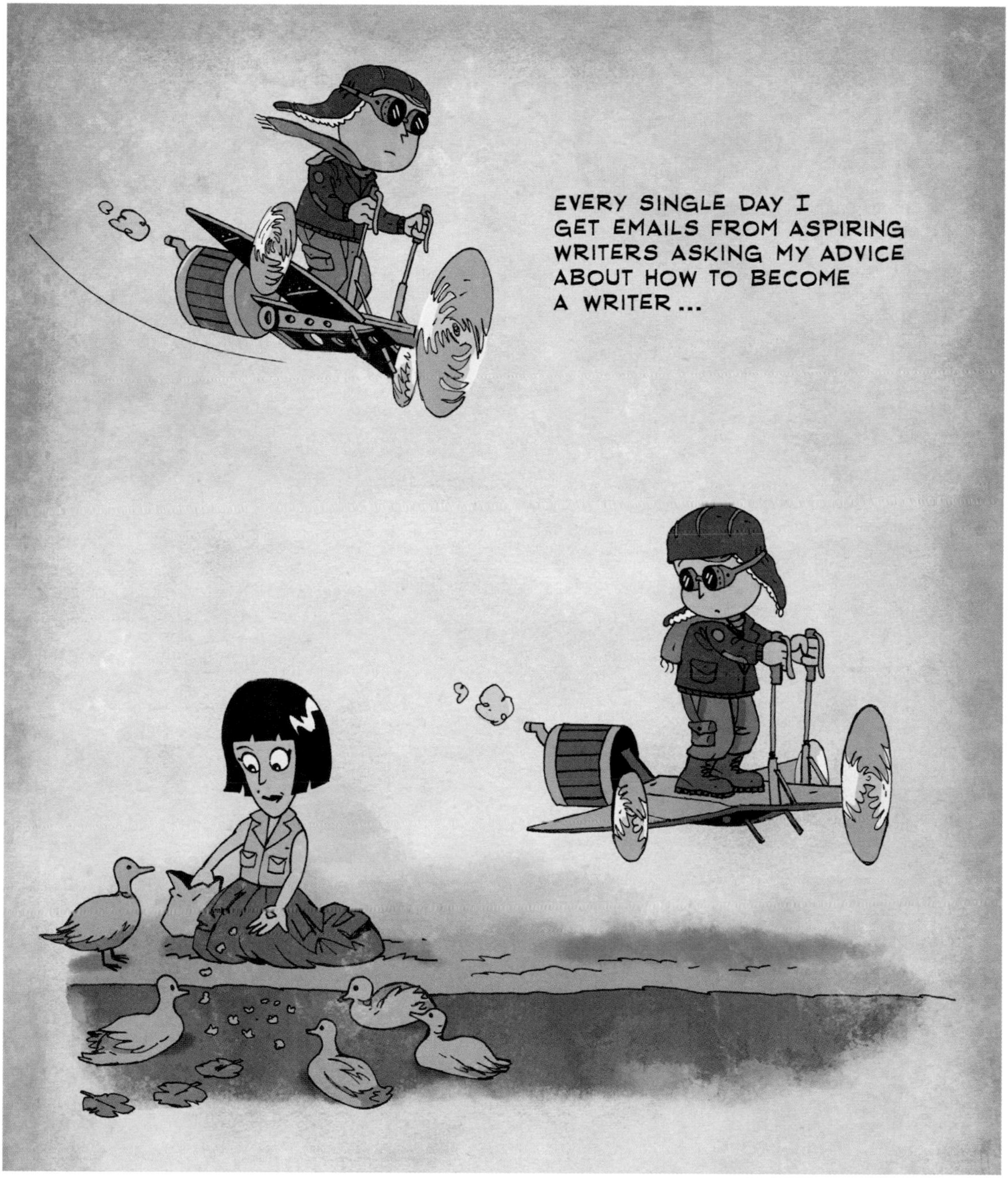
EVERY SINGLE DAY I GET EMAILS FROM ASPIRING WRITERS ASKING MY ADVICE ABOUT HOW TO BECOME A WRITER...

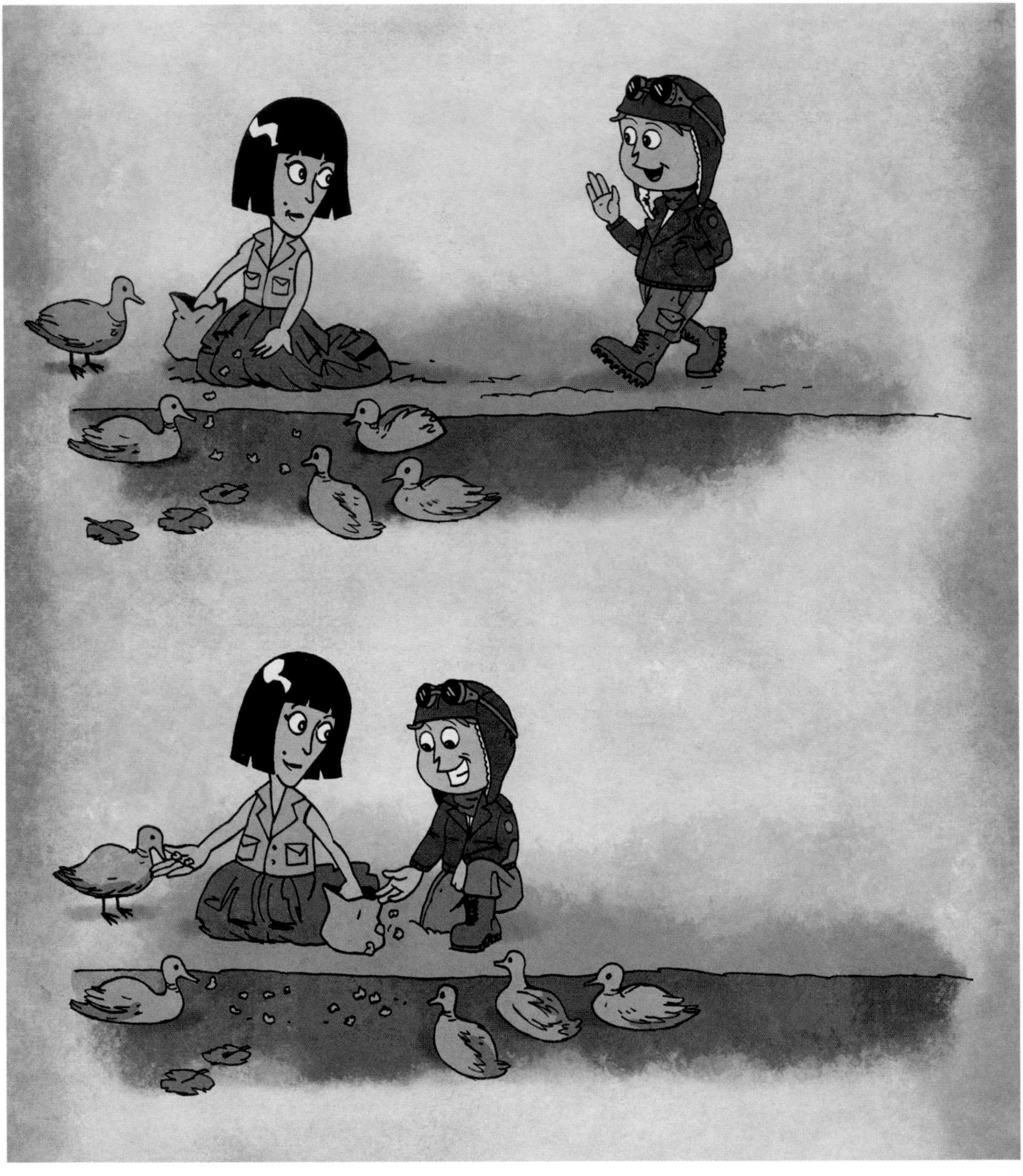

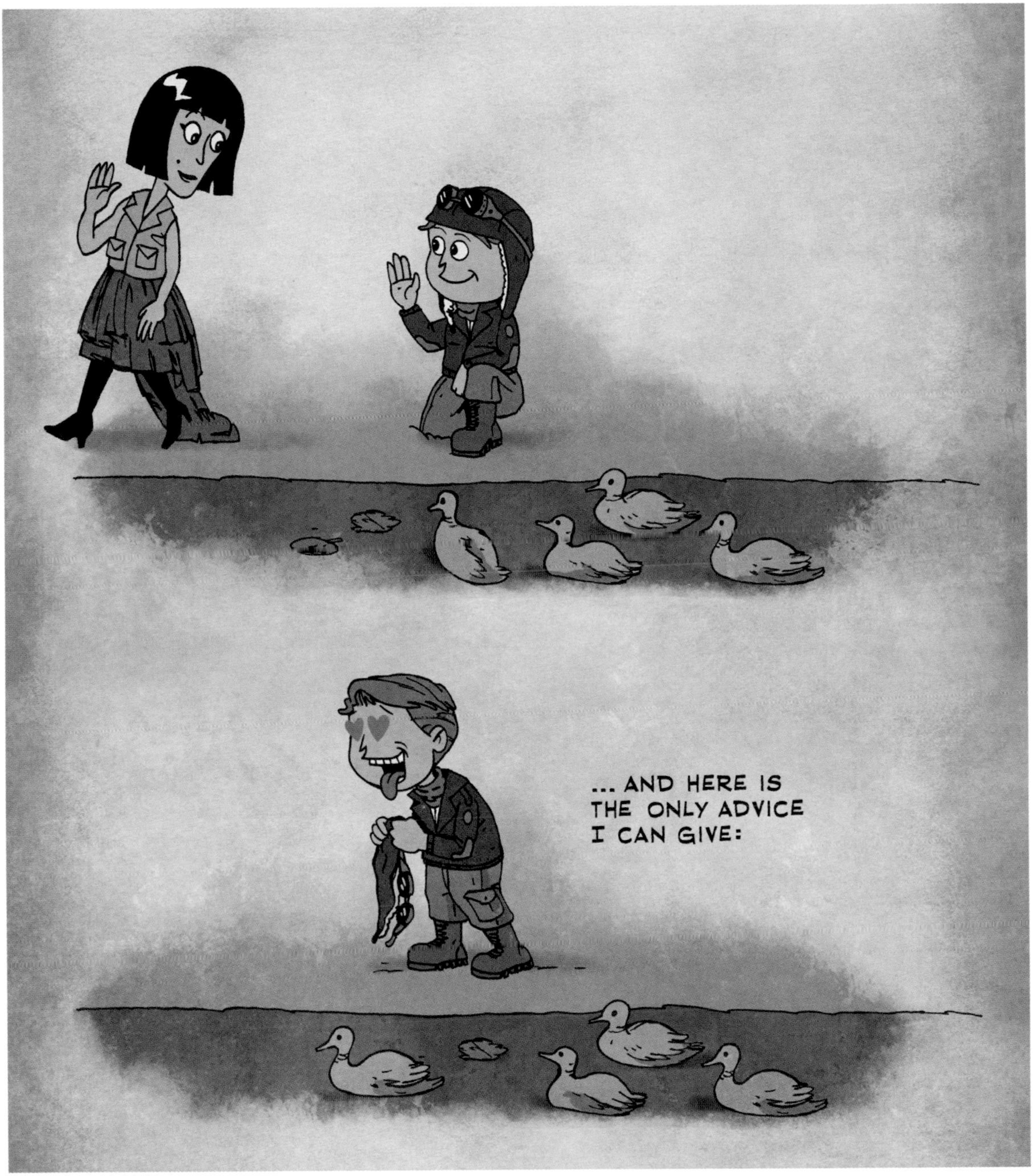
... AND HERE IS
THE ONLY ADVICE
I CAN GIVE:

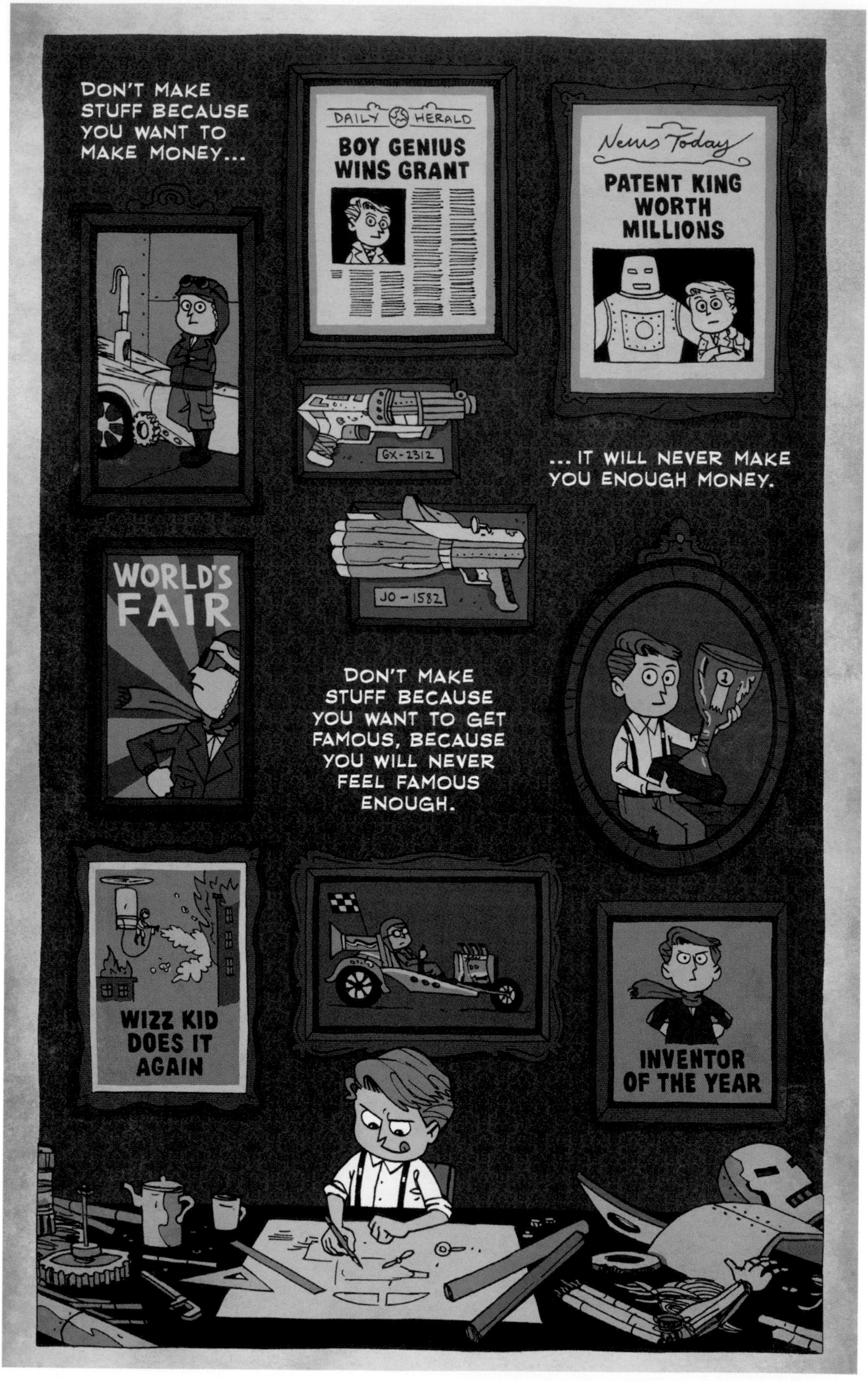
DON'T MAKE STUFF BECAUSE YOU WANT TO MAKE MONEY...
DAILY HERALD
BOY GENIUS WINS GRANT
News Today
PATENT KING WORTH MILLIONS
GX-2312
... IT WILL NEVER MAKE YOU ENOUGH MONEY.
JO-1582
WORLD'S FAIR
DON'T MAKE STUFF BECAUSE YOU WANT TO GET FAMOUS, BECAUSE YOU WILL NEVER FEEL FAMOUS ENOUGH.
WIZZ KID DOES IT AGAIN
INVENTOR OF THE YEAR

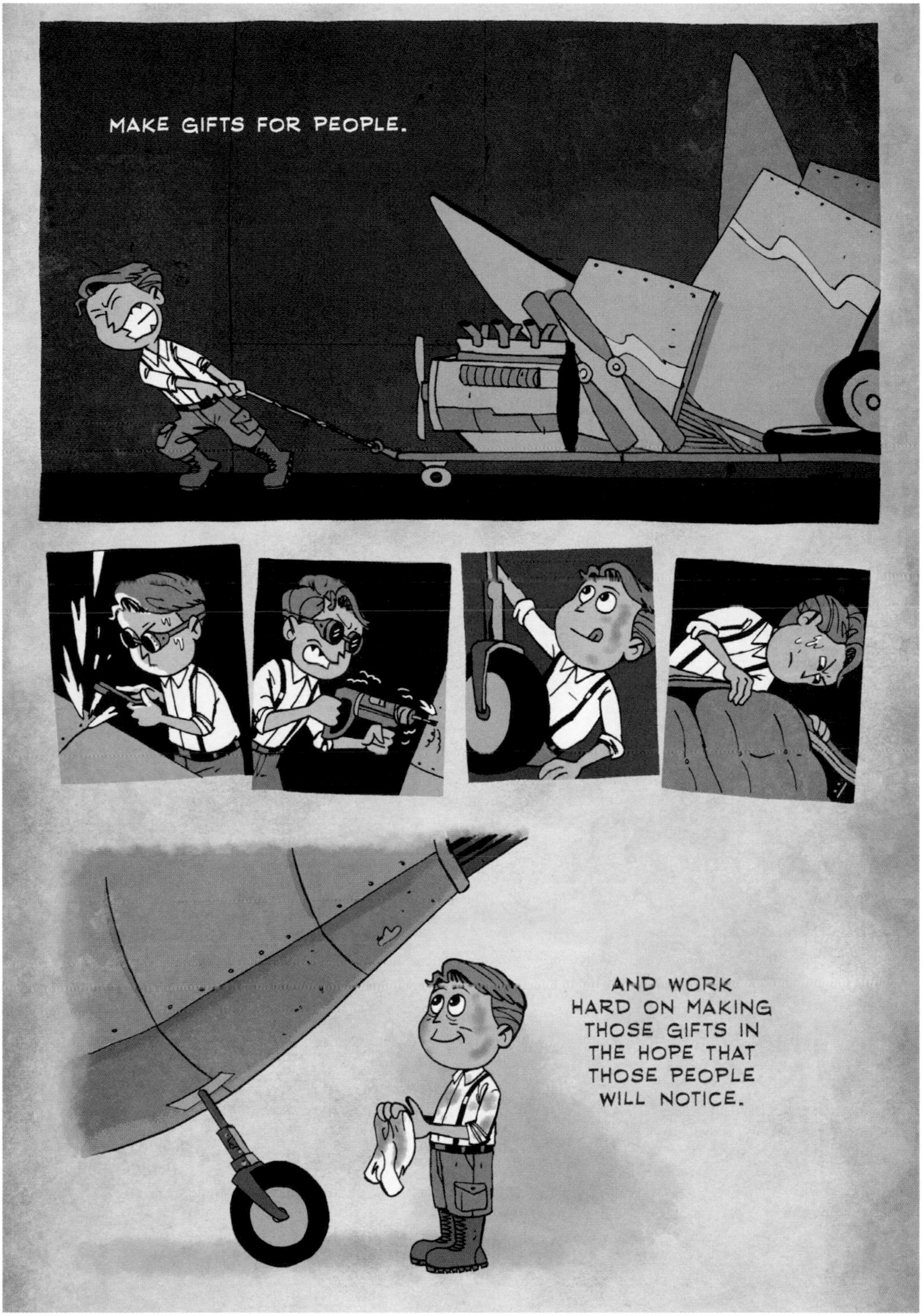
MAKE GIFTS FOR PEOPLE.
AND WORK HARD ON MAKING THOSE GIFTS IN THE HOPE THAT THOSE PEOPLE WILL NOTICE.

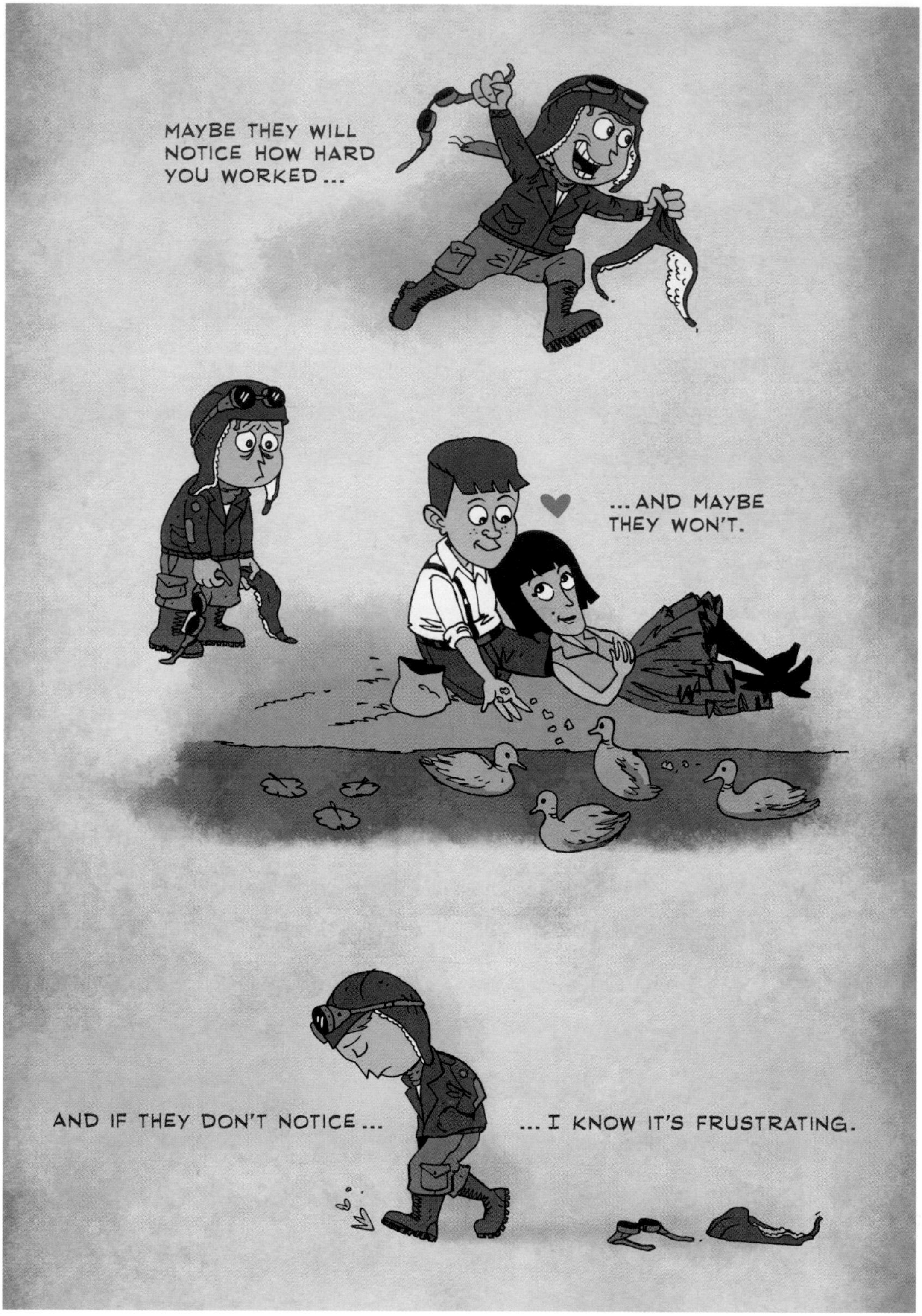

MAYBE THEY WILL NOTICE HOW HARD YOU WORKED...
...AND MAYBE THEY WON'T.
AND IF THEY DON'T NOTICE...
...I KNOW IT'S FRUSTRATING.

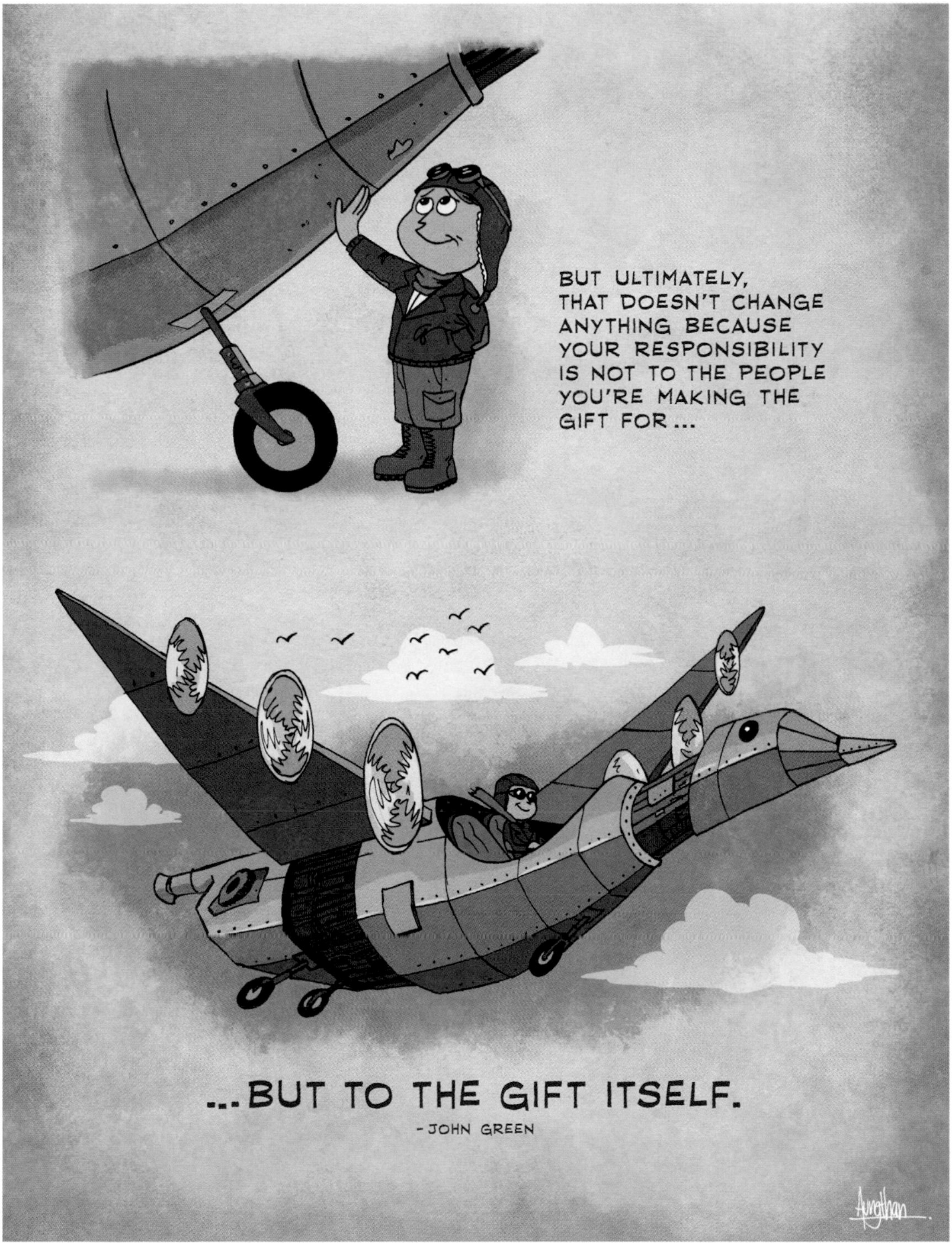
BUT ULTIMATELY, THAT DOESN'T CHANGE ANYTHING BECAUSE YOUR RESPONSIBILITY IS NOT TO THE PEOPLE YOU'RE MAKING THE GIFT FOR...
...BUT TO THE GIFT ITSELF.
-JOHN GREEN

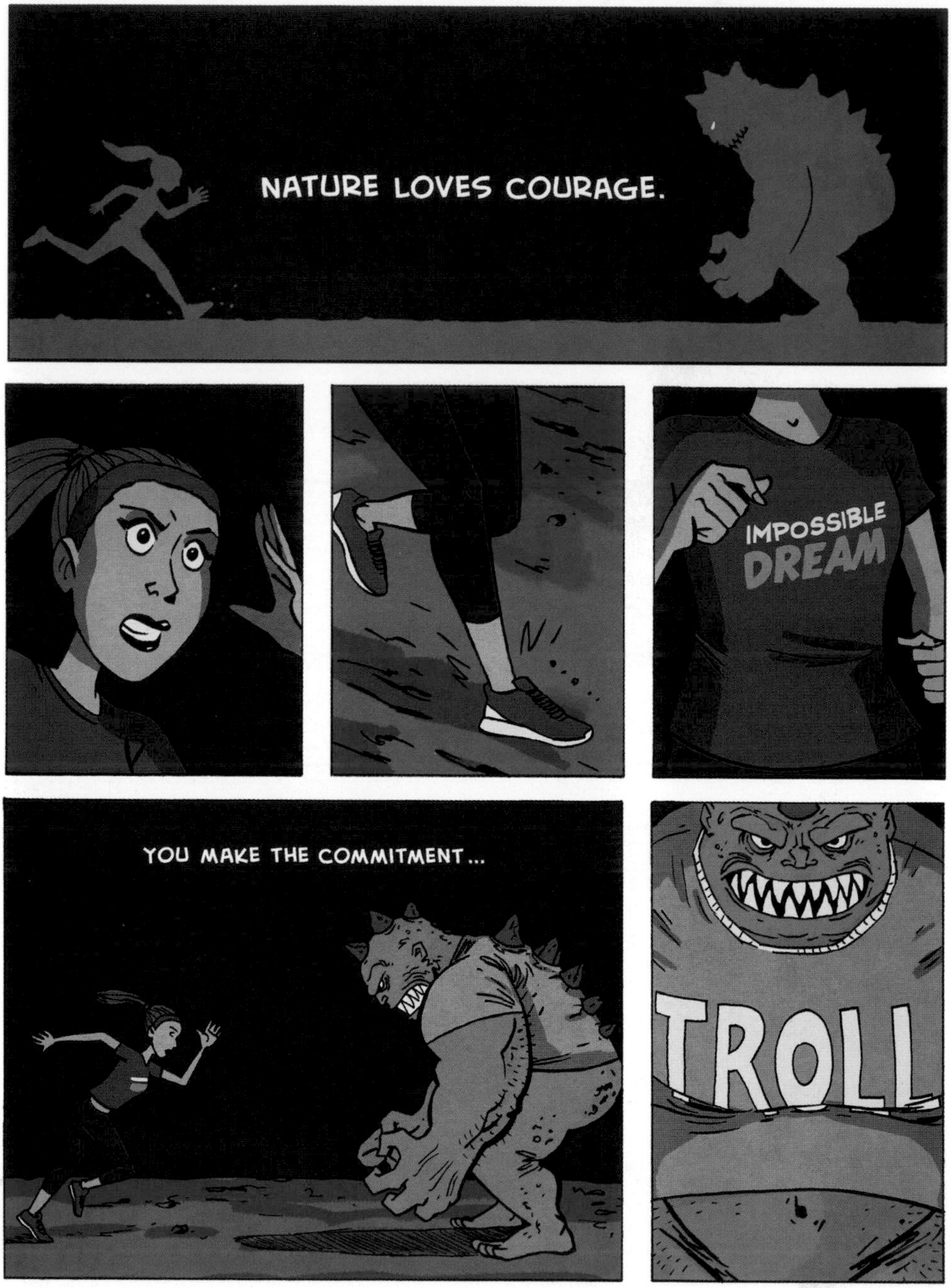
NATURE LOVES COURAGE.
IMPOSSIBLE DREAM
YOU MAKE THE COMMITMENT...
TROLL

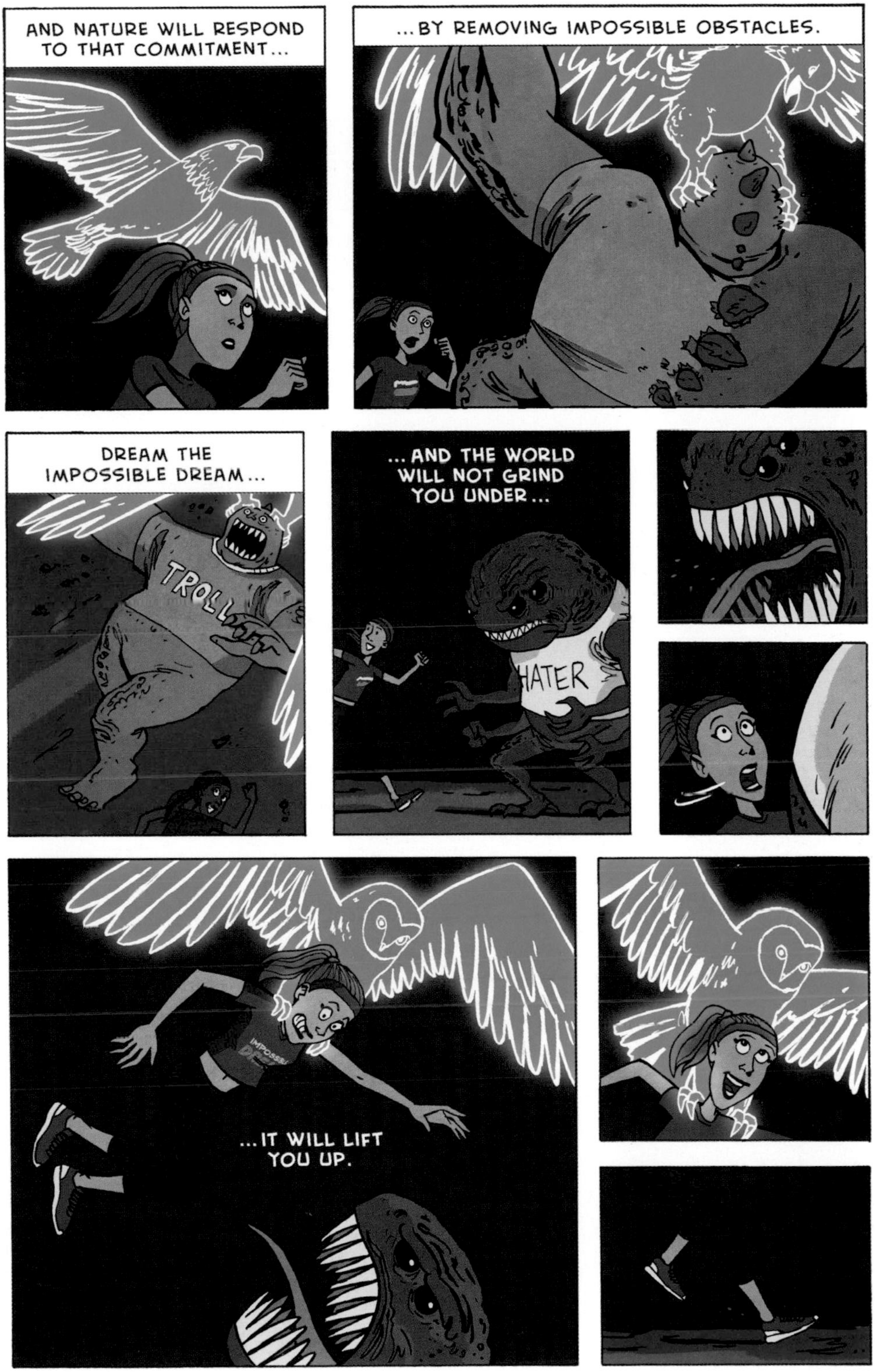

AND NATURE WILL RESPOND TO THAT COMMITMENT...
...BY REMOVING IMPOSSIBLE OBSTACLES.
DREAM THE IMPOSSIBLE DREAM...
TROLL
...AND THE WORLD WILL NOT GRIND YOU UNDER...
HATER
...IT WILL LIFT YOU UP.

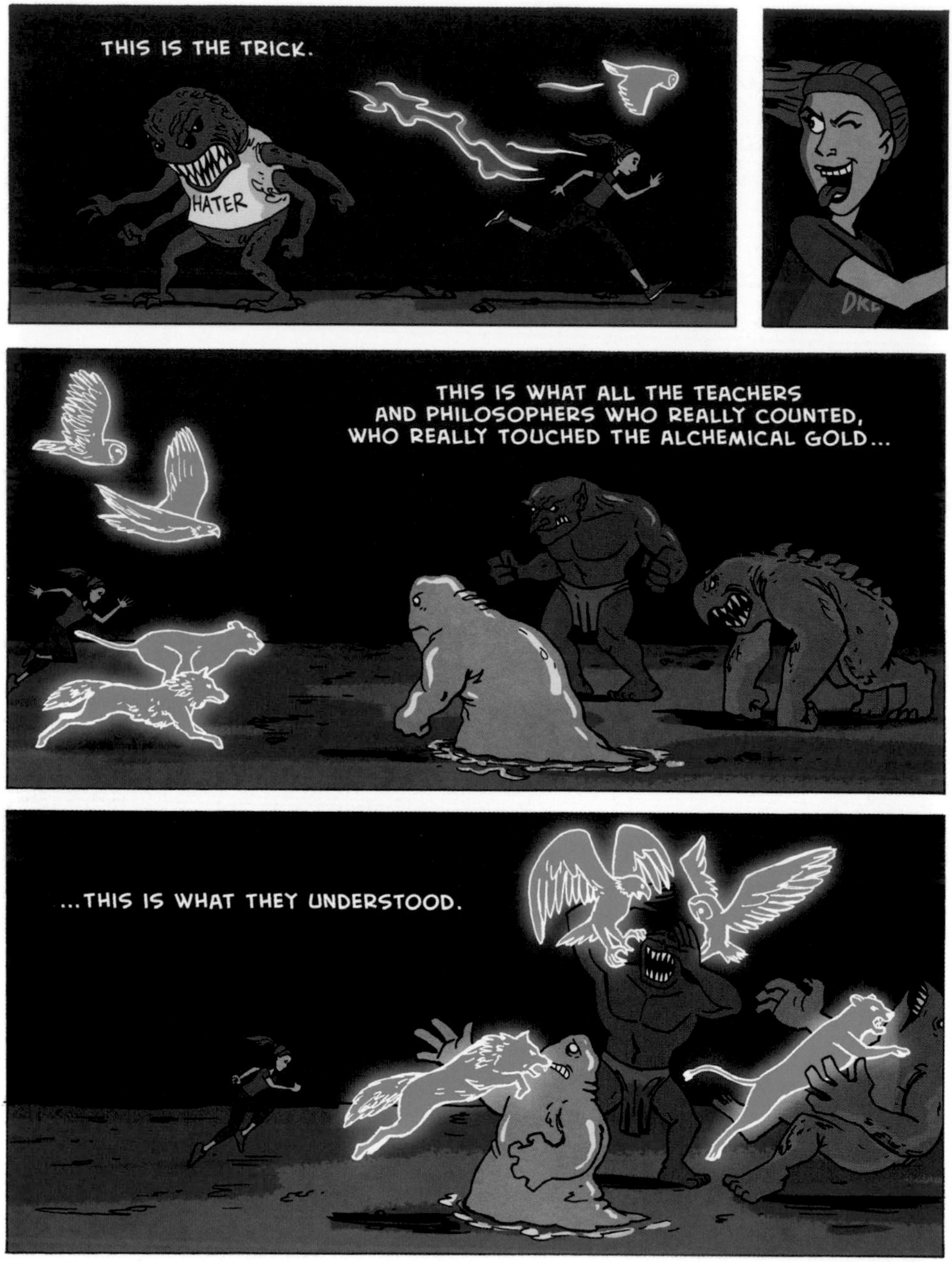
THIS IS THE TRICK.
HATER
THIS IS WHAT ALL THE TEACHERS AND PHILOSOPHERS WHO REALLY COUNTED, WHO REALLY TOUCHED THE ALCHEMICAL GOLD...
...THIS IS WHAT THEY UNDERSTOOD.

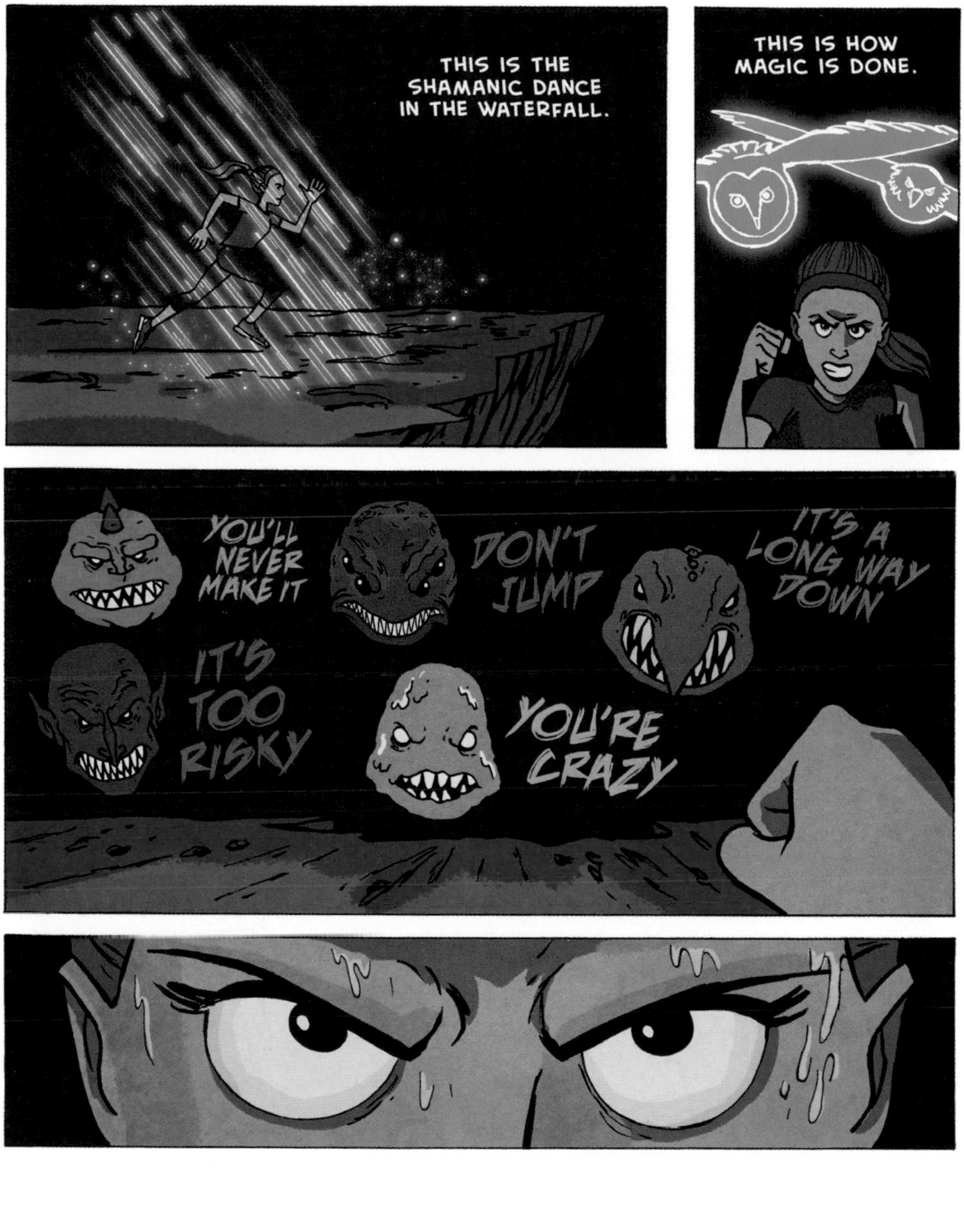
THIS IS THE SHAMANIC DANCE IN THE WATERFALL.
THIS IS HOW MAGIC IS DONE.
YOU'LL NEVER MAKE IT
DON'T JUMP
IT'S A LONG WAY DOWN
IT'S TOO RISKY
YOU'RE CRAZY

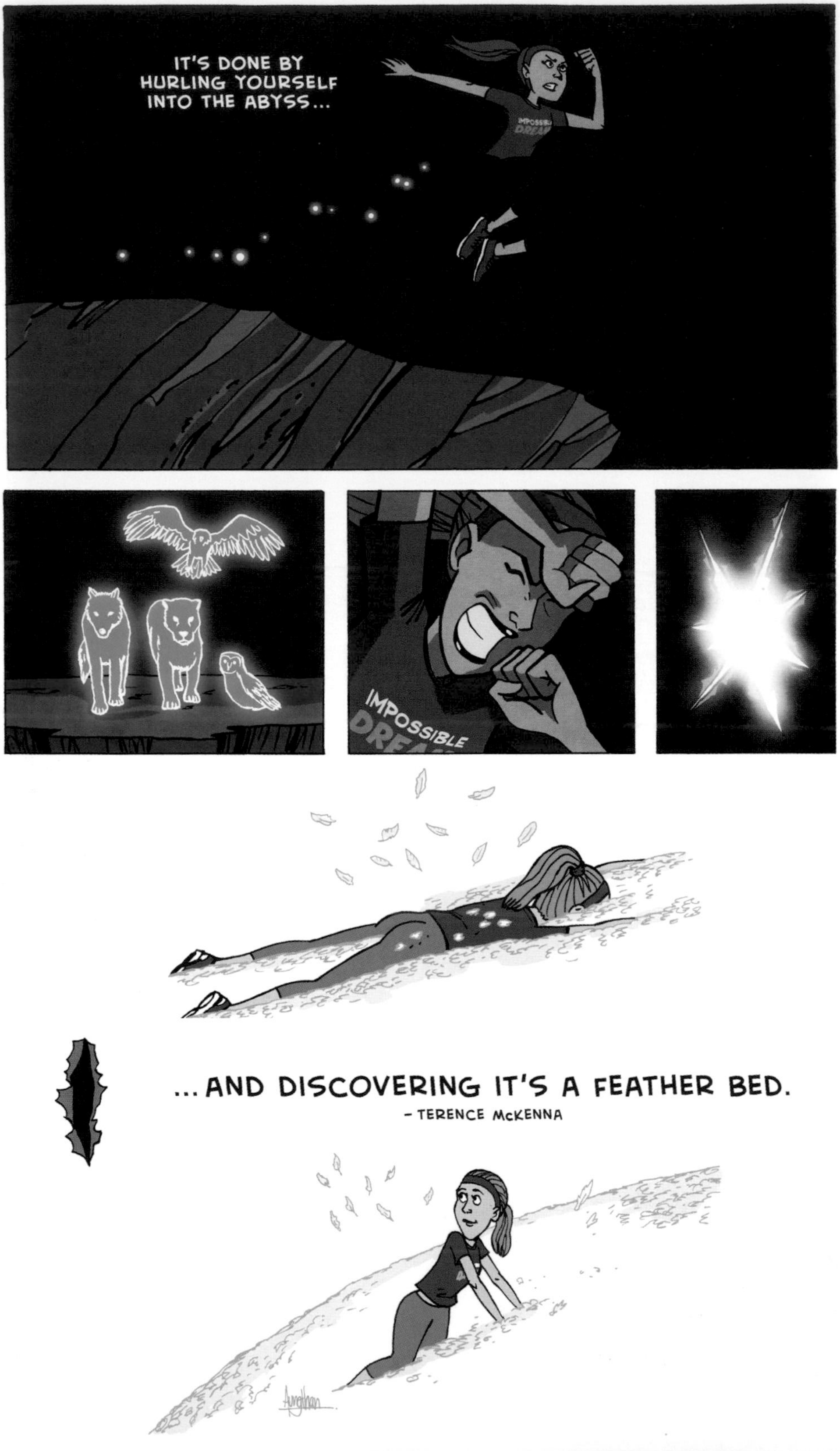
IT'S DONE BY HURLING YOURSELF INTO THE ABYSS...
IMPOSSIBLE
...AND DISCOVERING IT'S A FEATHER BED.
– TERENCE McKENNA

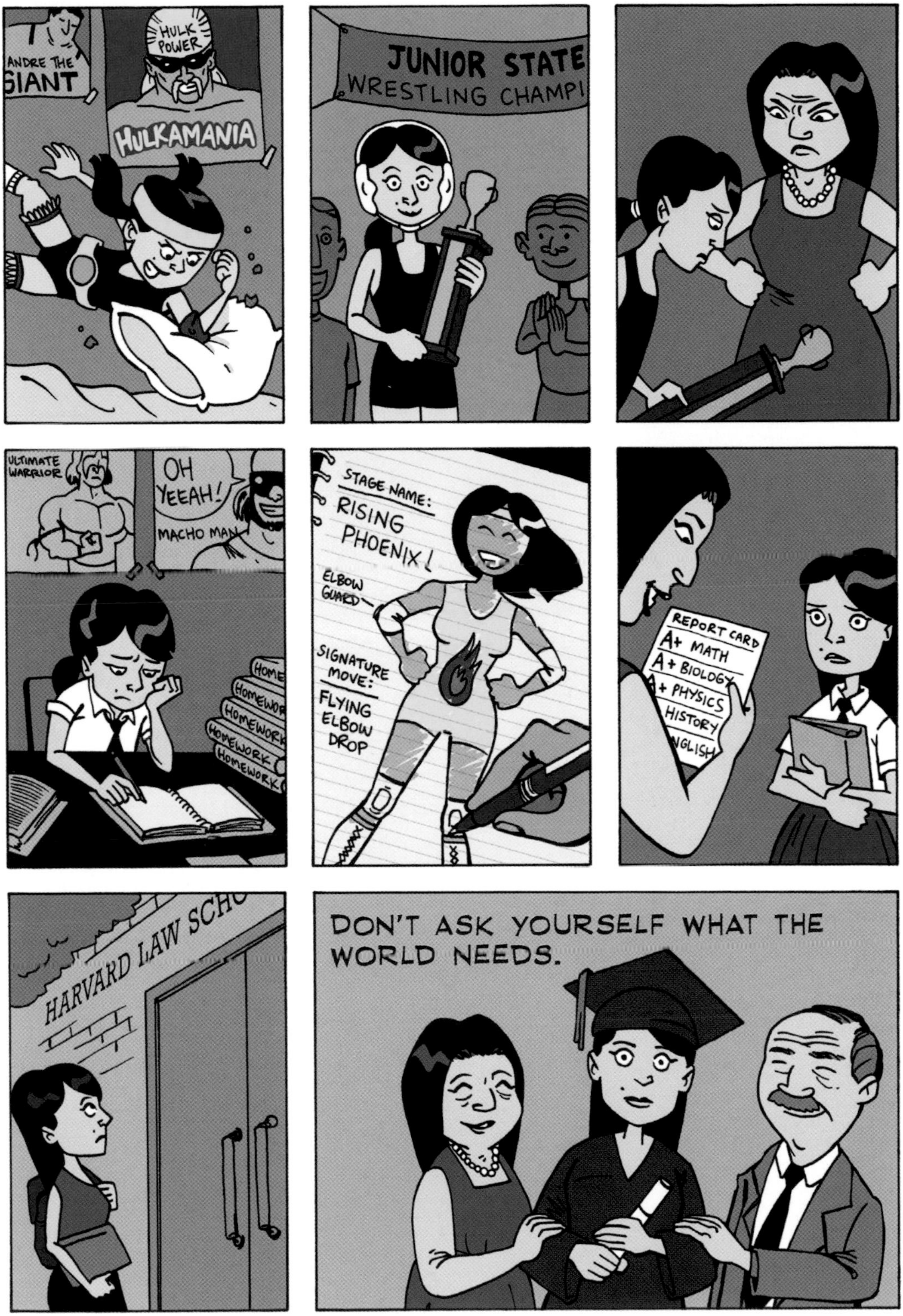
ANDRE THE GIANT
HULK POWER
HULKAMANIA
JUNIOR STATE WRESTLING CHAMPI
ULTIMATE WARRIOR
OH YEEAH!
MACHO MAN
HOMEWORK
HOMEWORK
HOMEWORK
HOMEWORK
HOMEWORK
STAGE NAME:
RISING PHOENIX!
ELBOW GUARD
SIGNATURE MOVE:
FLYING ELBOW DROP
REPORT CARD
A+ MATH
A+ BIOLOGY
A+ PHYSICS
HISTORY
ENGLISH
HARVARD LAW SCHO
DON'T ASK YOURSELF WHAT THE WORLD NEEDS.

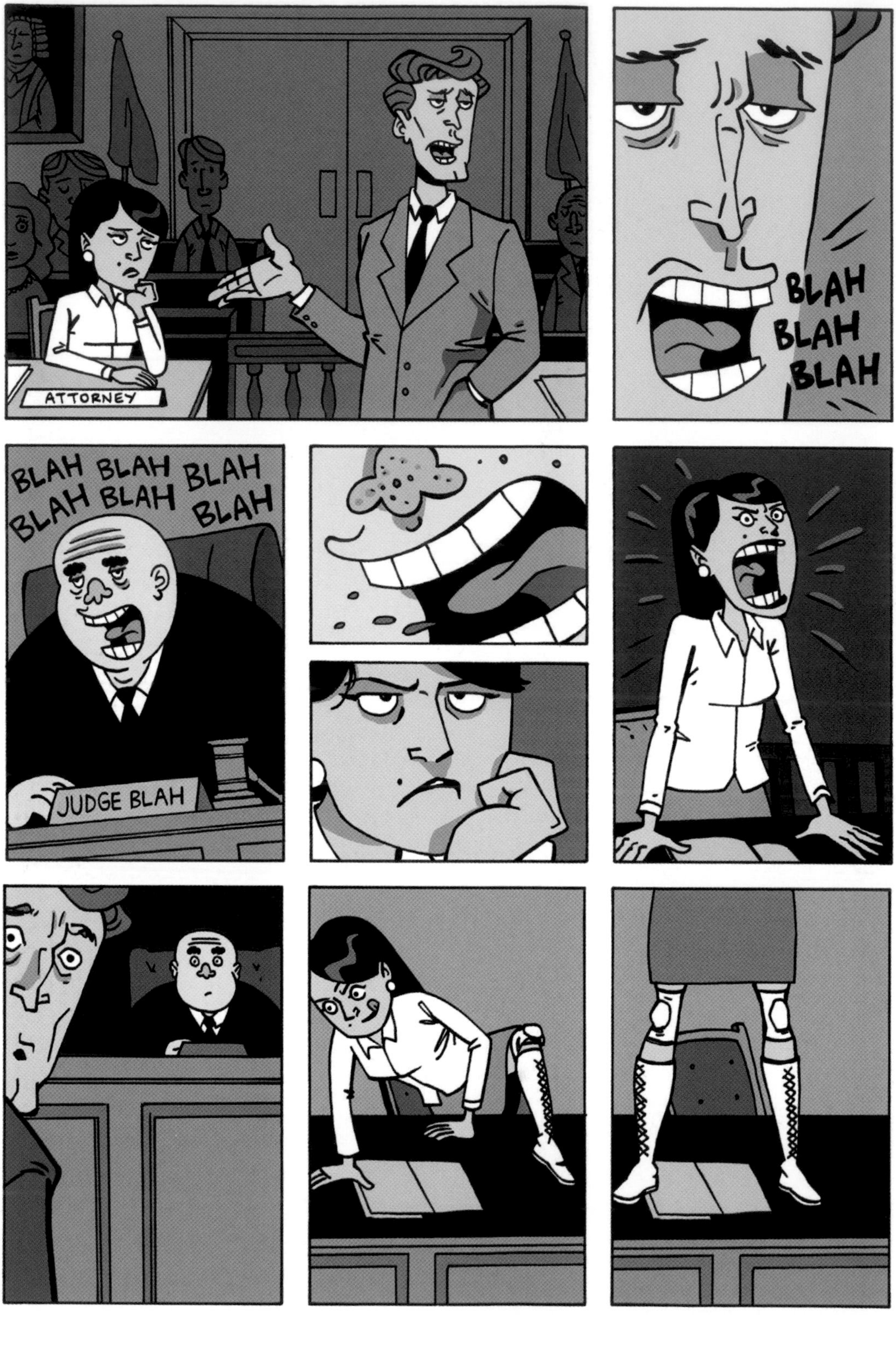
ATTORNEY
BLAH
BLAH
BLAH
BLAH BLAH BLAH
BLAH BLAH BLAH
JUDGE BLAH

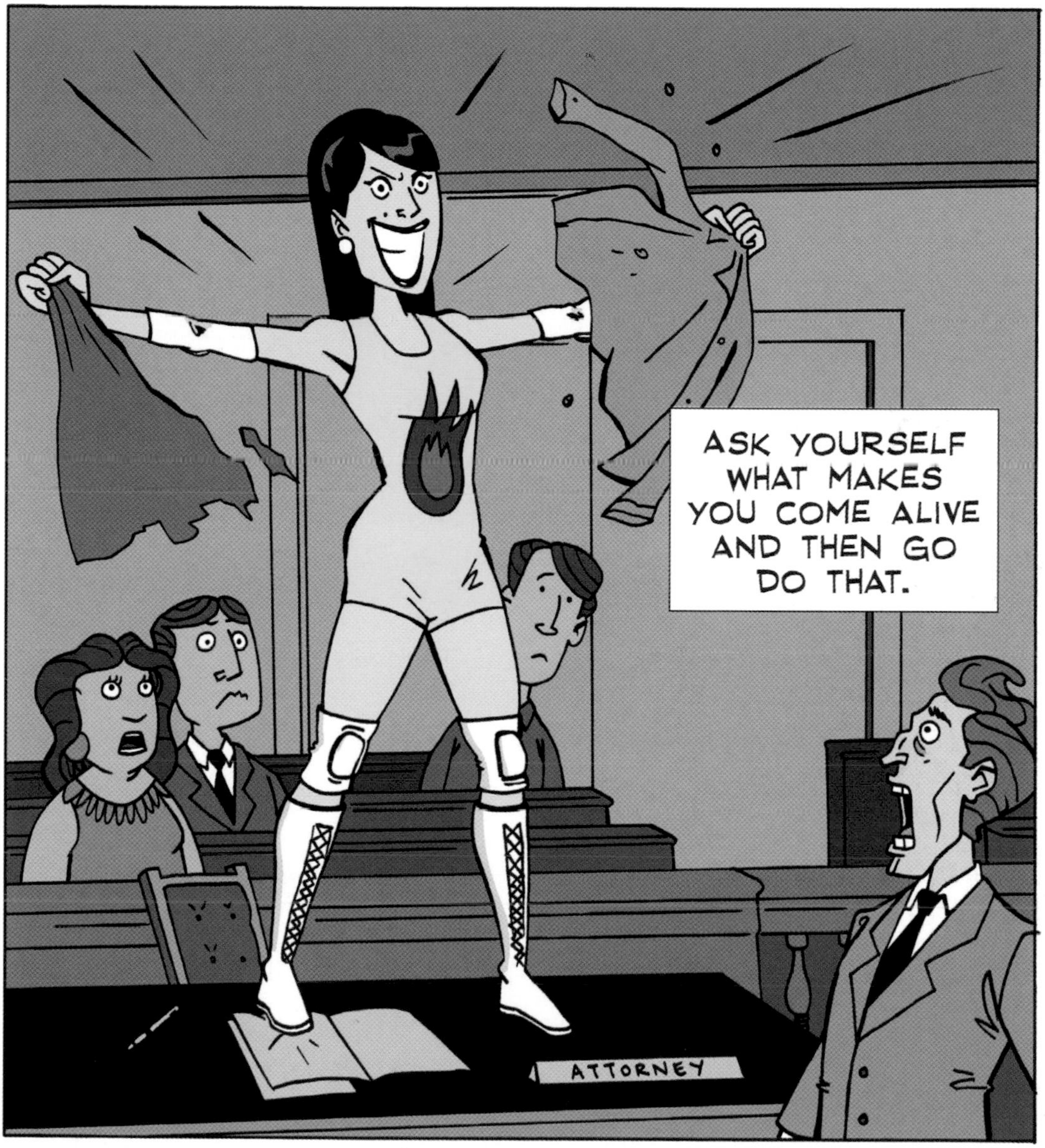
ASK YOURSELF WHAT MAKES YOU COME ALIVE AND THEN GO DO THAT.
ATTORNEY

BECAUSE WHAT
THE WORLD NEEDS
IS PEOPLE WHO
HAVE COME ALIVE.

- HOWARD THURMAN

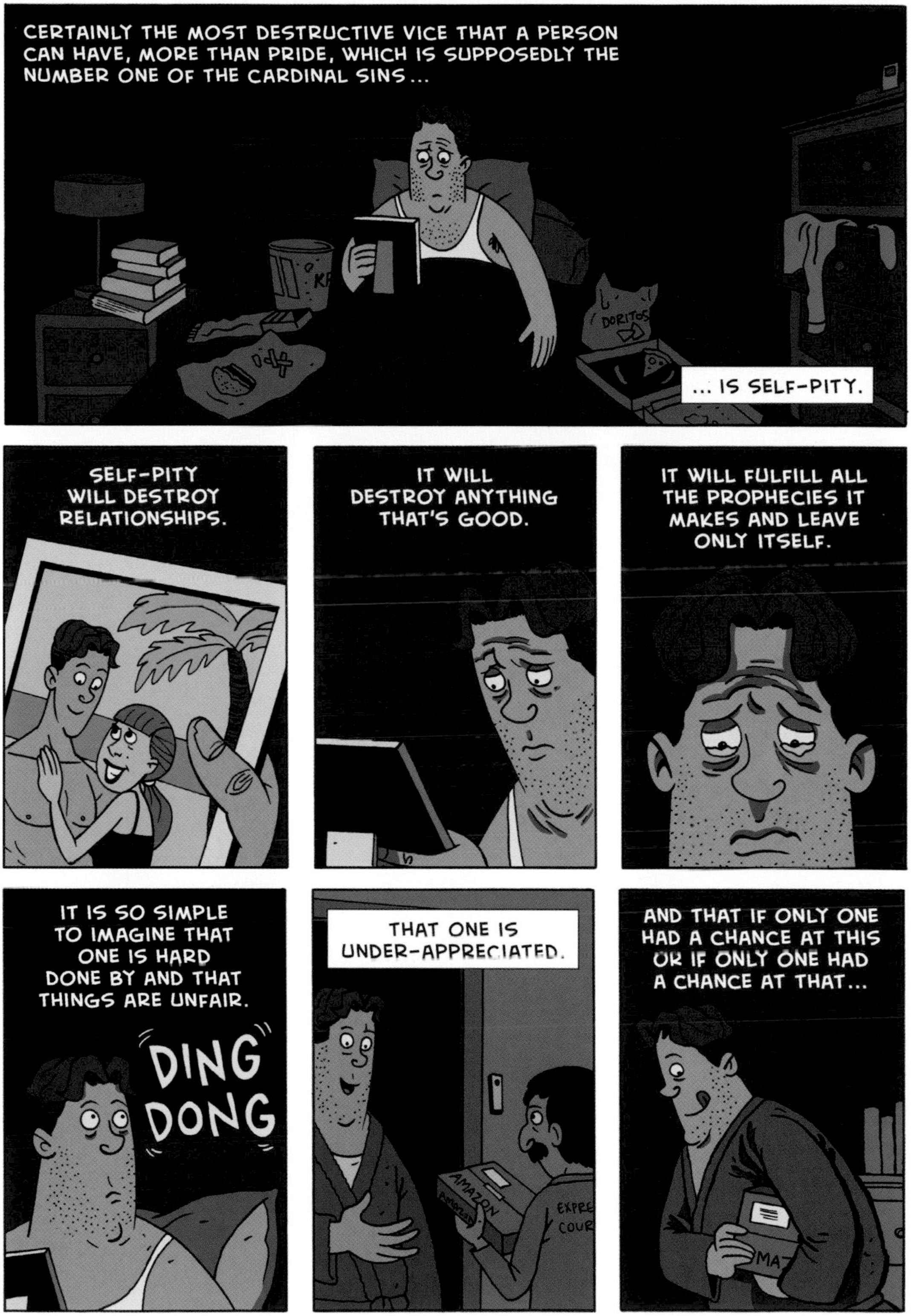
CERTAINLY THE MOST DESTRUCTIVE VICE THAT A PERSON CAN HAVE, MORE THAN PRIDE, WHICH IS SUPPOSEDLY THE NUMBER ONE OF THE CARDINAL SINS...
DORITOS
... IS SELF-PITY.
SELF-PITY WILL DESTROY RELATIONSHIPS.
IT WILL DESTROY ANYTHING THAT'S GOOD.
IT WILL FULFILL ALL THE PROPHECIES IT MAKES AND LEAVE ONLY ITSELF.
IT IS SO SIMPLE TO IMAGINE THAT ONE IS HARD DONE BY AND THAT THINGS ARE UNFAIR.
DING DONG
THAT ONE IS UNDER-APPRECIATED.
AMAZON
AND THAT IF ONLY ONE HAD A CHANCE AT THIS OR IF ONLY ONE HAD A CHANCE AT THAT...

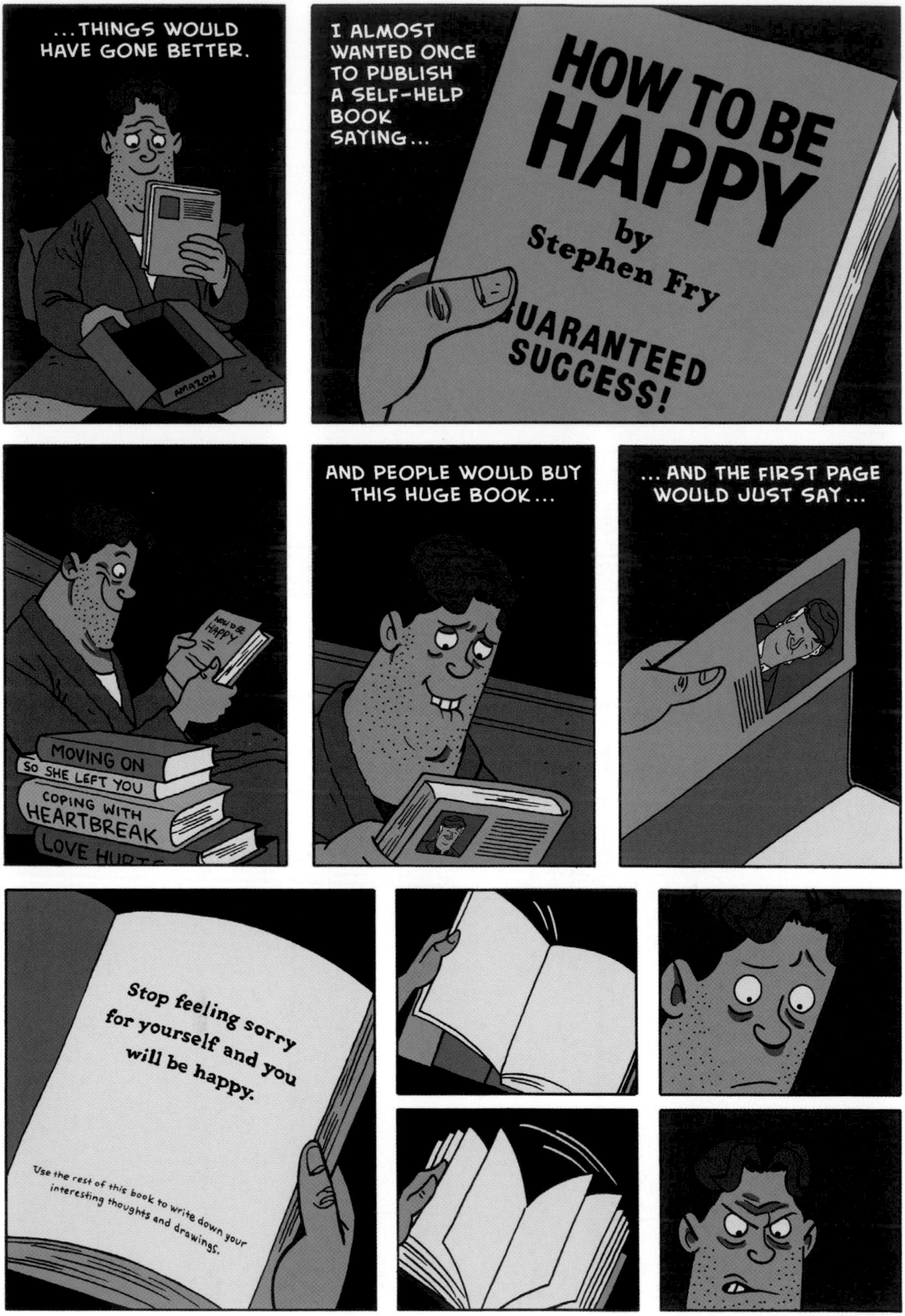
...THINGS WOULD HAVE GONE BETTER.
AMAZON
I ALMOST WANTED ONCE TO PUBLISH A SELF-HELP BOOK SAYING...
HOW TO BE HAPPY
by Stephen Fry
GUARANTEED SUCCESS!
HOW TO BE HAPPY
MOVING ON
SO SHE LEFT YOU
COPING WITH HEARTBREAK
AND PEOPLE WOULD BUY THIS HUGE BOOK...
...AND THE FIRST PAGE WOULD JUST SAY...
Stop feeling sorry for yourself and you will be happy.
Use the rest of this book to write down your interesting thoughts and drawings.

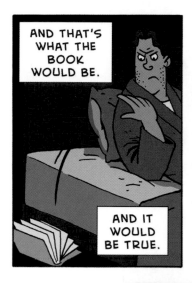

AND THAT'S WHAT THE BOOK WOULD BE.

AND IT WOULD BE TRUE.

IT SOUNDS LIKE "OH, THAT'S SO SIMPLE."

BUT, OF COURSE, IT'S NOT SIMPLE TO STOP FEELING SORRY FOR YOURSELF.

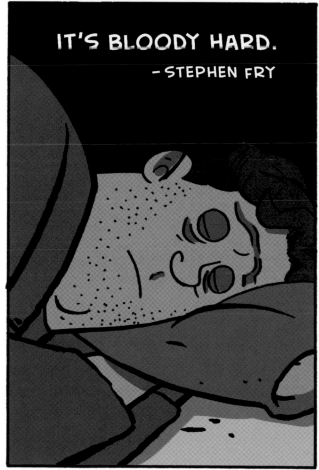

IT'S BLOODY HARD.

– STEPHEN FRY

Stop feeling sor
for yourself and y
will be happy.
UNIVERSITY
TRACK
TEAM
2004

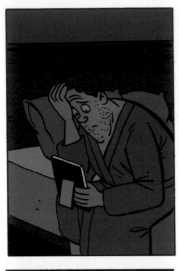

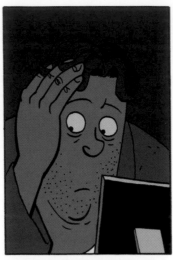

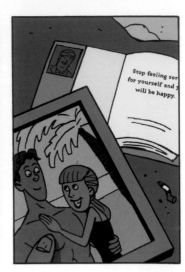

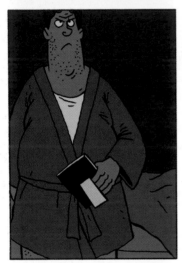

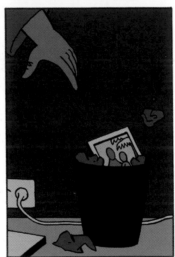

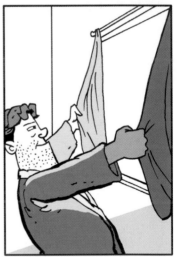

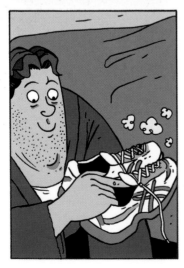

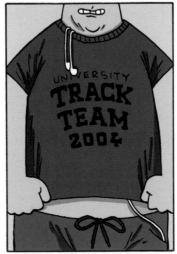

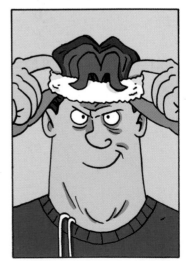

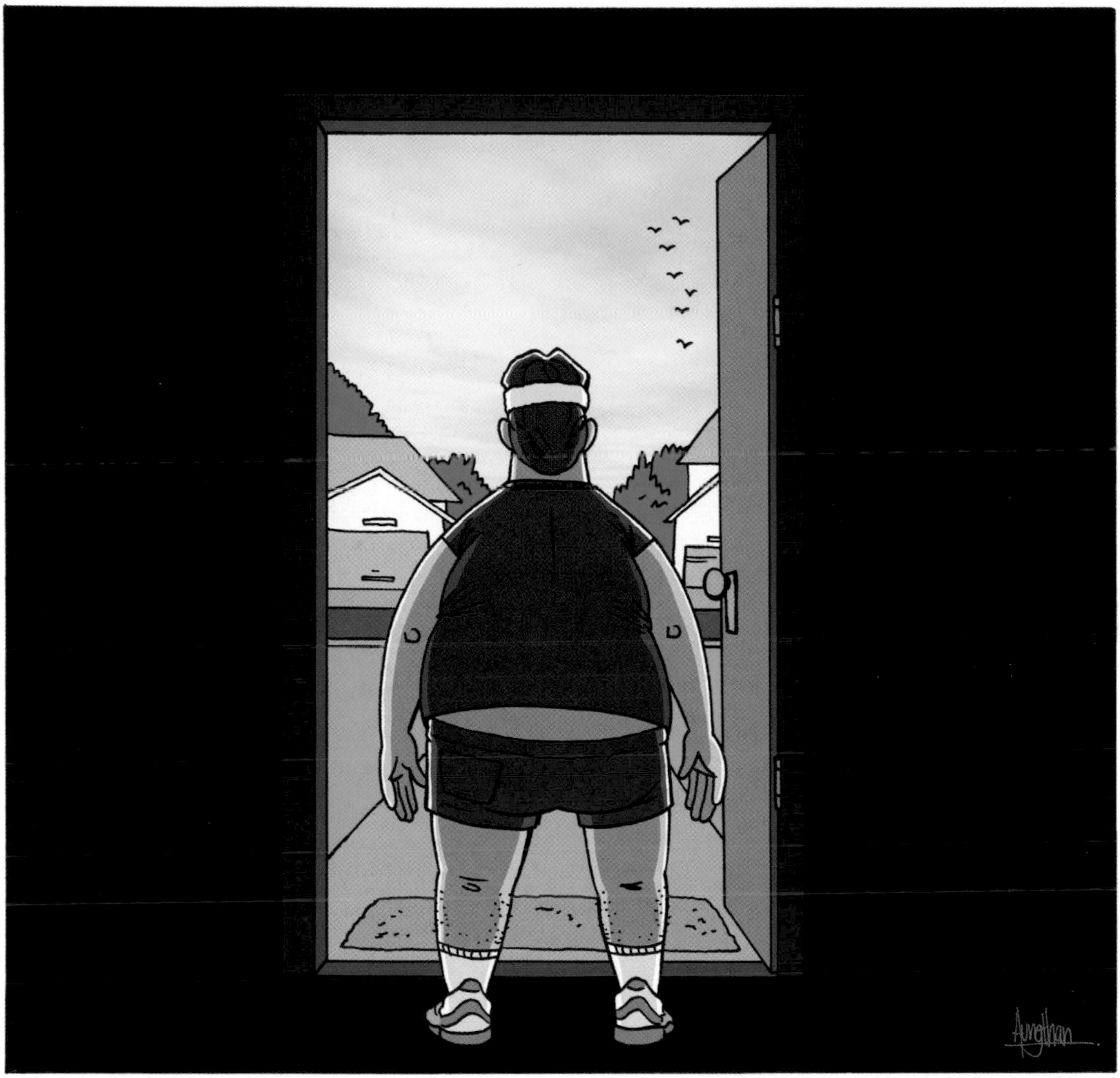

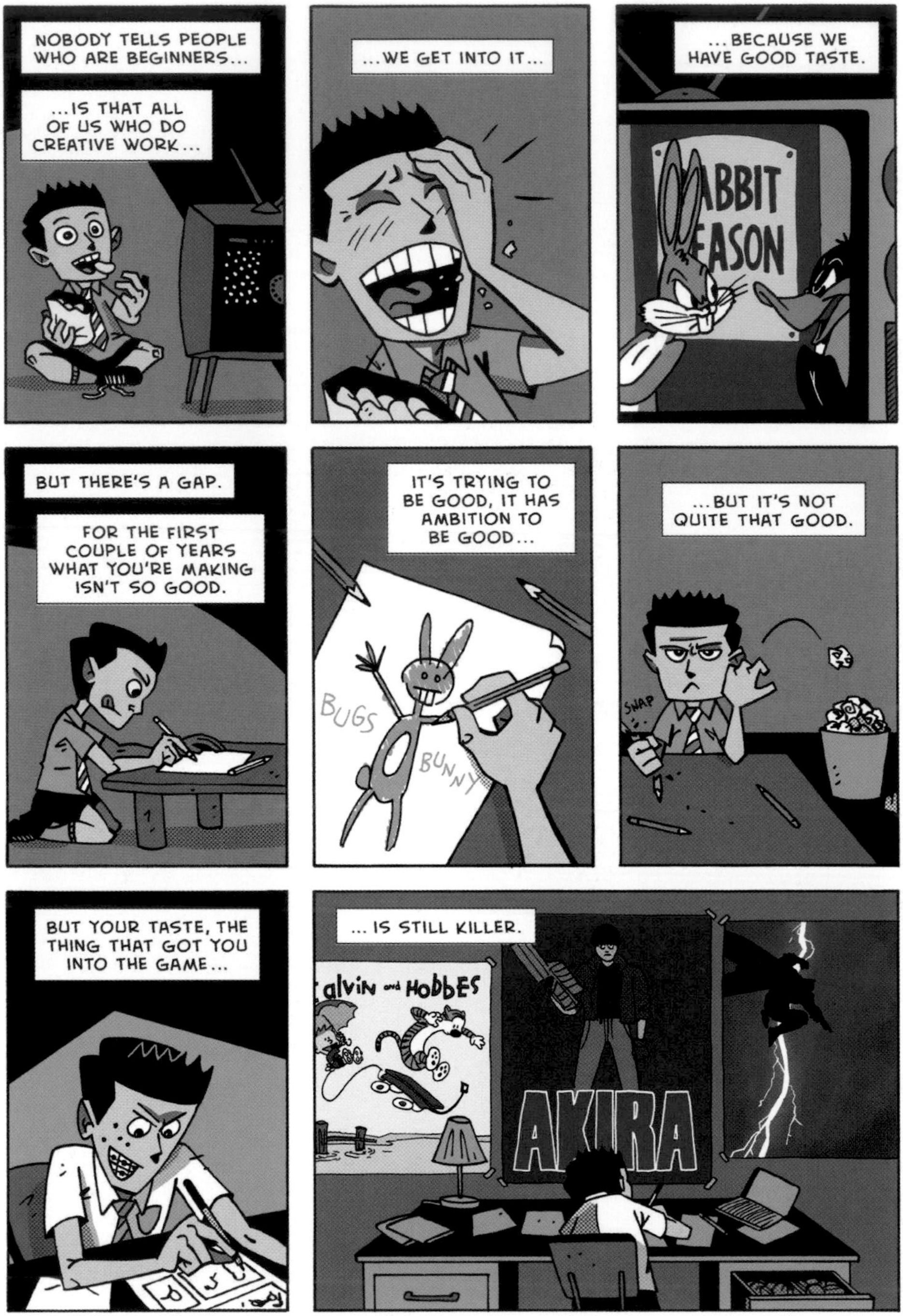
NOBODY TELLS PEOPLE WHO ARE BEGINNERS...
...IS THAT ALL OF US WHO DO CREATIVE WORK...
...WE GET INTO IT...
...BECAUSE WE HAVE GOOD TASTE.
ABBIT EASON
BUT THERE'S A GAP.
FOR THE FIRST COUPLE OF YEARS WHAT YOU'RE MAKING ISN'T SO GOOD.
IT'S TRYING TO BE GOOD, IT HAS AMBITION TO BE GOOD...
BUGS
BUNNY
...BUT IT'S NOT QUITE THAT GOOD.
SNAP
BUT YOUR TASTE, THE THING THAT GOT YOU INTO THE GAME...
...IS STILL KILLER.
Calvin and HOBBES
AKIRA

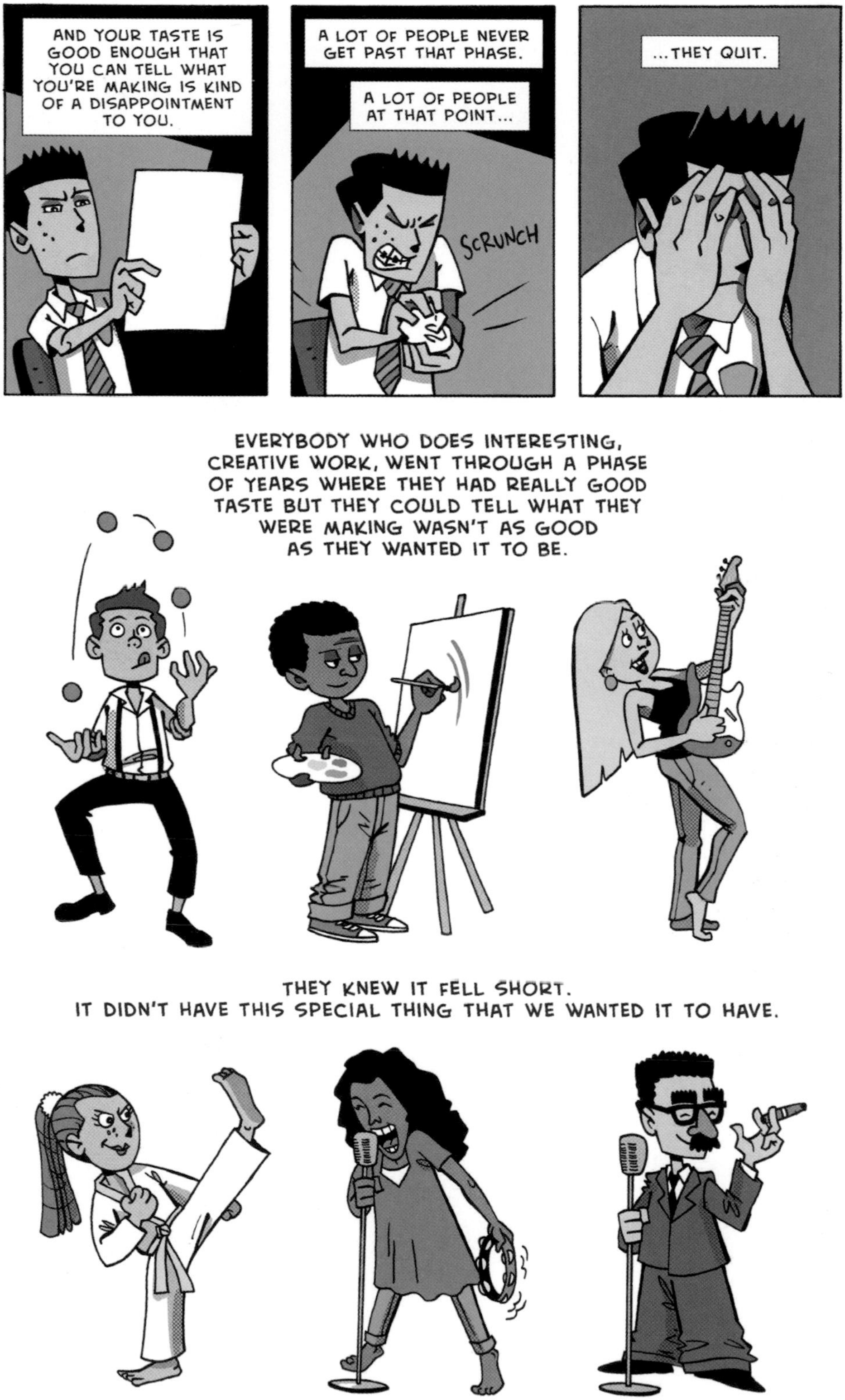
AND YOUR TASTE IS GOOD ENOUGH THAT YOU CAN TELL WHAT YOU'RE MAKING IS KIND OF A DISAPPOINTMENT TO YOU.
A LOT OF PEOPLE NEVER GET PAST THAT PHASE.
A LOT OF PEOPLE AT THAT POINT...
SCRUNCH
...THEY QUIT.
EVERYBODY WHO DOES INTERESTING, CREATIVE WORK, WENT THROUGH A PHASE OF YEARS WHERE THEY HAD REALLY GOOD TASTE BUT THEY COULD TELL WHAT THEY WERE MAKING WASN'T AS GOOD AS THEY WANTED IT TO BE.
THEY KNEW IT FELL SHORT.
IT DIDN'T HAVE THIS SPECIAL THING THAT WE WANTED IT TO HAVE.

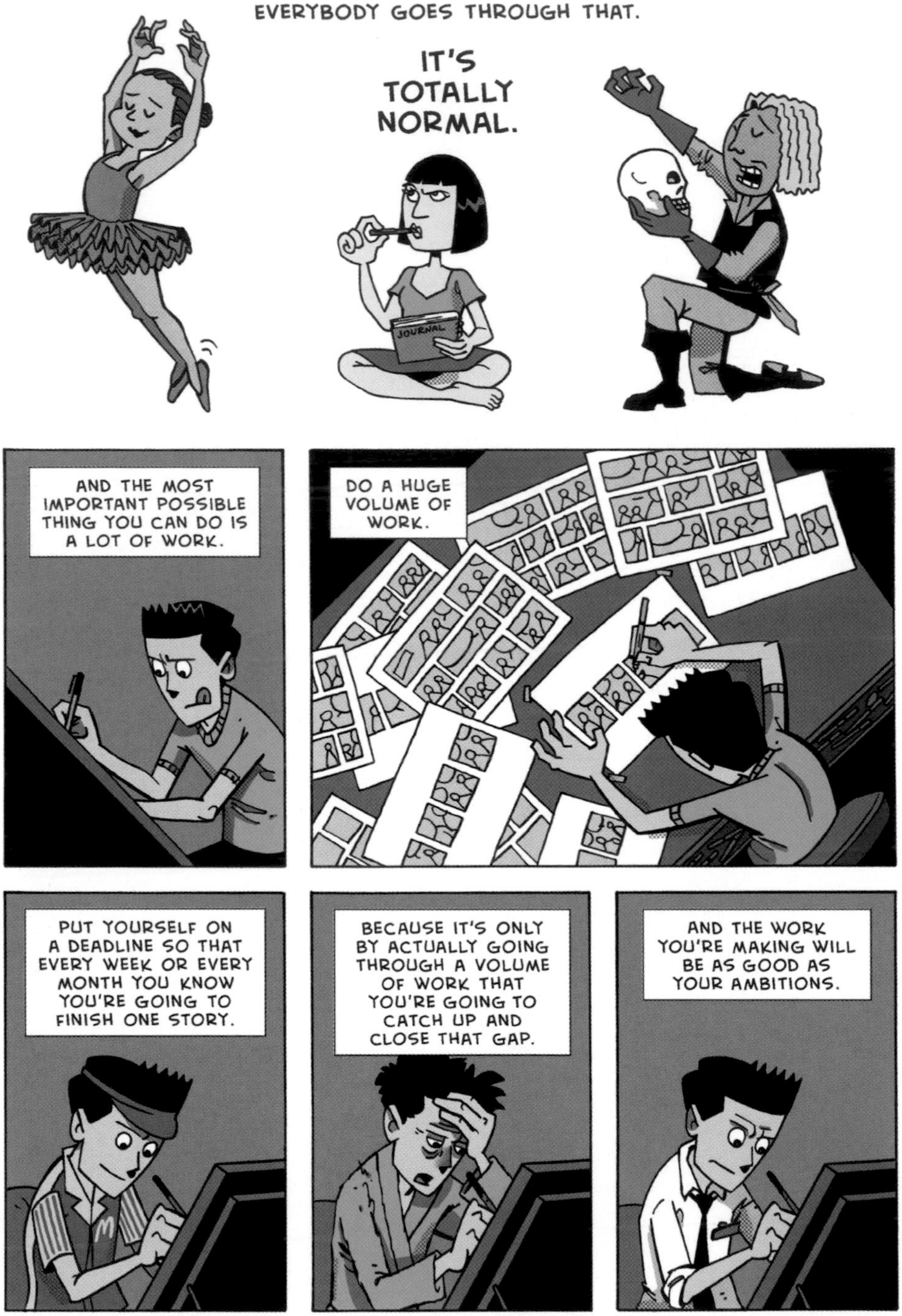
EVERYBODY GOES THROUGH THAT.
IT'S TOTALLY NORMAL.
JOURNAL
AND THE MOST IMPORTANT POSSIBLE THING YOU CAN DO IS A LOT OF WORK.
DO A HUGE VOLUME OF WORK.
PUT YOURSELF ON A DEADLINE SO THAT EVERY WEEK OR EVERY MONTH YOU KNOW YOU'RE GOING TO FINISH ONE STORY.
BECAUSE IT'S ONLY BY ACTUALLY GOING THROUGH A VOLUME OF WORK THAT YOU'RE GOING TO CATCH UP AND CLOSE THAT GAP.
AND THE WORK YOU'RE MAKING WILL BE AS GOOD AS YOUR AMBITIONS.

IT'S GOING TO TAKE YOU AWHILE.

IT'S NORMAL
TO TAKE AWHILE.

YOU JUST HAVE TO FIGHT YOUR WAY THROUGH.

—IRA GLASS

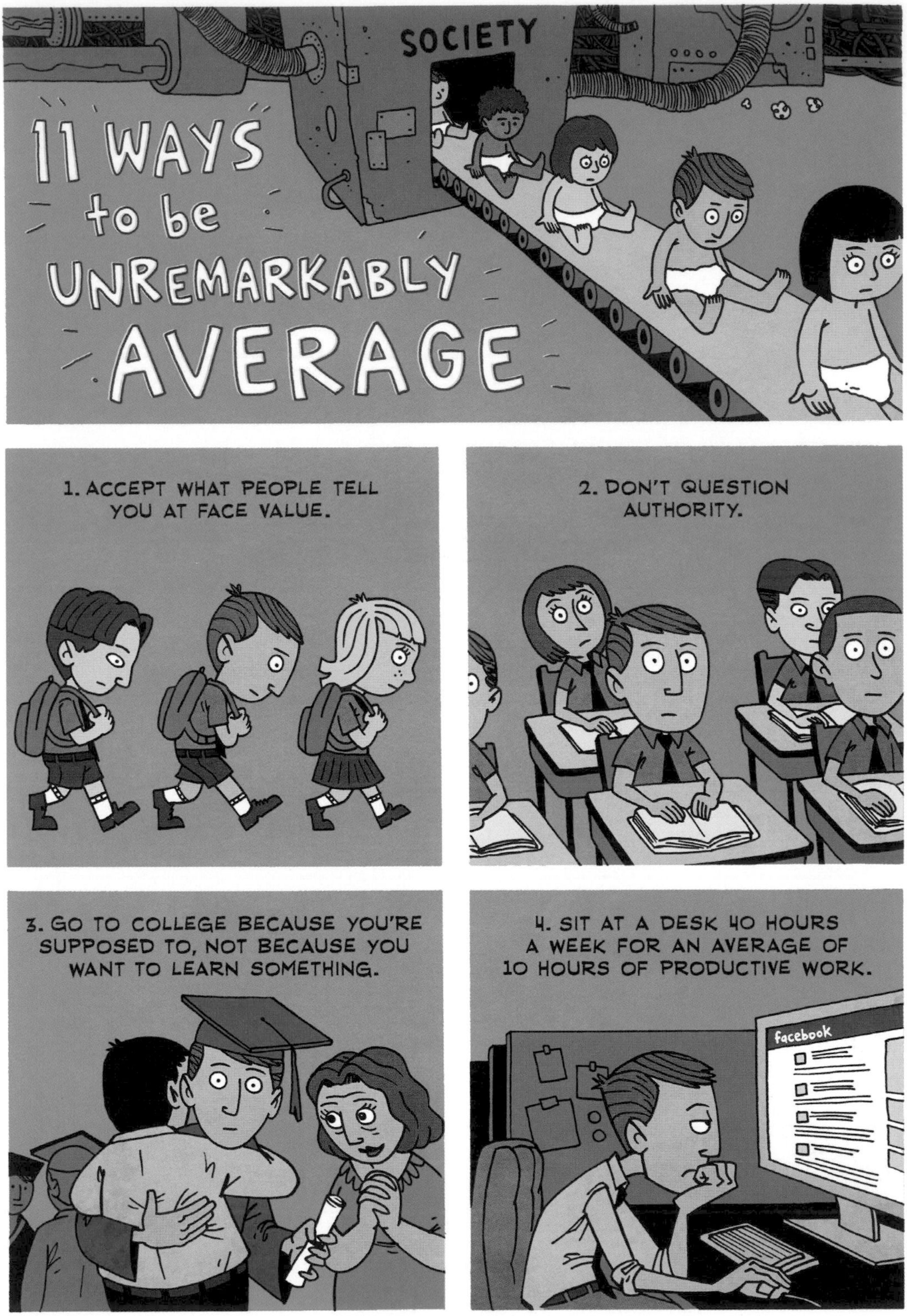
SOCIETY
11 WAYS to be UNREMARKABLY AVERAGE
1. ACCEPT WHAT PEOPLE TELL YOU AT FACE VALUE.
2. DON'T QUESTION AUTHORITY.
3. GO TO COLLEGE BECAUSE YOU'RE SUPPOSED TO, NOT BECAUSE YOU WANT TO LEARN SOMETHING.
4. SIT AT A DESK 40 HOURS A WEEK FOR AN AVERAGE OF 10 HOURS OF PRODUCTIVE WORK.
facebook

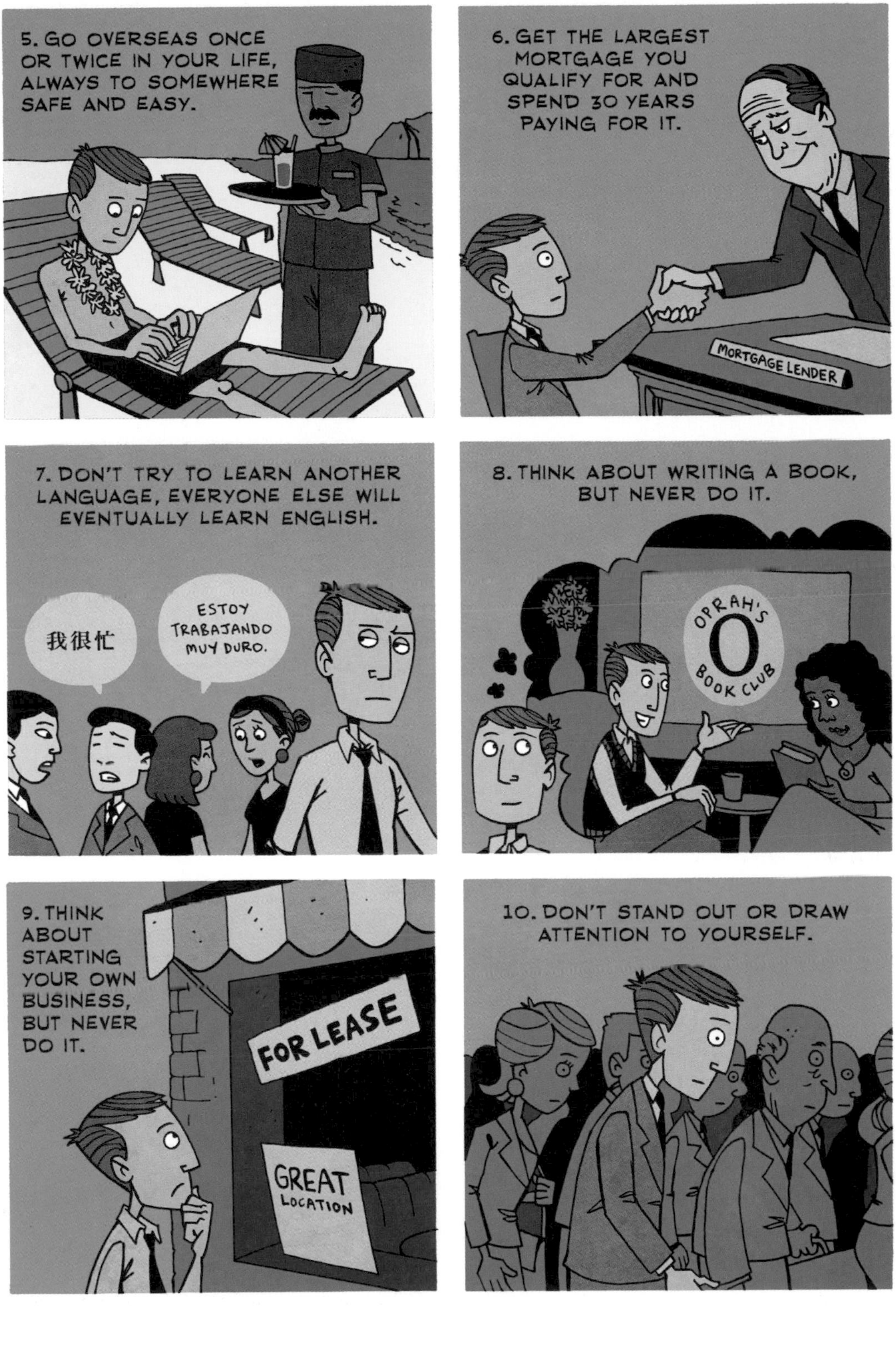
5. GO OVERSEAS ONCE OR TWICE IN YOUR LIFE, ALWAYS TO SOMEWHERE SAFE AND EASY.
6. GET THE LARGEST MORTGAGE YOU QUALIFY FOR AND SPEND 30 YEARS PAYING FOR IT.
MORTGAGE LENDER
7. DON'T TRY TO LEARN ANOTHER LANGUAGE, EVERYONE ELSE WILL EVENTUALLY LEARN ENGLISH.
我很忙
ESTOY TRABAJANDO MUY DURO.
8. THINK ABOUT WRITING A BOOK, BUT NEVER DO IT.
OPRAH'S O BOOK CLUB
9. THINK ABOUT STARTING YOUR OWN BUSINESS, BUT NEVER DO IT.
FOR LEASE
GREAT LOCATION
10. DON'T STAND OUT OR DRAW ATTENTION TO YOURSELF.

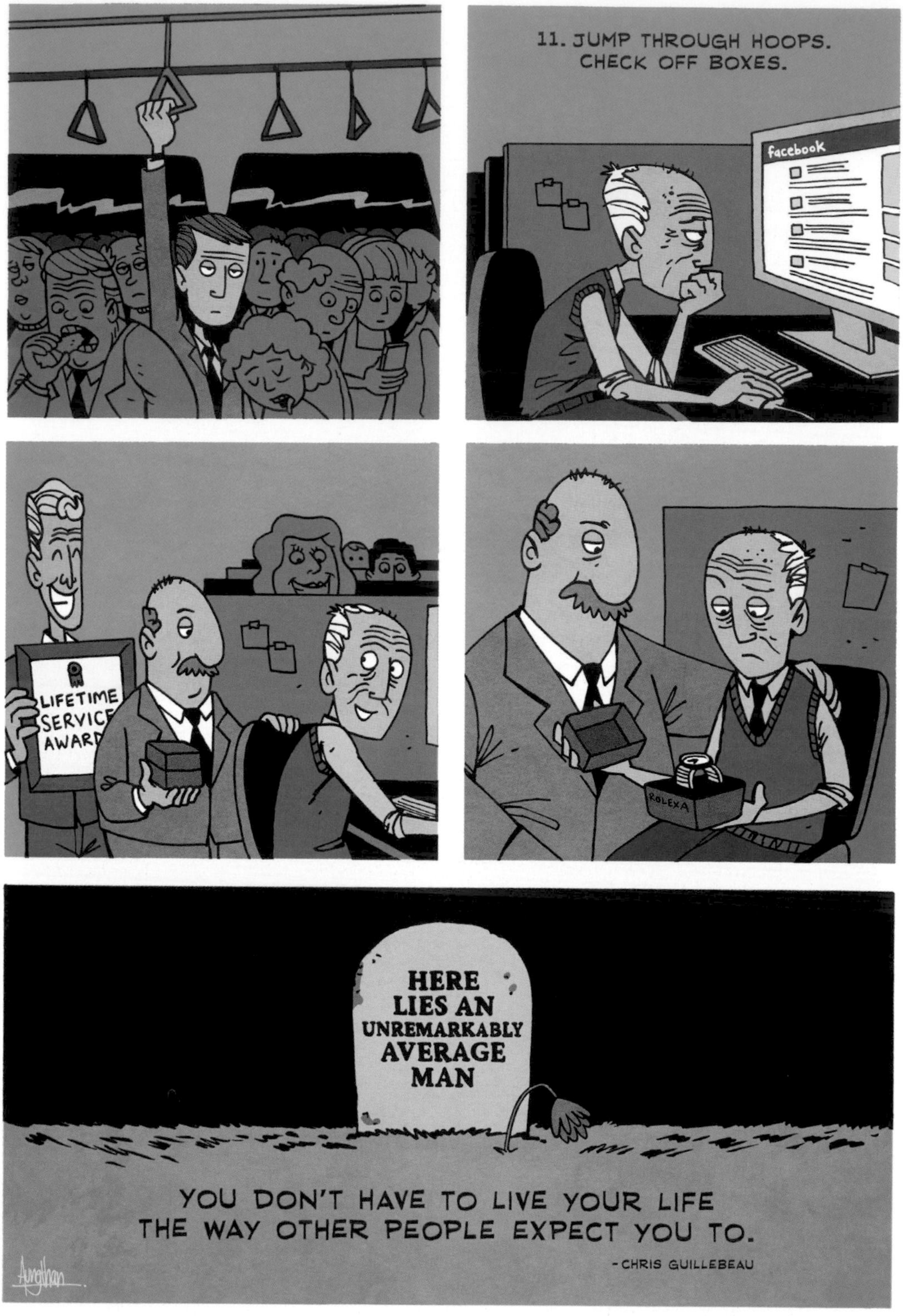

11. JUMP THROUGH HOOPS. CHECK OFF BOXES.
facebook
LIFETIME SERVICE AWARD
ROLEXA
HERE LIES AN UNREMARKABLY AVERAGE MAN
YOU DON'T HAVE TO LIVE YOUR LIFE THE WAY OTHER PEOPLE EXPECT YOU TO.
-CHRIS GUILLEBEAU

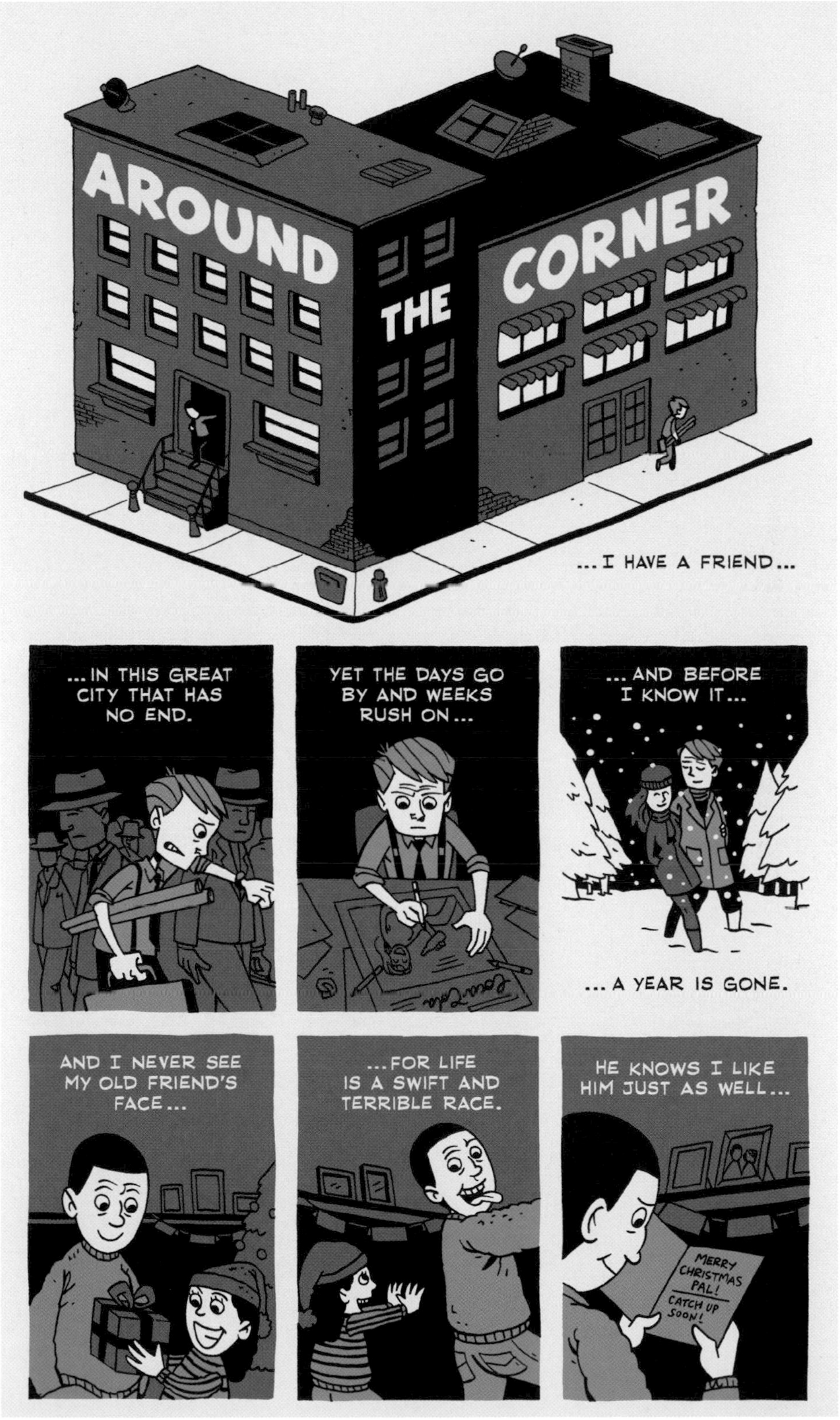
AROUND THE CORNER
...I HAVE A FRIEND...
...IN THIS GREAT CITY THAT HAS NO END.
YET THE DAYS GO BY AND WEEKS RUSH ON...
...AND BEFORE I KNOW IT...
...A YEAR IS GONE.
AND I NEVER SEE MY OLD FRIEND'S FACE...
...FOR LIFE IS A SWIFT AND TERRIBLE RACE.
HE KNOWS I LIKE HIM JUST AS WELL...
MERRY CHRISTMAS PAL!
CATCH UP SOON!

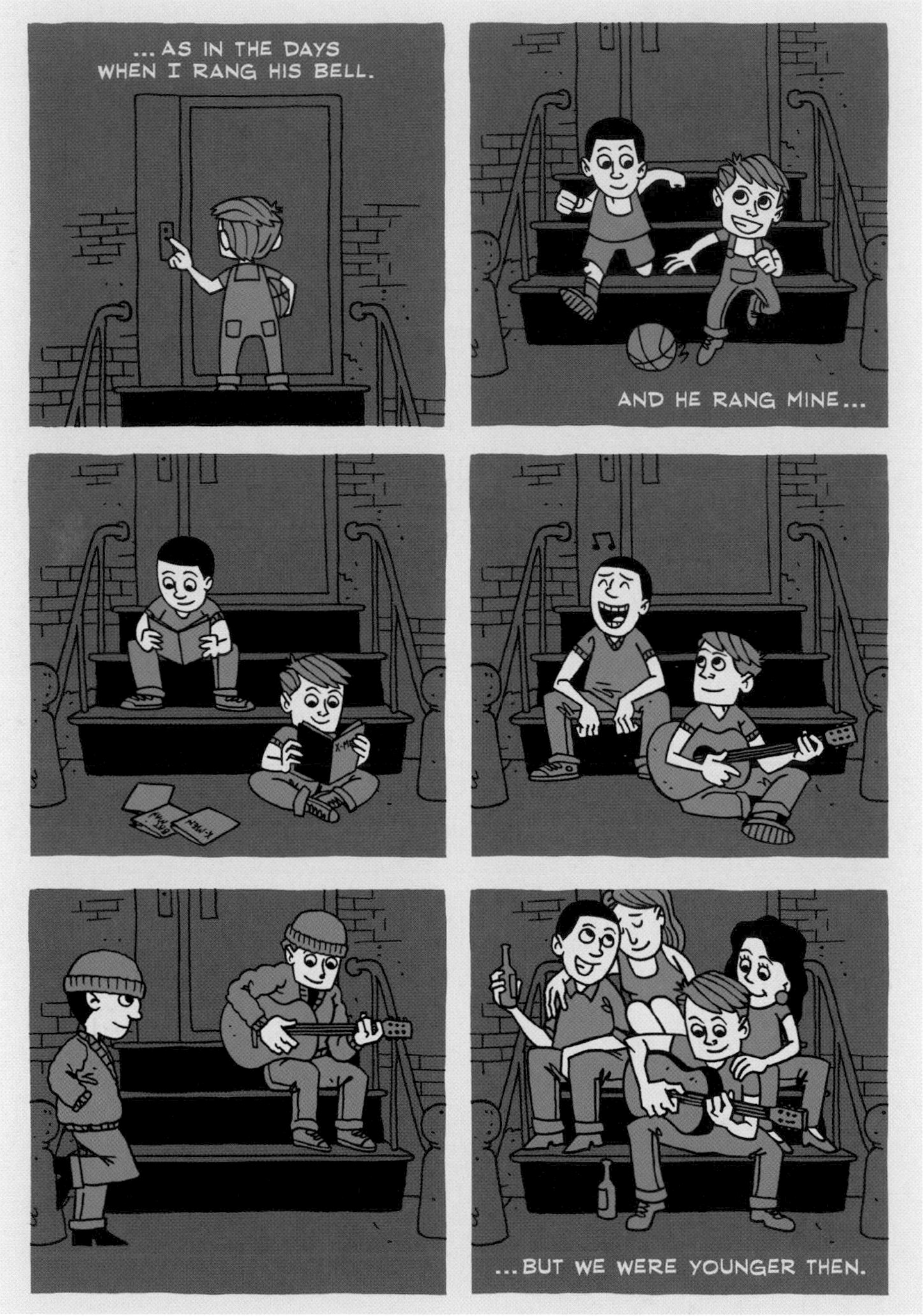

...AS IN THE DAYS WHEN I RANG HIS BELL.
AND HE RANG MINE...
...BUT WE WERE YOUNGER THEN.

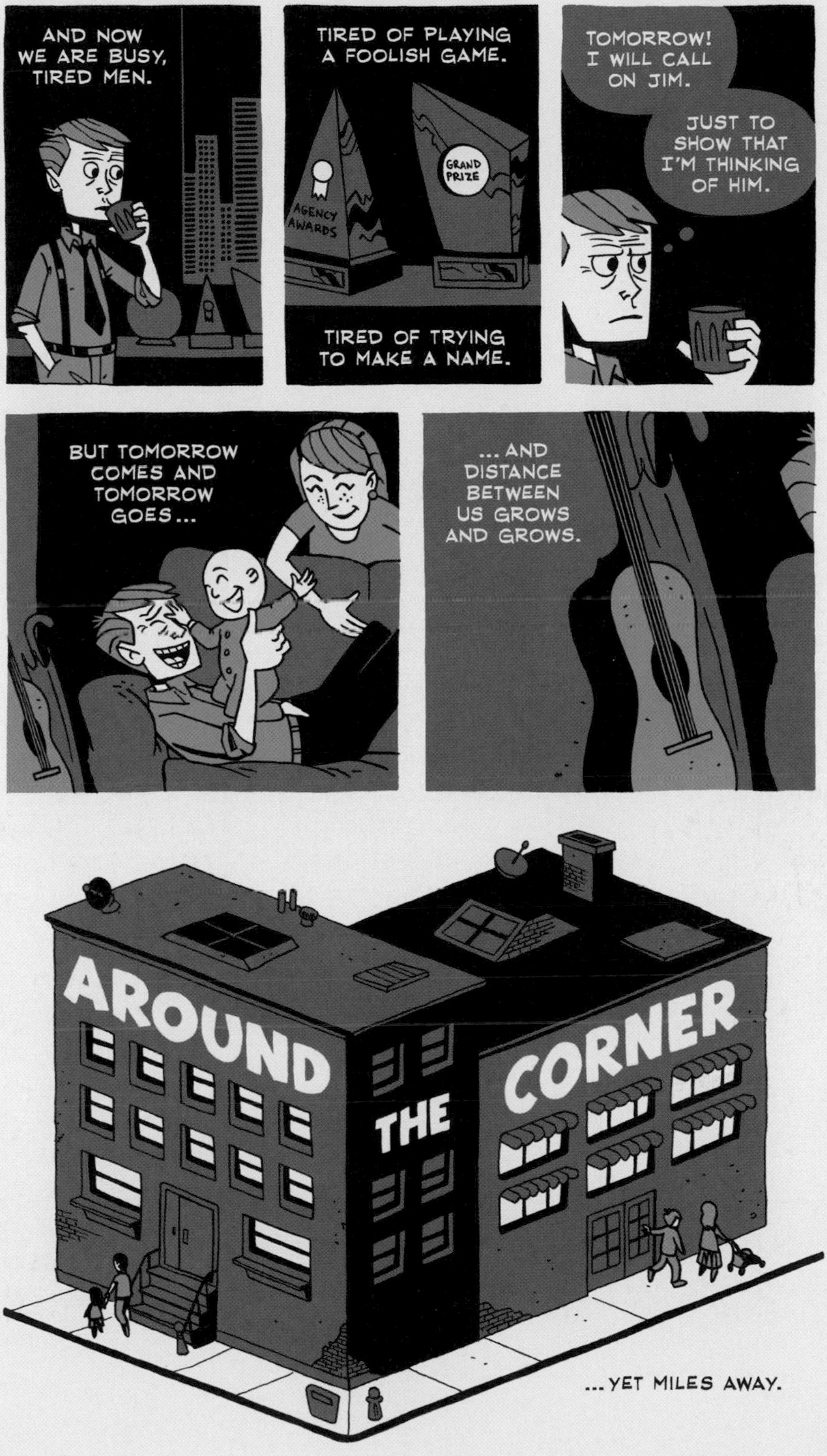
AND NOW WE ARE BUSY, TIRED MEN.
TIRED OF PLAYING A FOOLISH GAME.
AGENCY AWARDS
GRAND PRIZE
TIRED OF TRYING TO MAKE A NAME.
TOMORROW! I WILL CALL ON JIM.
JUST TO SHOW THAT I'M THINKING OF HIM.
BUT TOMORROW COMES AND TOMORROW GOES...
...AND DISTANCE BETWEEN US GROWS AND GROWS.
AROUND THE CORNER
...YET MILES AWAY.

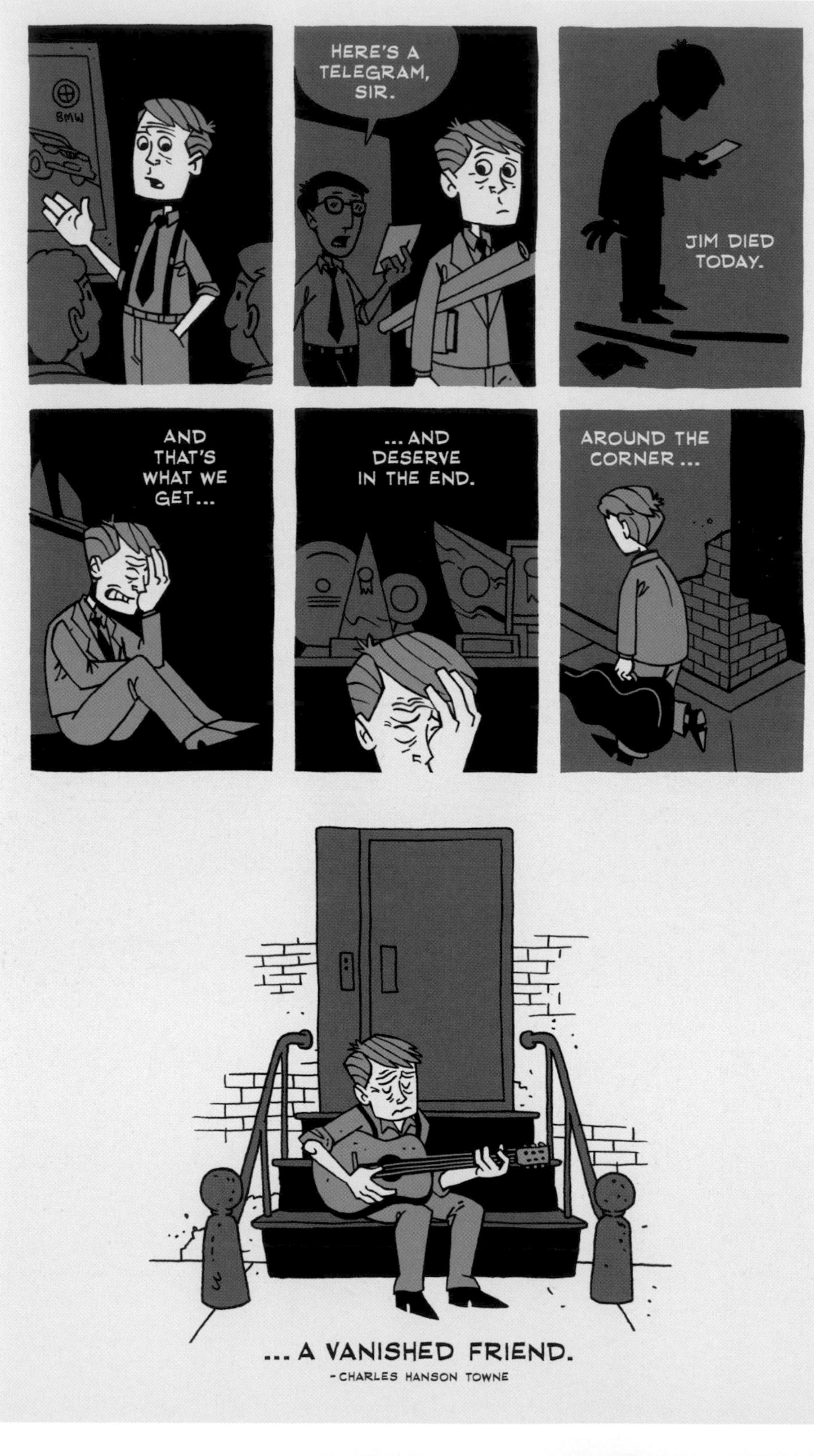
BMW
HERE'S A TELEGRAM, SIR.
JIM DIED TODAY.
AND THAT'S WHAT WE GET...
...AND DESERVE IN THE END.
AROUND THE CORNER...
...A VANISHED FRIEND.
-CHARLES HANSON TOWNE

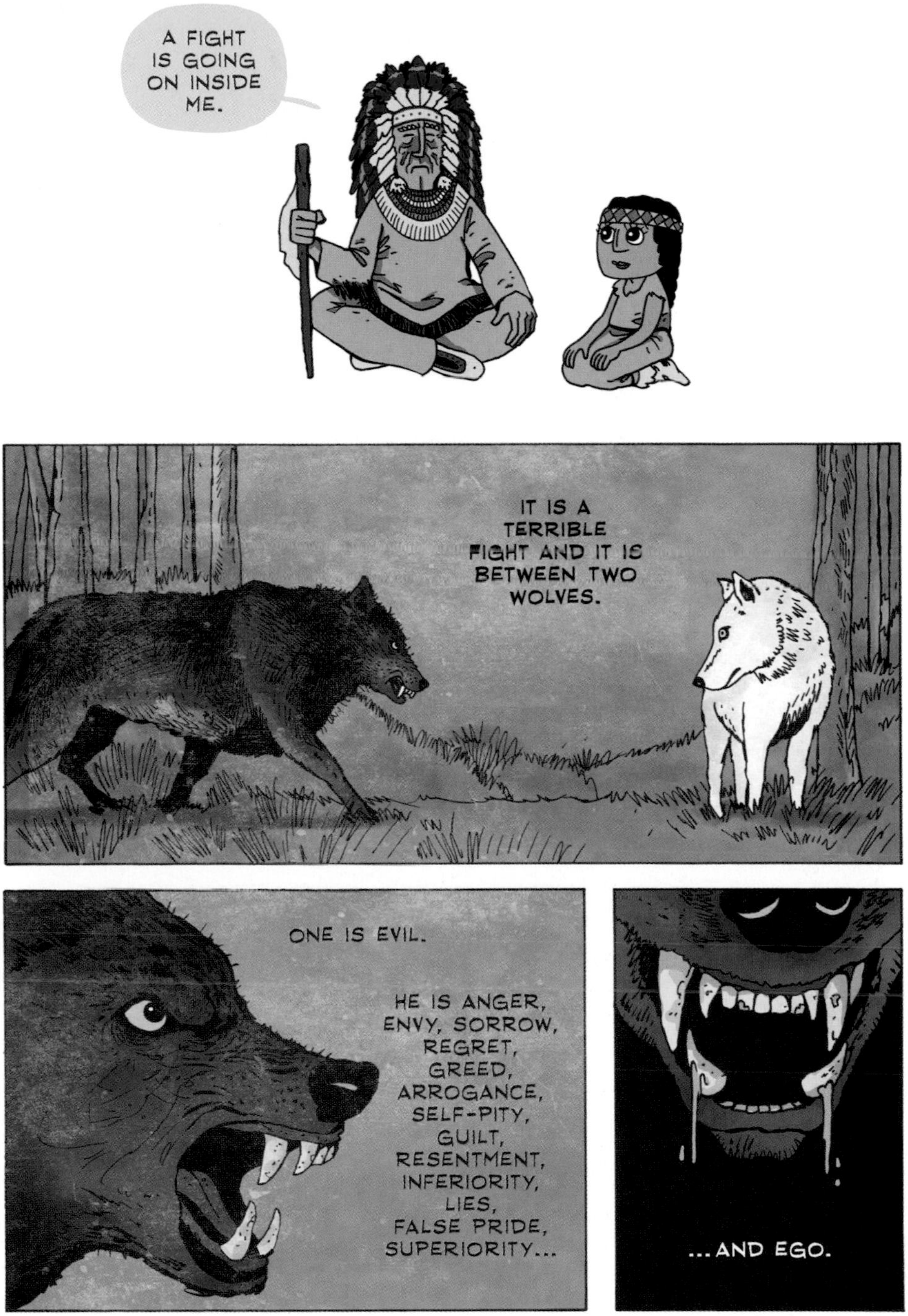
A FIGHT IS GOING ON INSIDE ME.
IT IS A TERRIBLE FIGHT AND IT IS BETWEEN TWO WOLVES.
ONE IS EVIL.
HE IS ANGER, ENVY, SORROW, REGRET, GREED, ARROGANCE, SELF-PITY, GUILT, RESENTMENT, INFERIORITY, LIES, FALSE PRIDE, SUPERIORITY...
...AND EGO.

THE OTHER
IS GOOD.

HE IS JOY,
PEACE, LOVE,
HOPE, SERENITY,
HUMILITY,
KINDNESS,
BENEVOLENCE,
EMPATHY,
GENEROSITY,
TRUTH,
COMPASSION...

...AND FAITH.

THE SAME
FIGHT IS
GOING ON
INSIDE YOU.

AND INSIDE
EVERY OTHER
PERSON, TOO.

WHICH
WOLF WILL
WIN?

THE
ONE YOU
FEED.

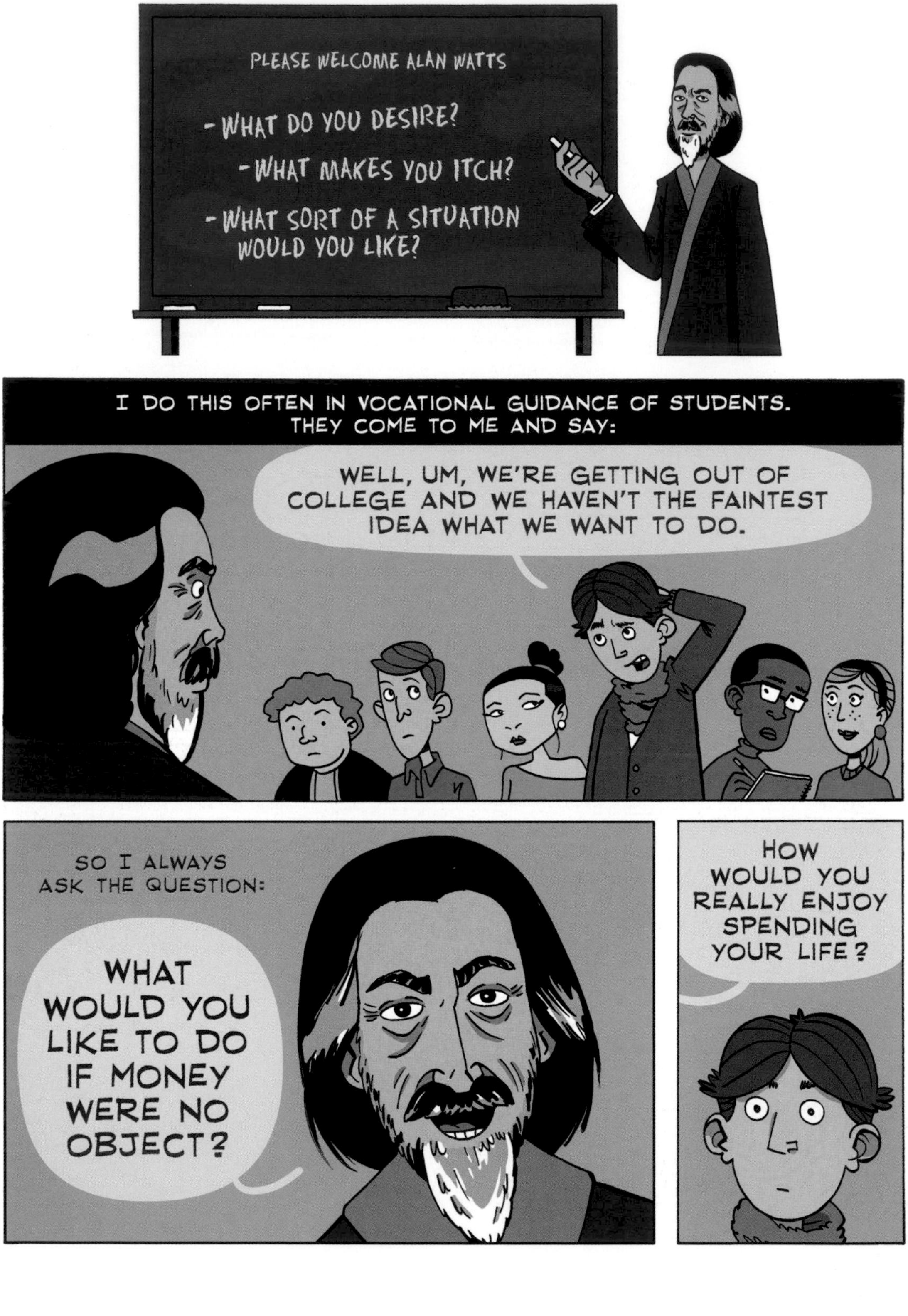
PLEASE WELCOME ALAN WATTS
- WHAT DO YOU DESIRE?
- WHAT MAKES YOU ITCH?
- WHAT SORT OF A SITUATION WOULD YOU LIKE?
I DO THIS OFTEN IN VOCATIONAL GUIDANCE OF STUDENTS. THEY COME TO ME AND SAY:
WELL, UM, WE'RE GETTING OUT OF COLLEGE AND WE HAVEN'T THE FAINTEST IDEA WHAT WE WANT TO DO.
SO I ALWAYS ASK THE QUESTION:
WHAT WOULD YOU LIKE TO DO IF MONEY WERE NO OBJECT?
HOW WOULD YOU REALLY ENJOY SPENDING YOUR LIFE?

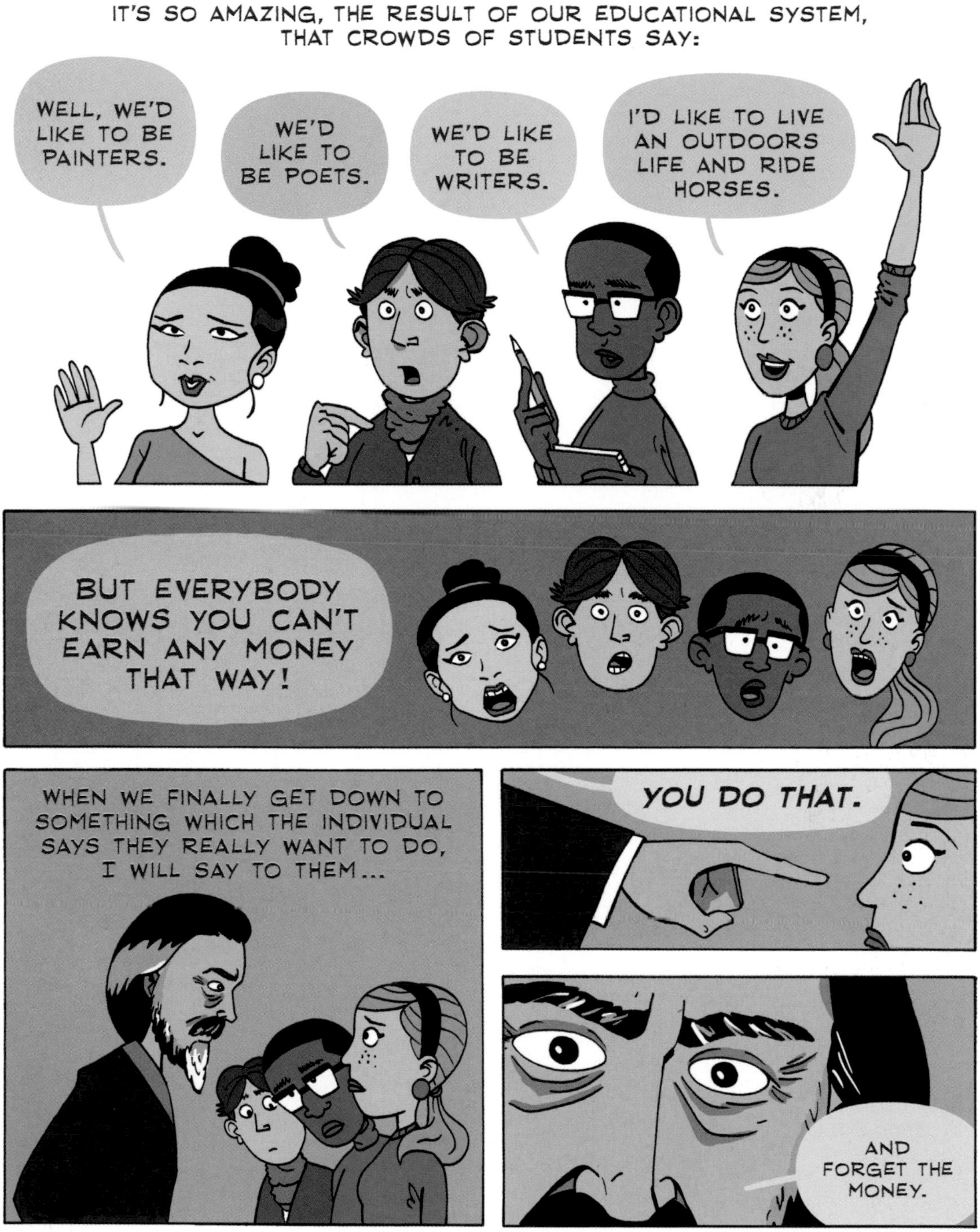
IT'S SO AMAZING, THE RESULT OF OUR EDUCATIONAL SYSTEM, THAT CROWDS OF STUDENTS SAY:
WELL, WE'D LIKE TO BE PAINTERS.
WE'D LIKE TO BE POETS.
WE'D LIKE TO BE WRITERS.
I'D LIKE TO LIVE AN OUTDOORS LIFE AND RIDE HORSES.
BUT EVERYBODY KNOWS YOU CAN'T EARN ANY MONEY THAT WAY!
WHEN WE FINALLY GET DOWN TO SOMETHING WHICH THE INDIVIDUAL SAYS THEY REALLY WANT TO DO, I WILL SAY TO THEM...
YOU DO THAT.
AND FORGET THE MONEY.

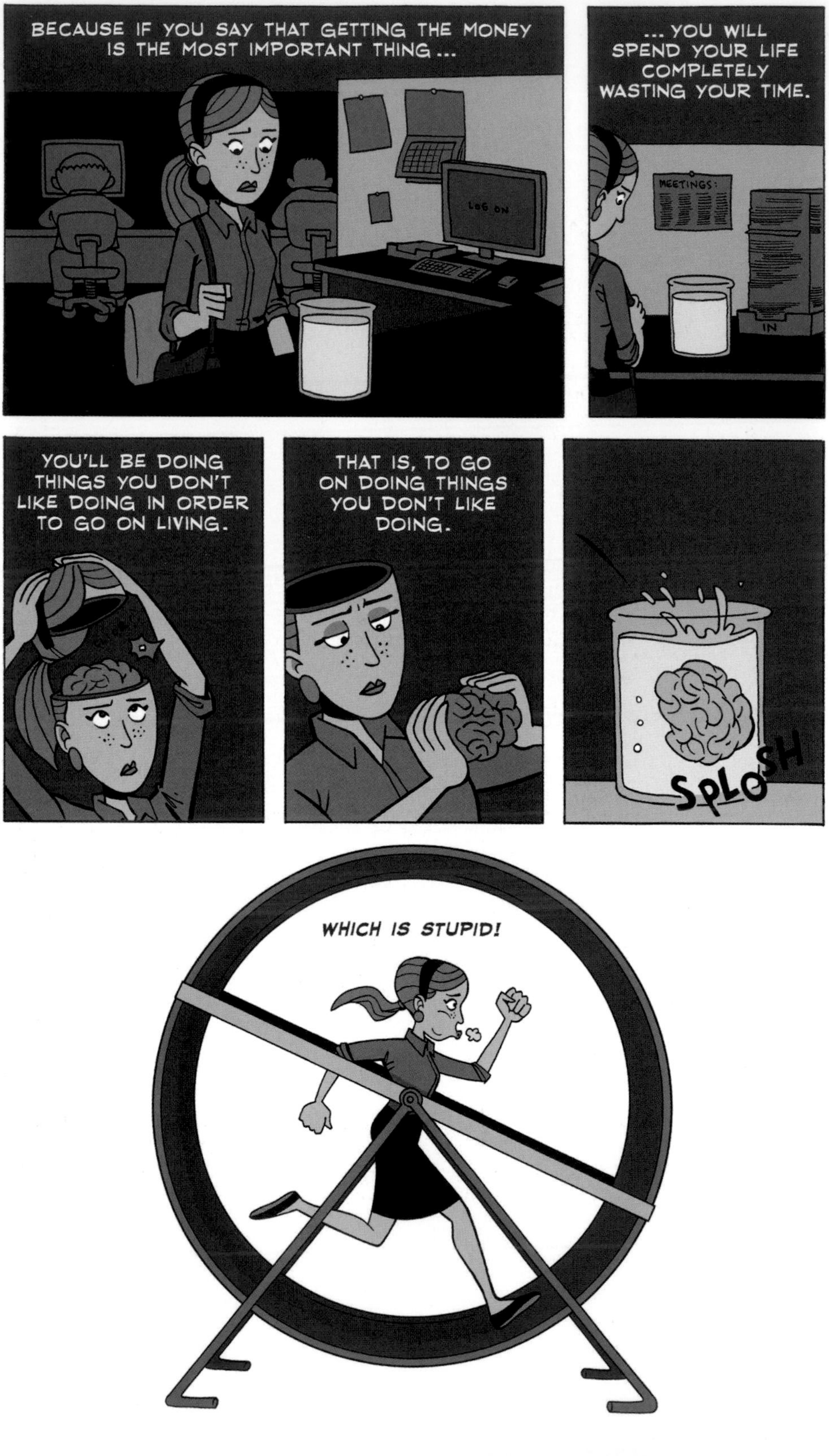
BECAUSE IF YOU SAY THAT GETTING THE MONEY IS THE MOST IMPORTANT THING...
LOG ON
... YOU WILL SPEND YOUR LIFE COMPLETELY WASTING YOUR TIME.
MEETINGS:
IN
YOU'LL BE DOING THINGS YOU DON'T LIKE DOING IN ORDER TO GO ON LIVING.
THAT IS, TO GO ON DOING THINGS YOU DON'T LIKE DOING.
SPLOSH
WHICH IS STUPID!

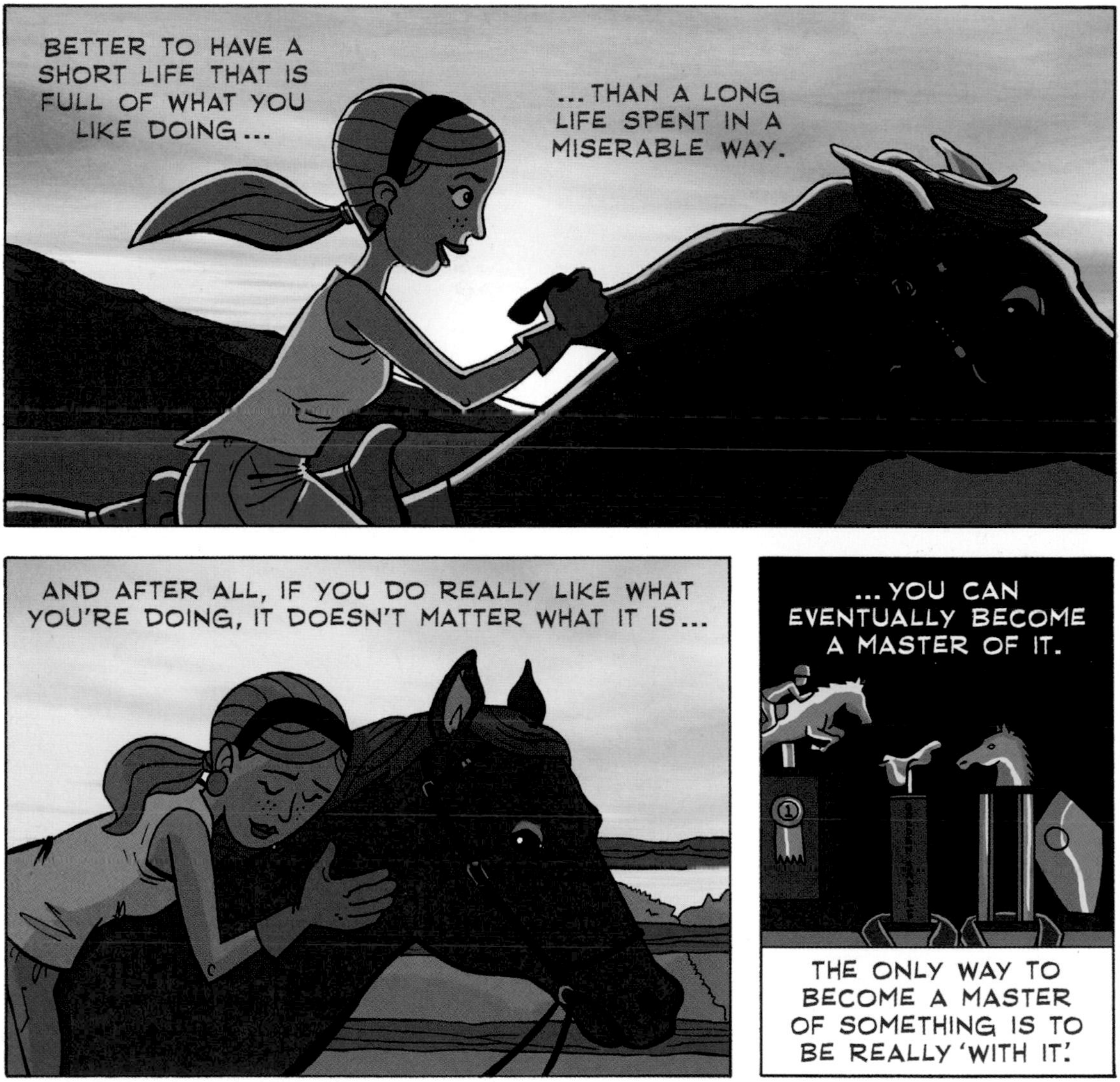
BETTER TO HAVE A SHORT LIFE THAT IS FULL OF WHAT YOU LIKE DOING...
...THAN A LONG LIFE SPENT IN A MISERABLE WAY.
AND AFTER ALL, IF YOU DO REALLY LIKE WHAT YOU'RE DOING, IT DOESN'T MATTER WHAT IT IS...
...YOU CAN EVENTUALLY BECOME A MASTER OF IT.
THE ONLY WAY TO BECOME A MASTER OF SOMETHING IS TO BE REALLY 'WITH IT.'

AND THEN YOU'LL BE ABLE TO GET A GOOD FEE FOR WHATEVER IT IS.

THEREFORE, IT'S SO IMPORTANT TO CONSIDER THIS QUESTION...

"WHAT DO I DESIRE?"
-ALAN WATTS

RIDING SCHOOL

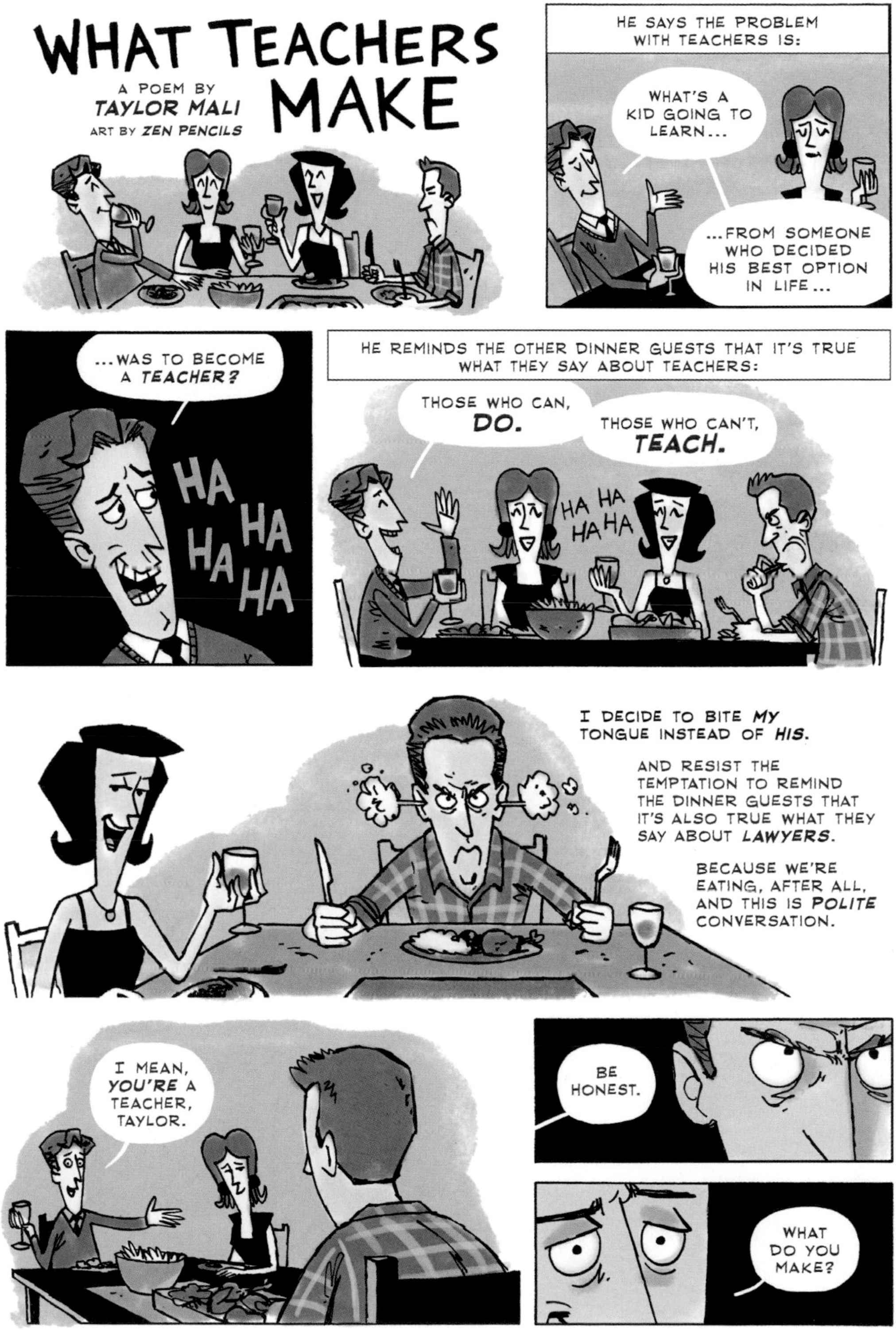
WHAT TEACHERS MAKE
A POEM BY TAYLOR MALI
ART BY ZEN PENCILS
HE SAYS THE PROBLEM WITH TEACHERS IS:
WHAT'S A KID GOING TO LEARN...
...FROM SOMEONE WHO DECIDED HIS BEST OPTION IN LIFE...
...WAS TO BECOME A TEACHER?
HA HA HA HA HA
HE REMINDS THE OTHER DINNER GUESTS THAT IT'S TRUE WHAT THEY SAY ABOUT TEACHERS:
THOSE WHO CAN, DO.
THOSE WHO CAN'T, TEACH.
HA HA HA HA
I DECIDE TO BITE MY TONGUE INSTEAD OF HIS.
AND RESIST THE TEMPTATION TO REMIND THE DINNER GUESTS THAT IT'S ALSO TRUE WHAT THEY SAY ABOUT LAWYERS.
BECAUSE WE'RE EATING, AFTER ALL, AND THIS IS POLITE CONVERSATION.
I MEAN, YOU'RE A TEACHER, TAYLOR.
BE HONEST.
WHAT DO YOU MAKE?

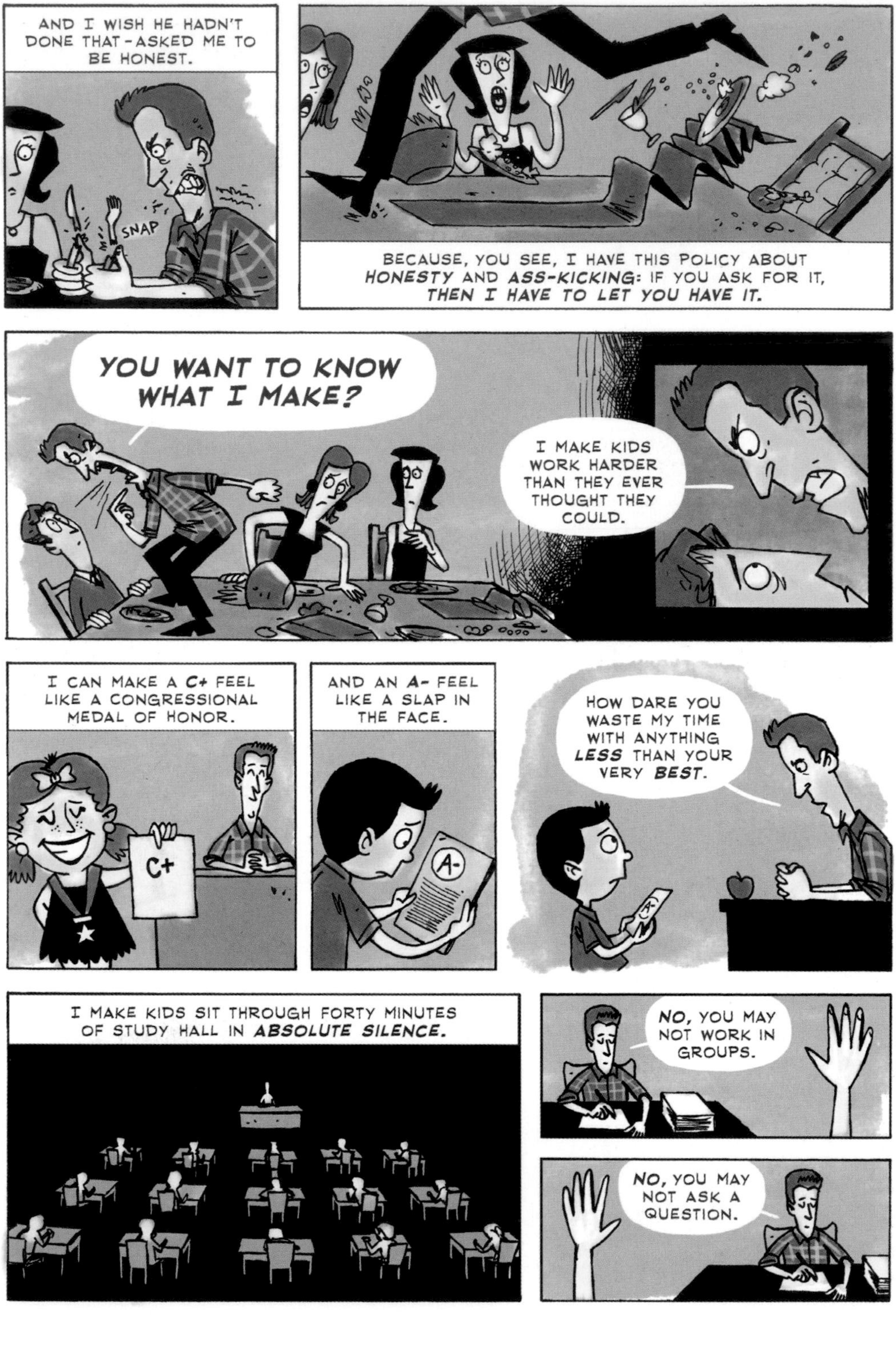
AND I WISH HE HADN'T DONE THAT - ASKED ME TO BE HONEST.
SNAP
BECAUSE, YOU SEE, I HAVE THIS POLICY ABOUT HONESTY AND ASS-KICKING: IF YOU ASK FOR IT, THEN I HAVE TO LET YOU HAVE IT.
YOU WANT TO KNOW WHAT I MAKE?
I MAKE KIDS WORK HARDER THAN THEY EVER THOUGHT THEY COULD.
I CAN MAKE A C+ FEEL LIKE A CONGRESSIONAL MEDAL OF HONOR.
C+
AND AN A- FEEL LIKE A SLAP IN THE FACE.
A-
HOW DARE YOU WASTE MY TIME WITH ANYTHING LESS THAN YOUR VERY BEST.
I MAKE KIDS SIT THROUGH FORTY MINUTES OF STUDY HALL IN ABSOLUTE SILENCE.
NO, YOU MAY NOT WORK IN GROUPS.
NO, YOU MAY NOT ASK A QUESTION.

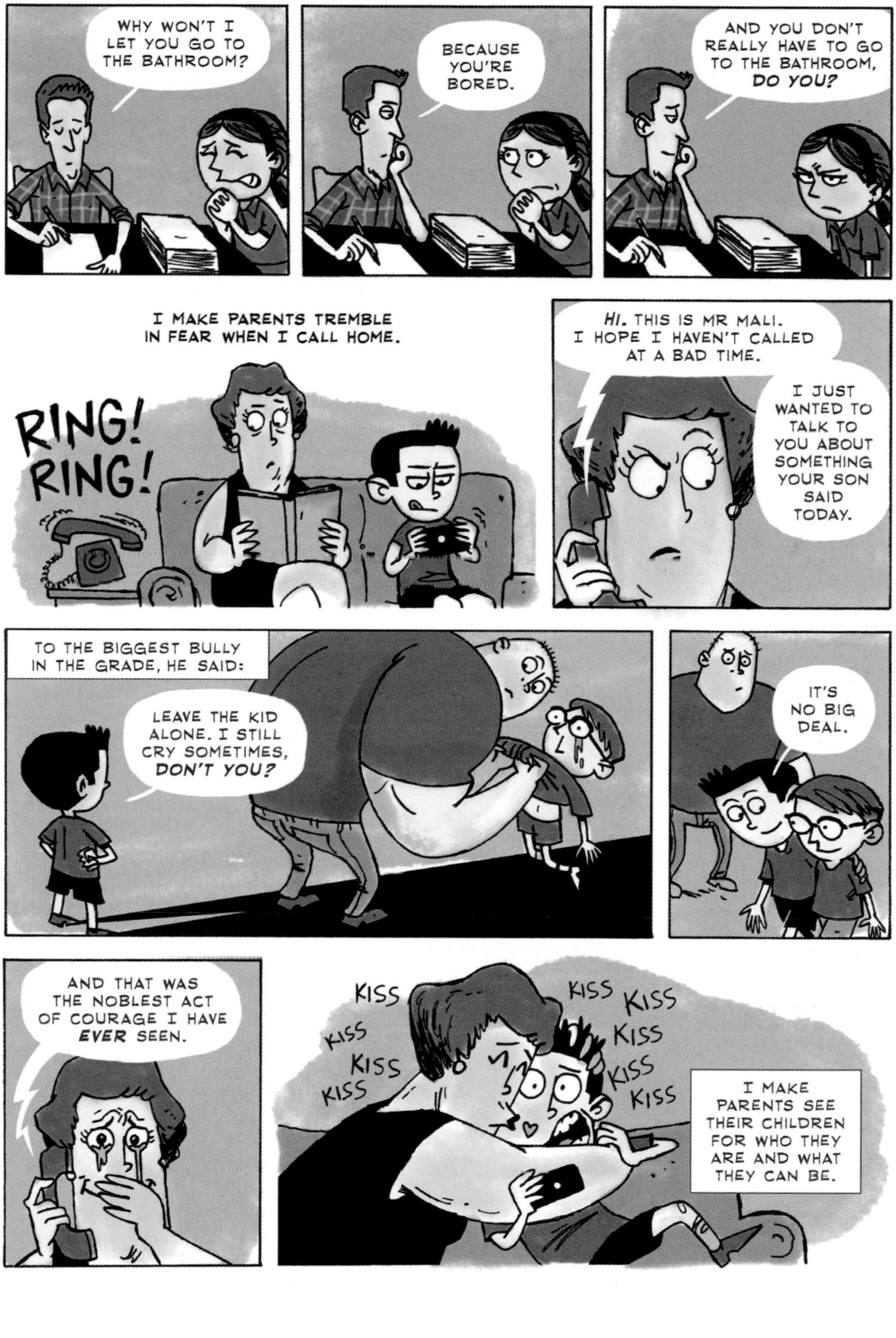
WHY WON'T I LET YOU GO TO THE BATHROOM?
BECAUSE YOU'RE BORED.
AND YOU DON'T REALLY HAVE TO GO TO THE BATHROOM, DO YOU?
I MAKE PARENTS TREMBLE IN FEAR WHEN I CALL HOME.
RING! RING!
HI. THIS IS MR MALI. I HOPE I HAVEN'T CALLED AT A BAD TIME.
I JUST WANTED TO TALK TO YOU ABOUT SOMETHING YOUR SON SAID TODAY.
TO THE BIGGEST BULLY IN THE GRADE, HE SAID:
LEAVE THE KID ALONE. I STILL CRY SOMETIMES, DON'T YOU?
IT'S NO BIG DEAL.
AND THAT WAS THE NOBLEST ACT OF COURAGE I HAVE EVER SEEN.
KISS KISS KISS KISS KISS KISS KISS KISS KISS
I MAKE PARENTS SEE THEIR CHILDREN FOR WHO THEY ARE AND WHAT THEY CAN BE.

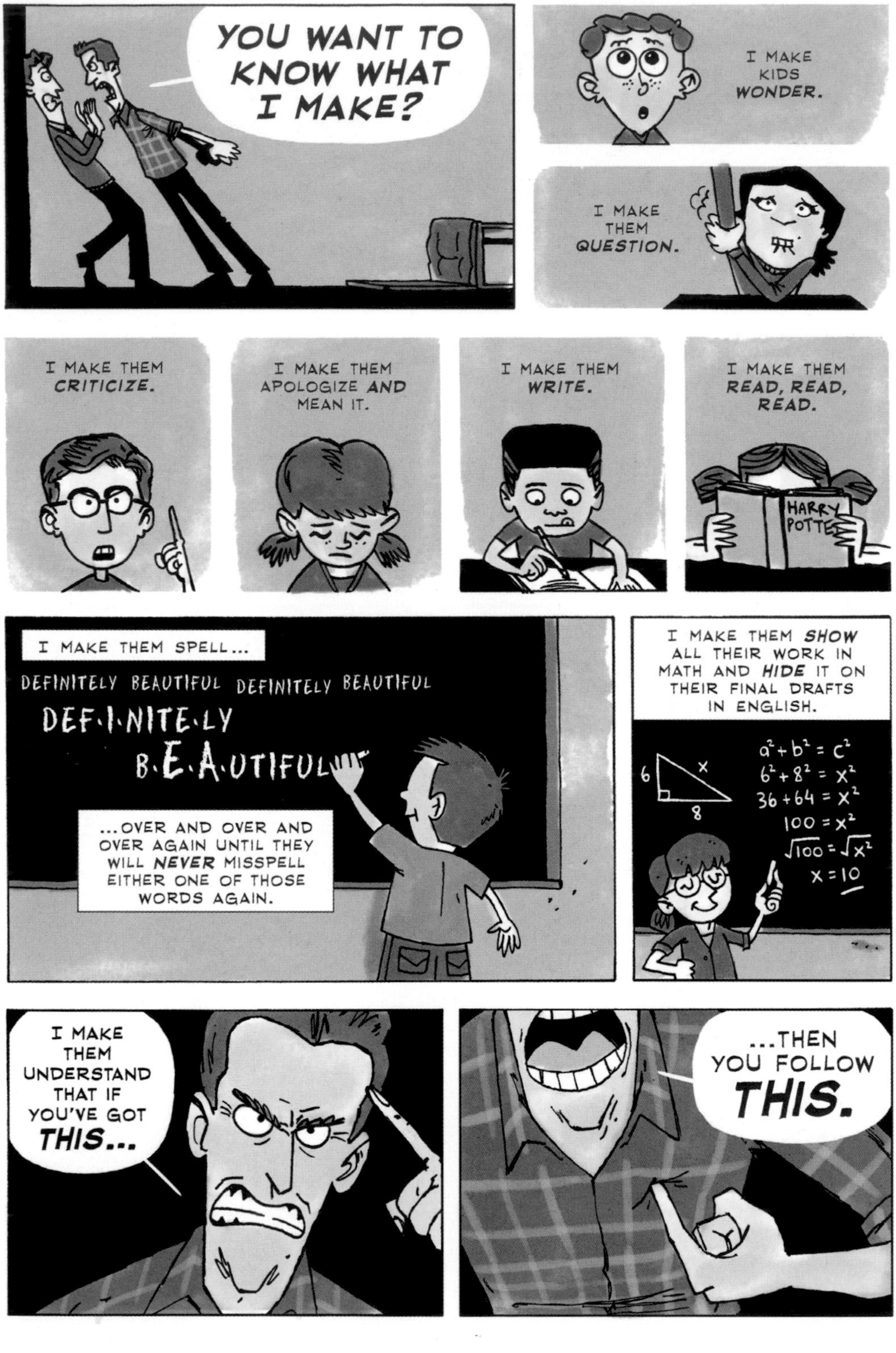
YOU WANT TO KNOW WHAT I MAKE?
I MAKE KIDS WONDER.
I MAKE THEM QUESTION.
I MAKE THEM CRITICIZE.
I MAKE THEM APOLOGIZE AND MEAN IT.
I MAKE THEM WRITE.
I MAKE THEM READ, READ, READ.
HARRY POTTE
I MAKE THEM SPELL...
DEFINITELY BEAUTIFUL DEFINITELY BEAUTIFUL
DEF·I·NITE·LY
B·E·A·UTIFUL
...OVER AND OVER AND OVER AGAIN UNTIL THEY WILL NEVER MISSPELL EITHER ONE OF THOSE WORDS AGAIN.
I MAKE THEM SHOW ALL THEIR WORK IN MATH AND HIDE IT ON THEIR FINAL DRAFTS IN ENGLISH.
6
X
8
a²+b² = c²
6²+8² = x²
36+64 = x²
100 = x²
√100 = √x²
x = 10
I MAKE THEM UNDERSTAND THAT IF YOU'VE GOT THIS...
...THEN YOU FOLLOW THIS.

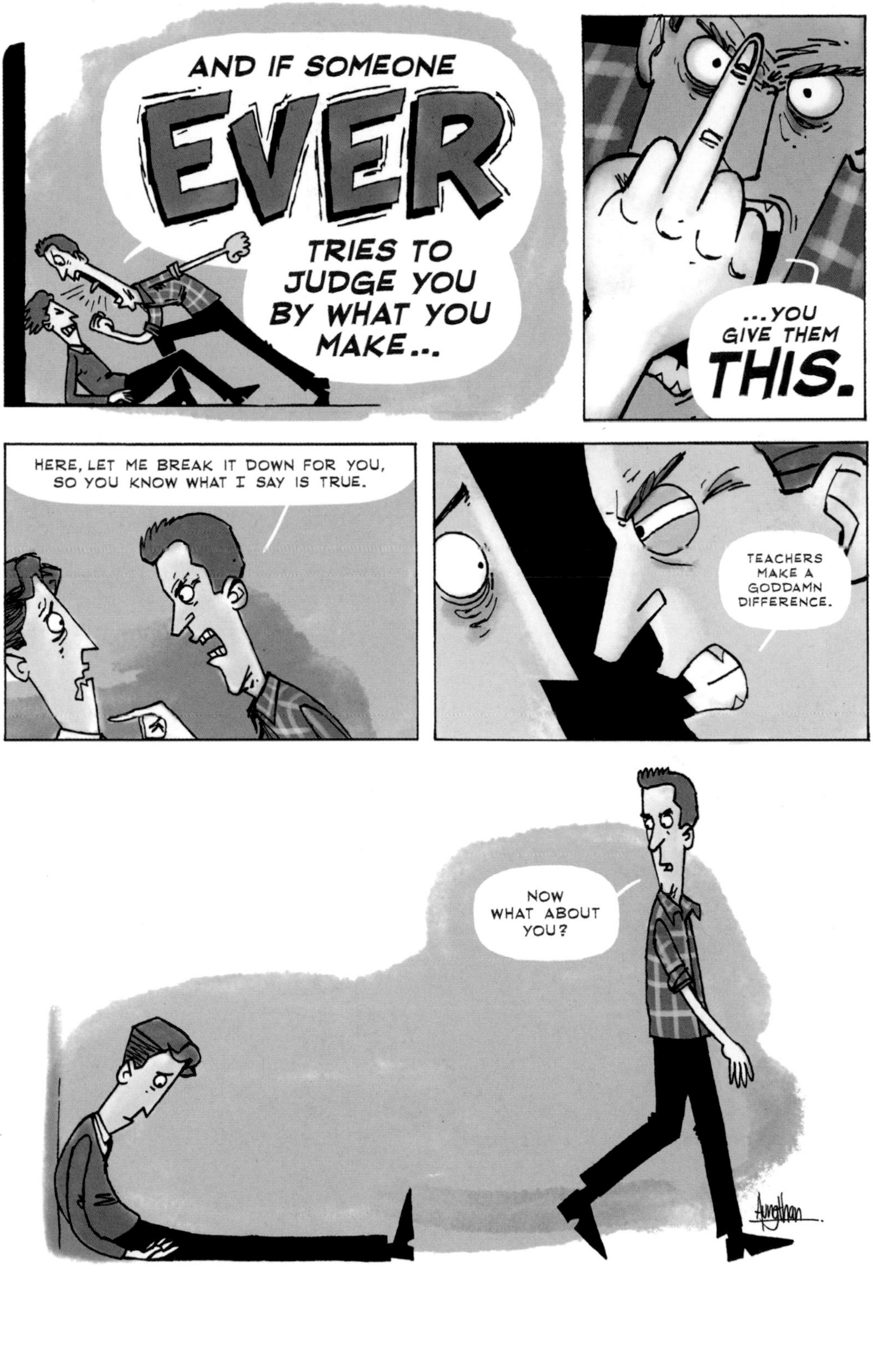
AND IF SOMEONE
EVER
TRIES TO JUDGE YOU BY WHAT YOU MAKE...
...YOU GIVE THEM THIS.
HERE, LET ME BREAK IT DOWN FOR YOU, SO YOU KNOW WHAT I SAY IS TRUE.
TEACHERS MAKE A GODDAMN DIFFERENCE.
NOW WHAT ABOUT YOU?

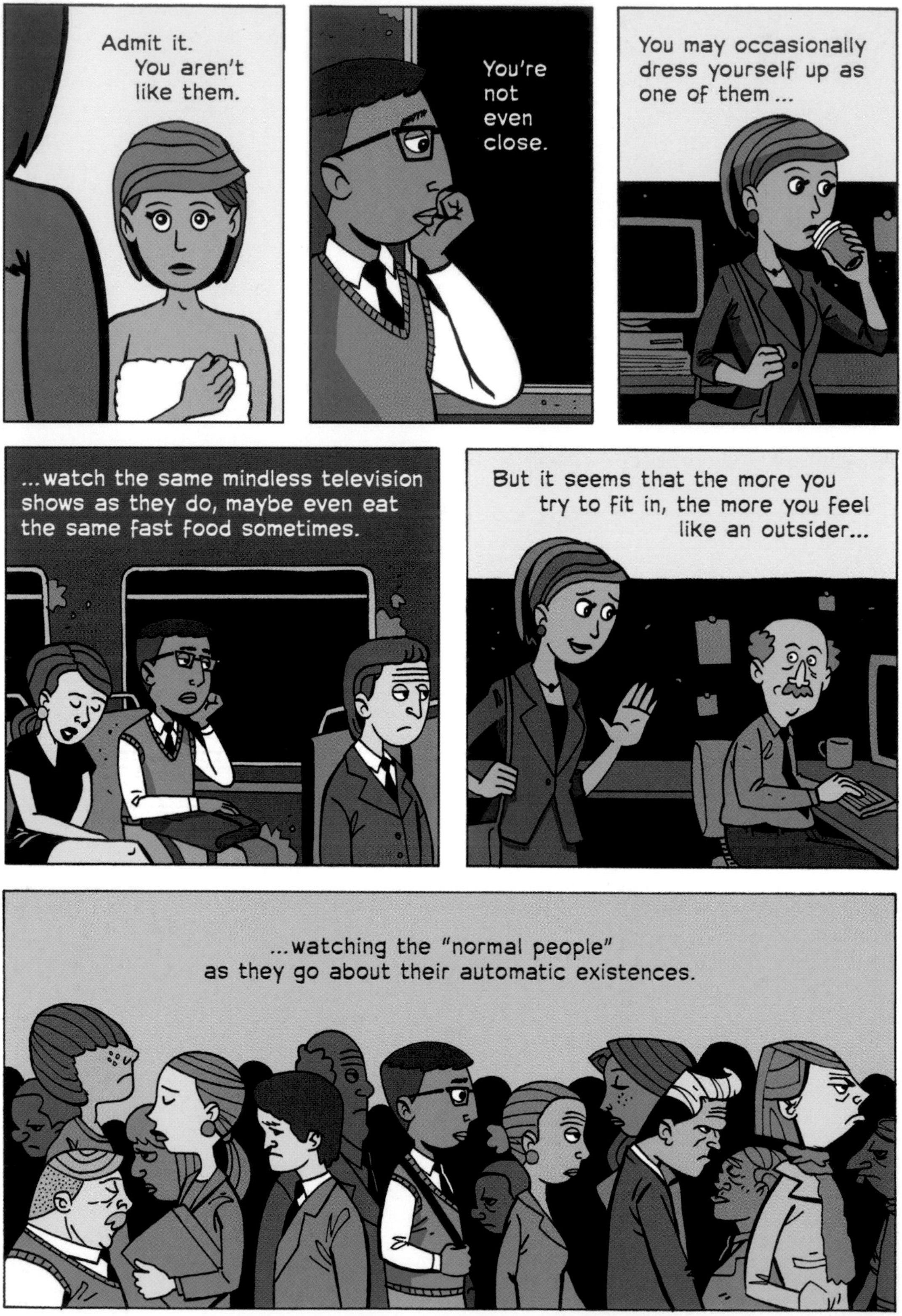
Admit it. You aren't like them.
You're not even close.
You may occasionally dress yourself up as one of them ...
...watch the same mindless television shows as they do, maybe even eat the same fast food sometimes.
But it seems that the more you try to fit in, the more you feel like an outsider...
...watching the "normal people" as they go about their automatic existences.

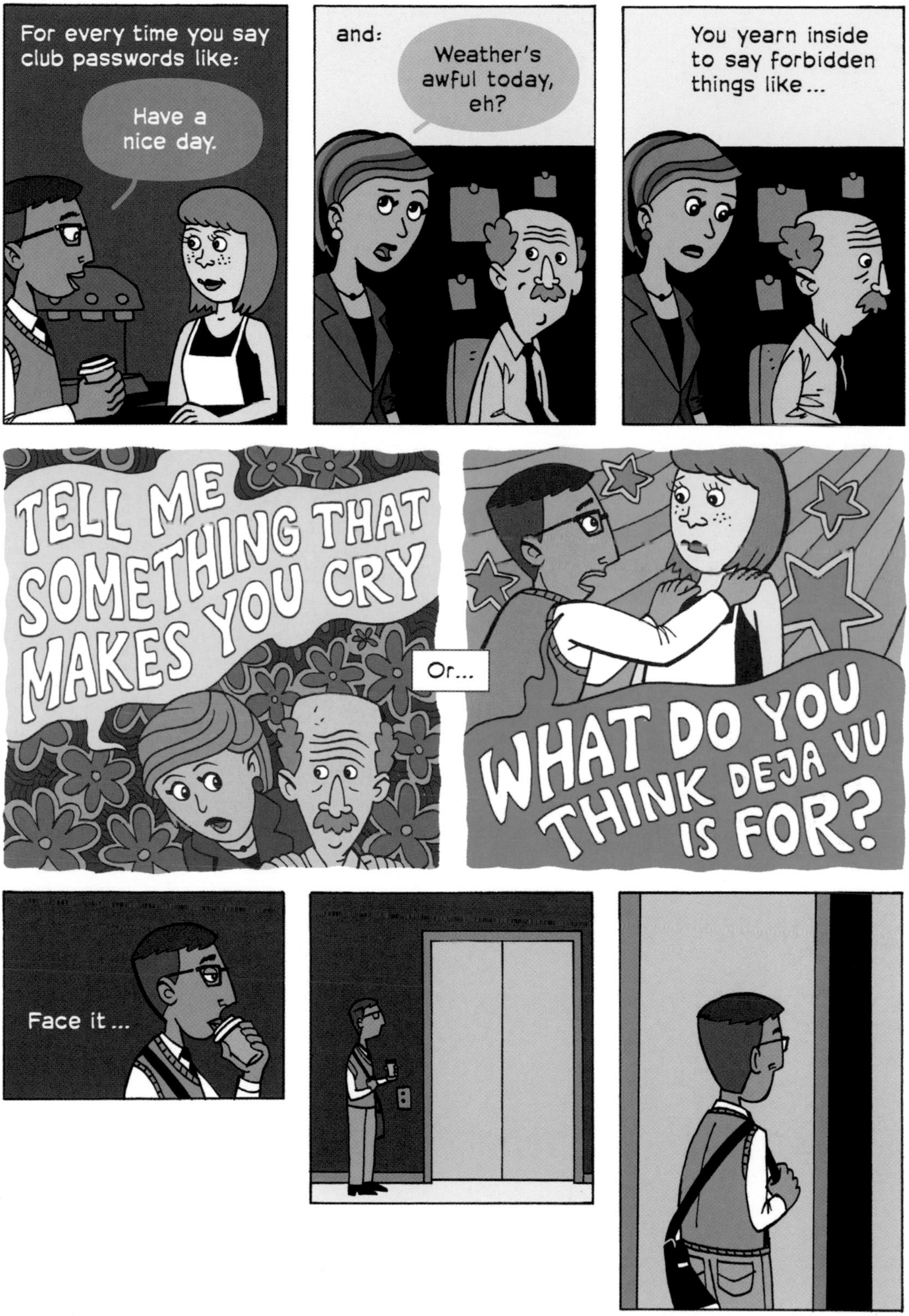

For every time you say club passwords like:
Have a nice day.
and:
Weather's awful today, eh?
You yearn inside to say forbidden things like...
TELL ME SOMETHING THAT MAKES YOU CRY
Or...
WHAT DO YOU THINK DEJA VU IS FOR?
Face it...

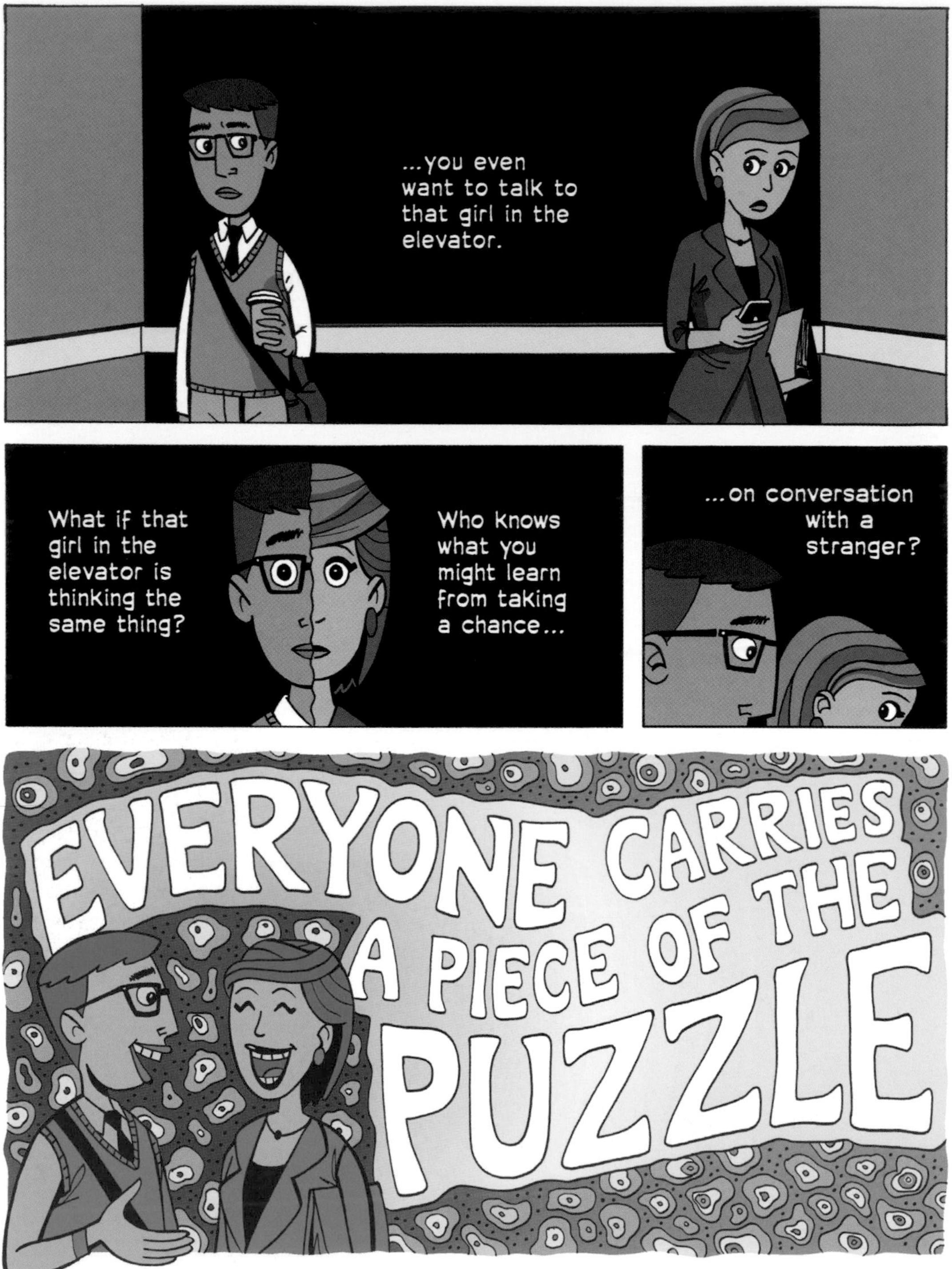
...you even want to talk to that girl in the elevator.
What if that girl in the elevator is thinking the same thing?
Who knows what you might learn from taking a chance...
...on conversation with a stranger?
EVERYONE CARRIES A PIECE OF THE PUZZLE

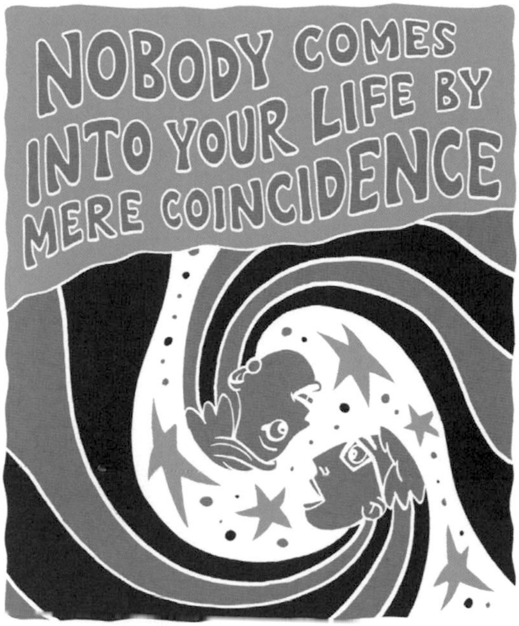
NOBODY COMES INTO YOUR LIFE BY MERE COINCIDENCE

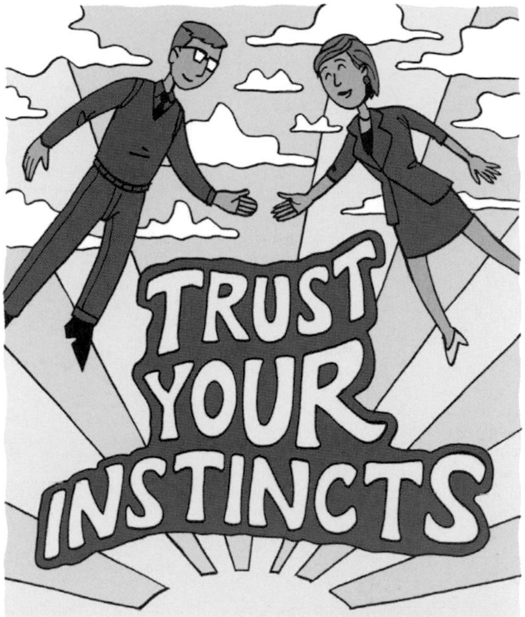
TRUST YOUR INSTINCTS

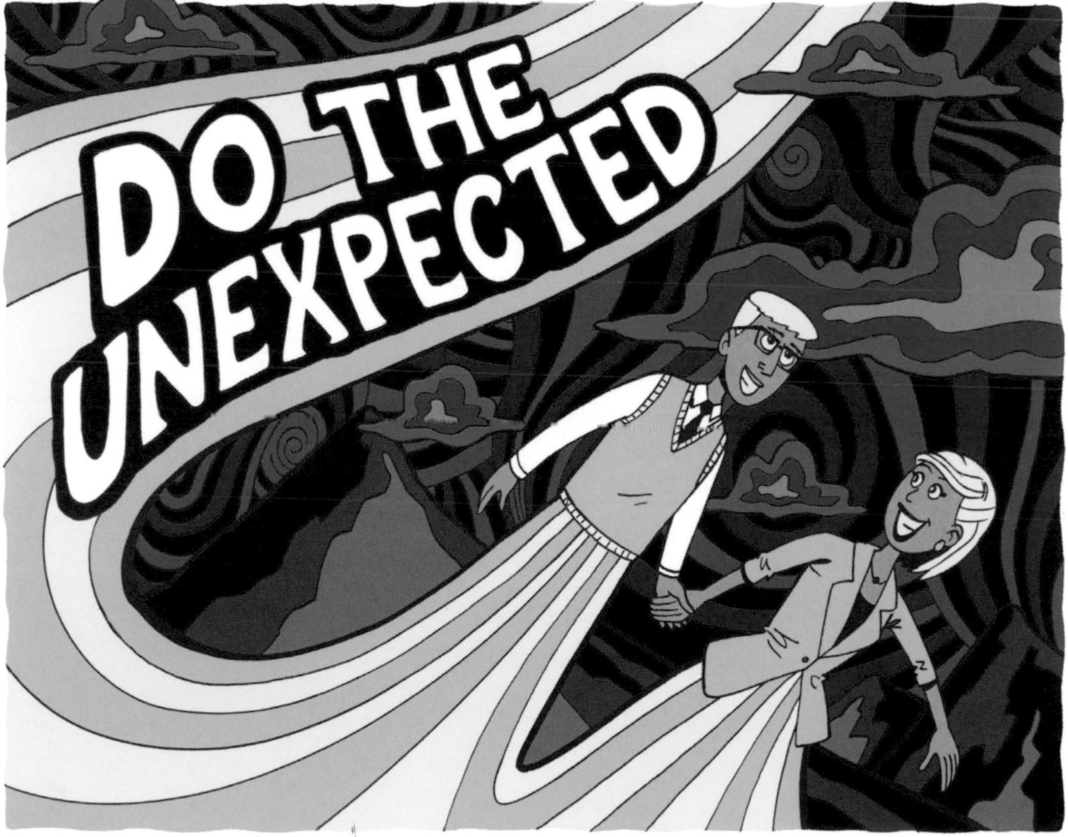
DO THE UNEXPECTED

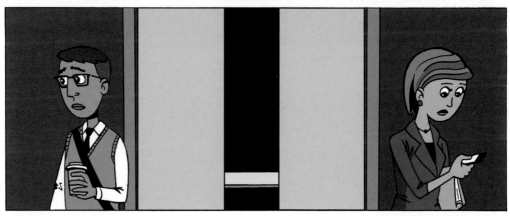

Find the others.

—Timothy Leary

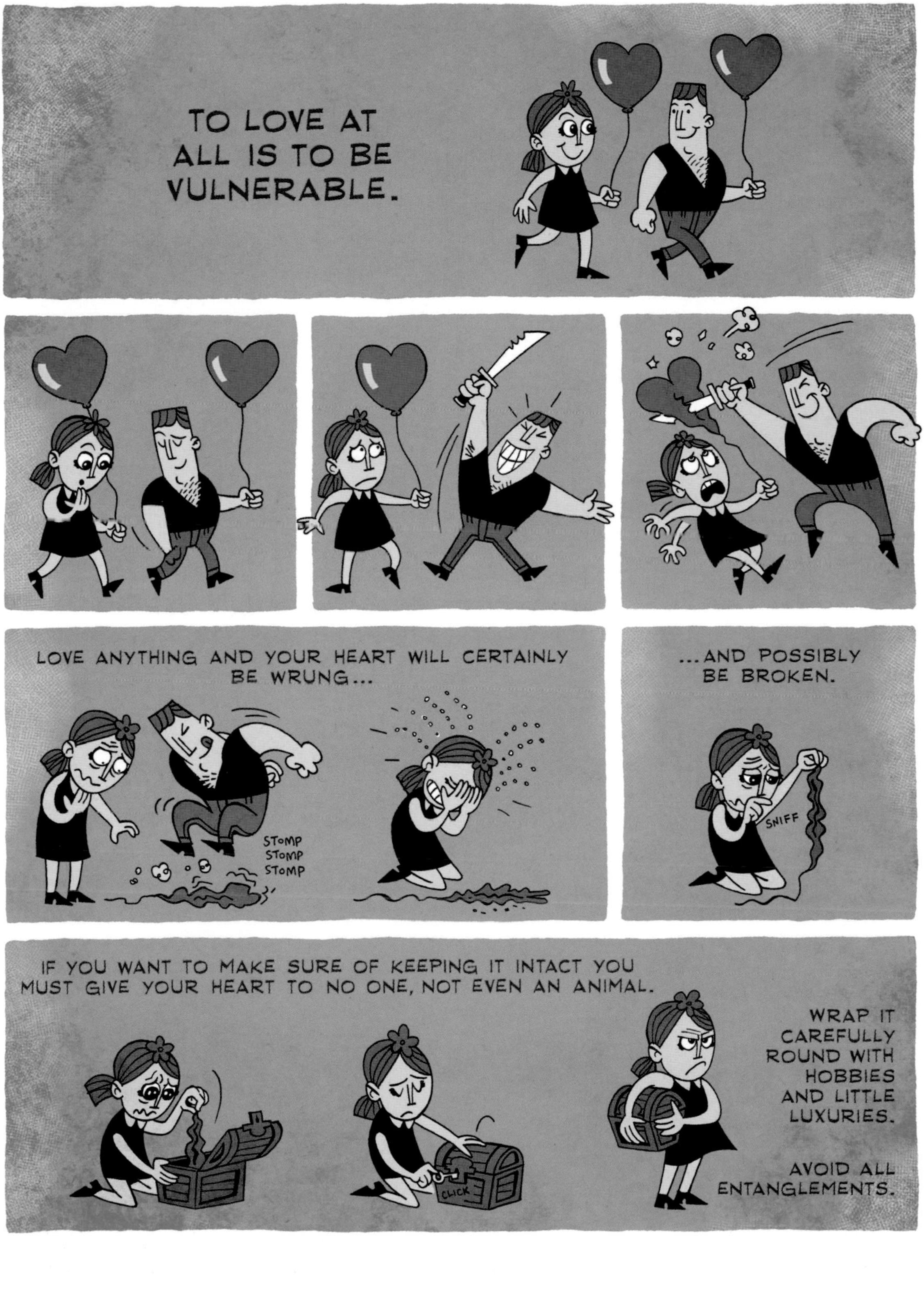
TO LOVE AT ALL IS TO BE VULNERABLE.
LOVE ANYTHING AND YOUR HEART WILL CERTAINLY BE WRUNG...
STOMP STOMP STOMP
...AND POSSIBLY BE BROKEN.
SNIFF
IF YOU WANT TO MAKE SURE OF KEEPING IT INTACT YOU MUST GIVE YOUR HEART TO NO ONE, NOT EVEN AN ANIMAL.
CLICK
WRAP IT CAREFULLY ROUND WITH HOBBIES AND LITTLE LUXURIES.
AVOID ALL ENTANGLEMENTS.

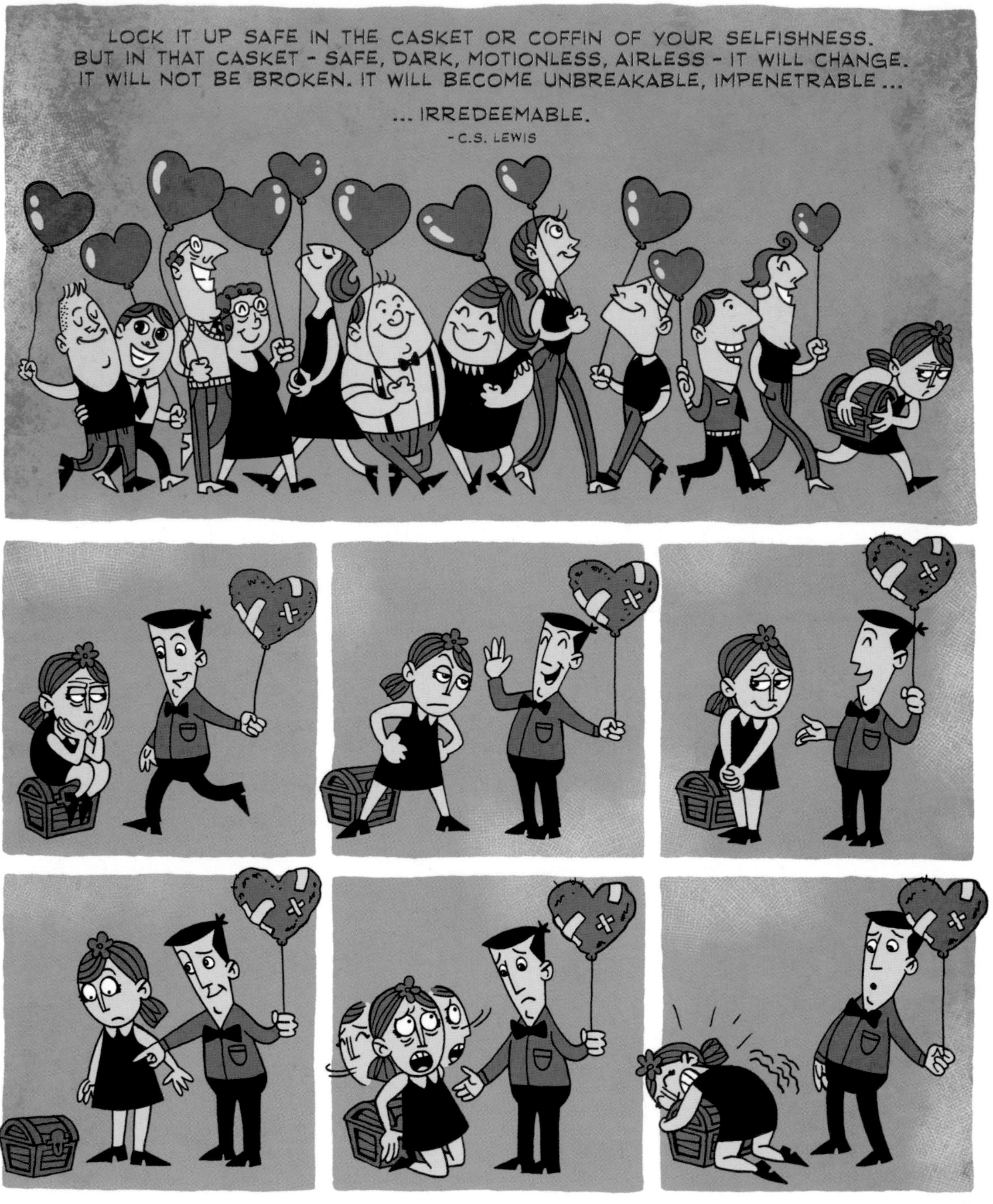
LOCK IT UP SAFE IN THE CASKET OR COFFIN OF YOUR SELFISHNESS.
BUT IN THAT CASKET - SAFE, DARK, MOTIONLESS, AIRLESS - IT WILL CHANGE.
IT WILL NOT BE BROKEN. IT WILL BECOME UNBREAKABLE, IMPENETRABLE ...
... IRREDEEMABLE.
- C.S. LEWIS

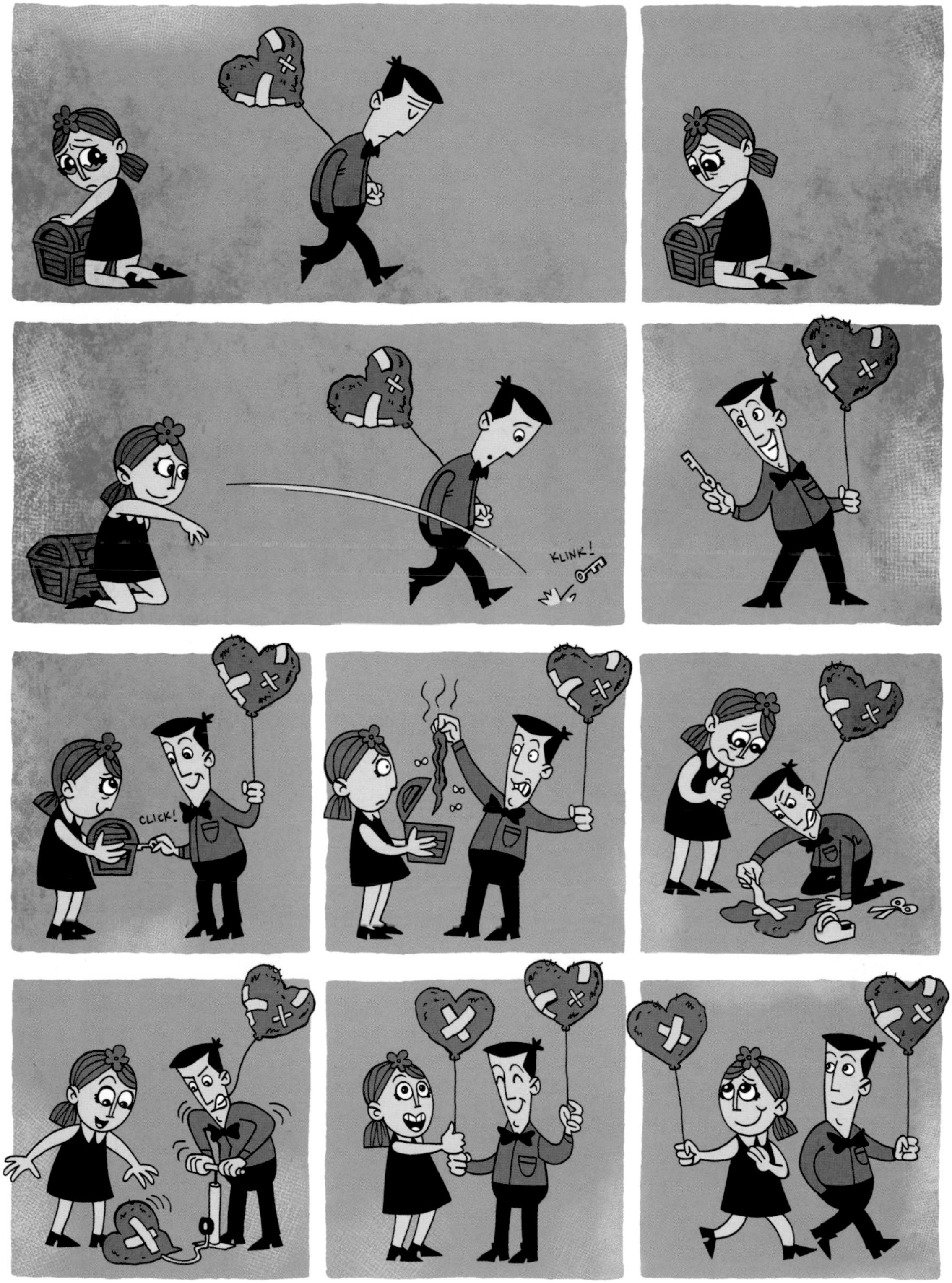
KLINK!
CLICK!

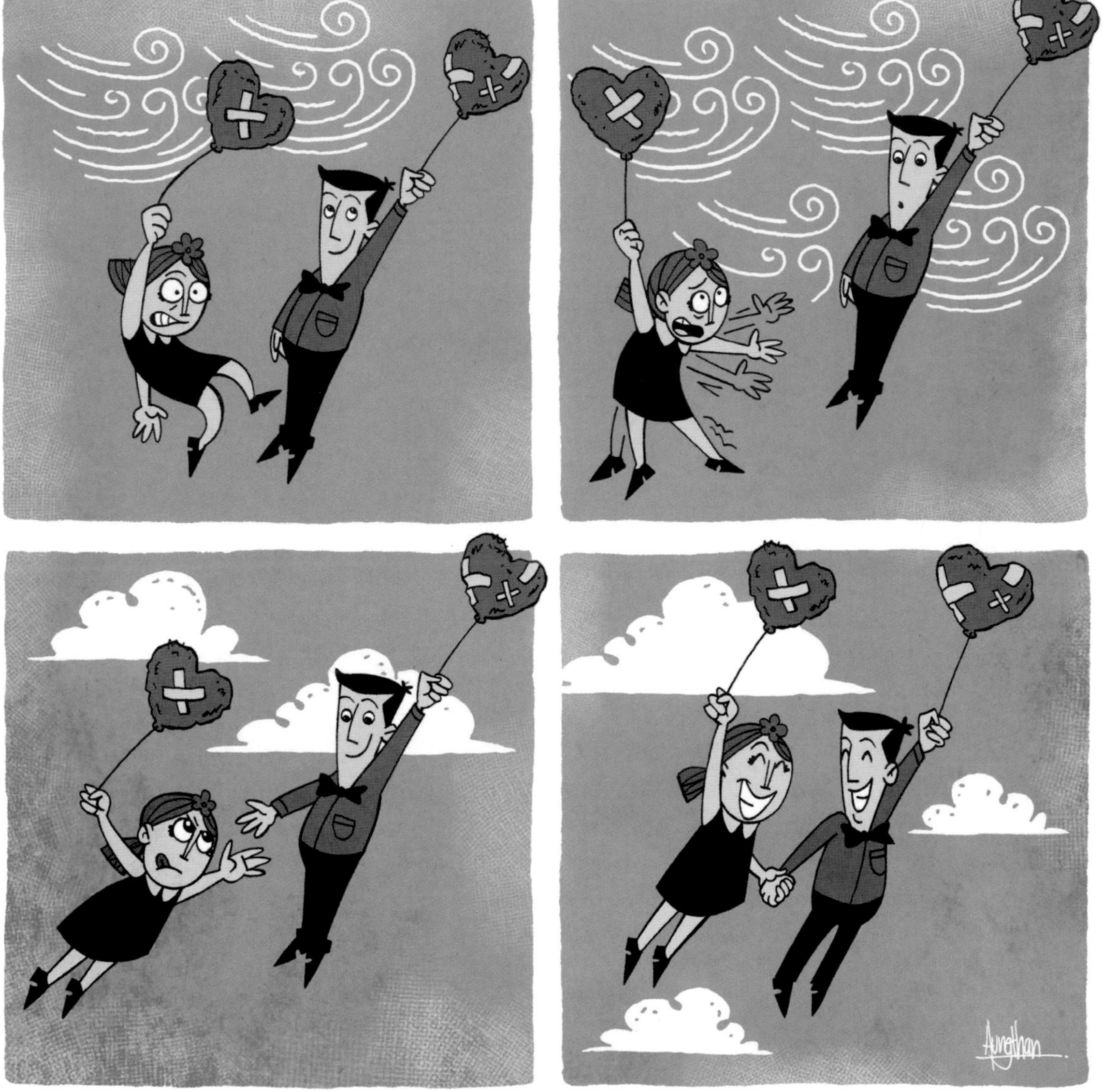

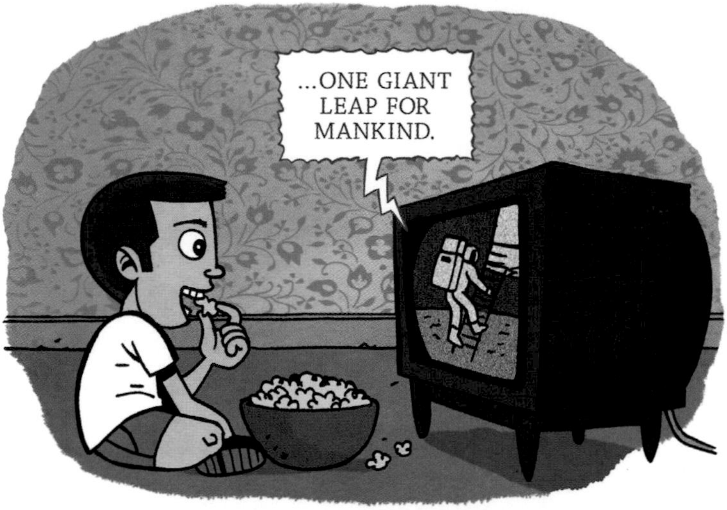
...ONE GIANT LEAP FOR MANKIND.

DECIDE IN YOUR HEART OF HEARTS WHAT REALLY EXCITES AND CHALLENGES YOU...

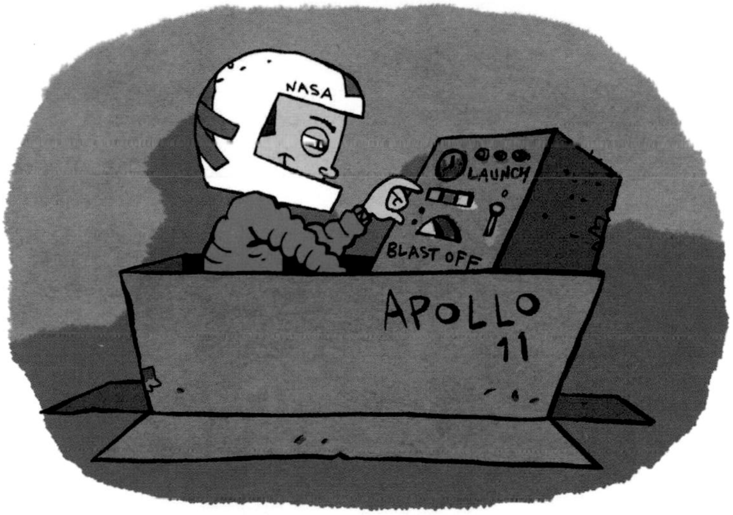
NASA
LAUNCH
BLAST OFF
APOLLO 11

...AND START MOVING YOUR LIFE IN THAT DIRECTION.

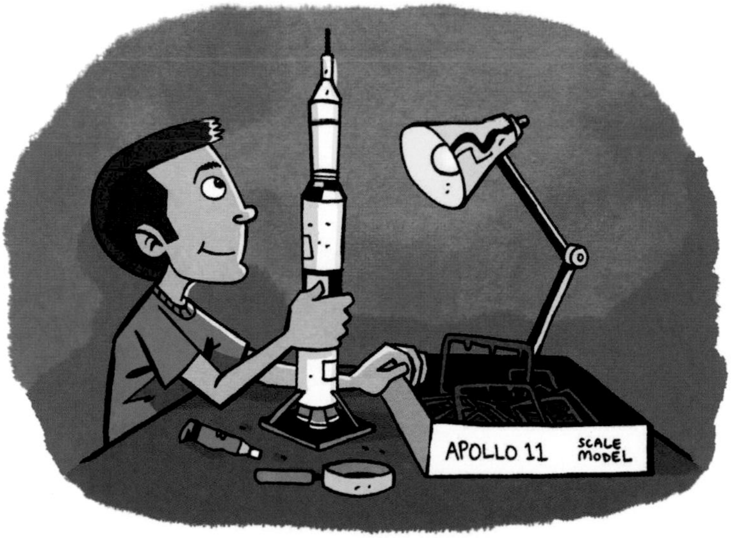
APOLLO 11
SCALE MODEL

EVERY DECISION YOU MAKE, FROM WHAT YOU EAT TO WHAT YOU DO WITH YOUR TIME TONIGHT...

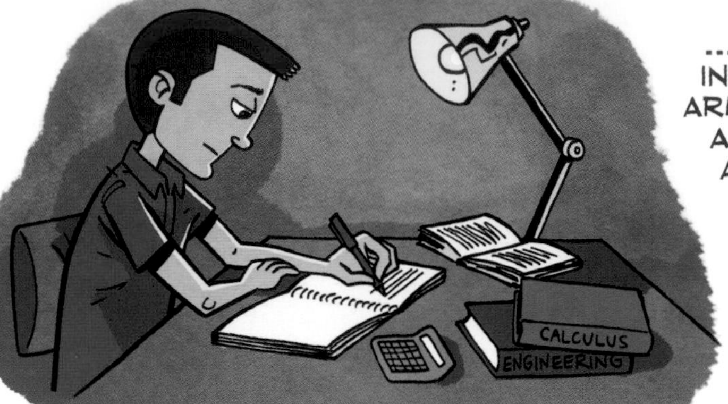
CALCULUS
ENGINEERING

...TURNS YOU INTO WHO YOU ARE TOMORROW, AND THE DAY AFTER THAT.

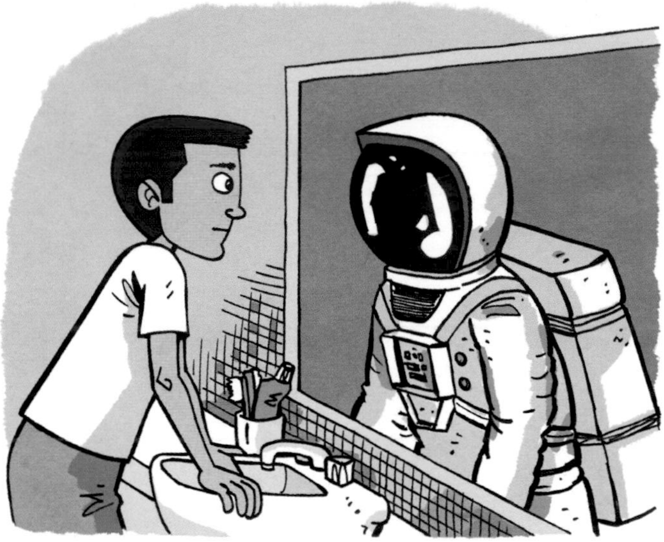

LOOK AT WHO YOU WANT TO BE, AND START SCULPTING YOURSELF INTO THAT PERSON.

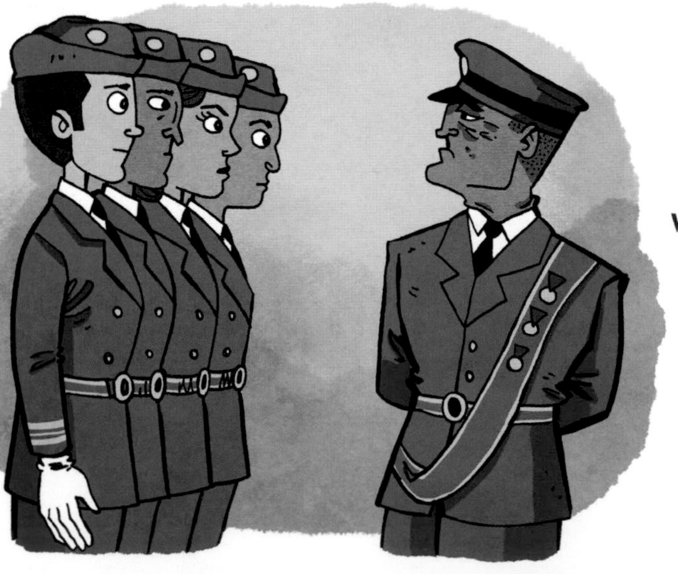

YOU MAY NOT GET EXACTLY WHERE YOU THOUGHT YOU'D BE...

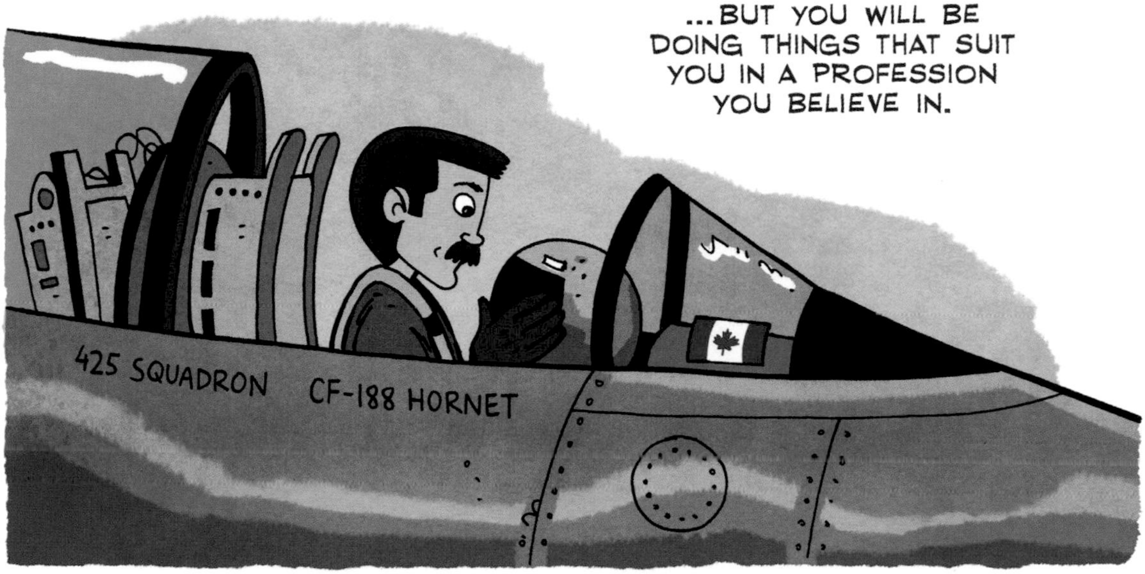
...BUT YOU WILL BE DOING THINGS THAT SUIT YOU IN A PROFESSION YOU BELIEVE IN.
425 SQUADRON
CF-188 HORNET

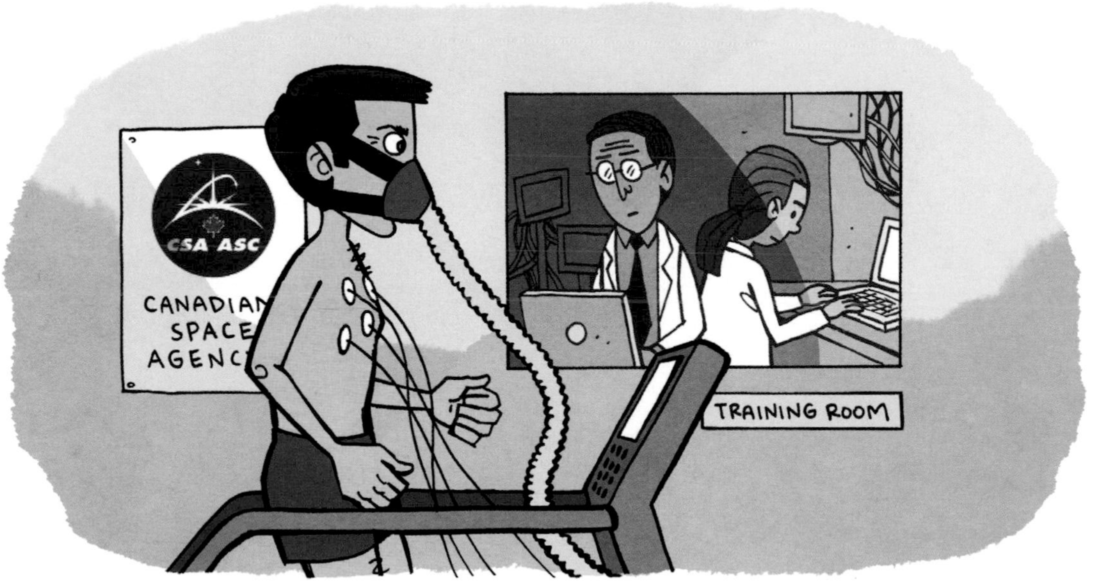
CSA ASC
CANADIAN SPACE AGENC
TRAINING ROOM

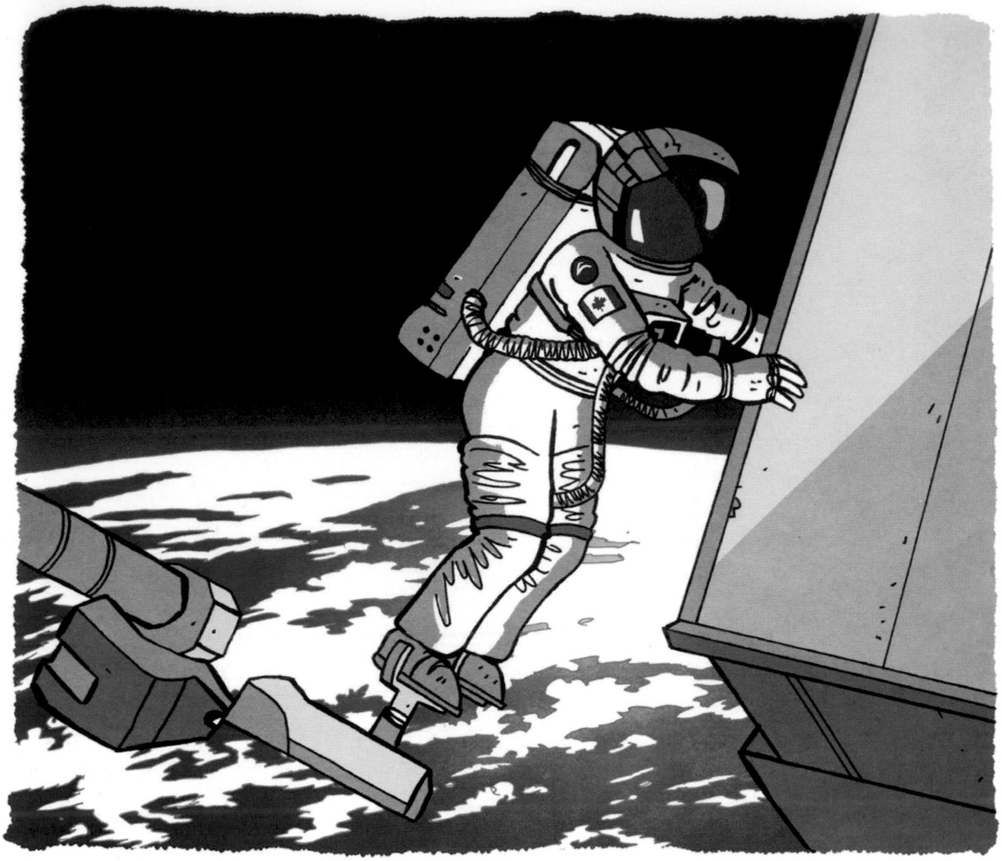

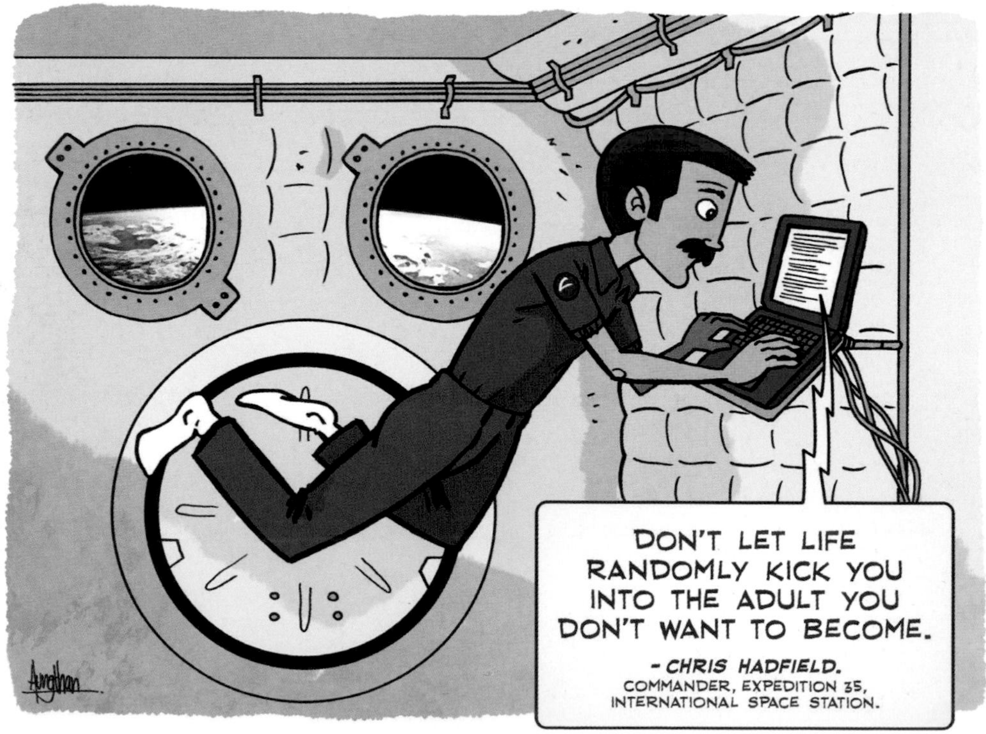
DON'T LET LIFE RANDOMLY KICK YOU INTO THE ADULT YOU DON'T WANT TO BECOME.
- CHRIS HADFIELD.
COMMANDER, EXPEDITION 35, INTERNATIONAL SPACE STATION.

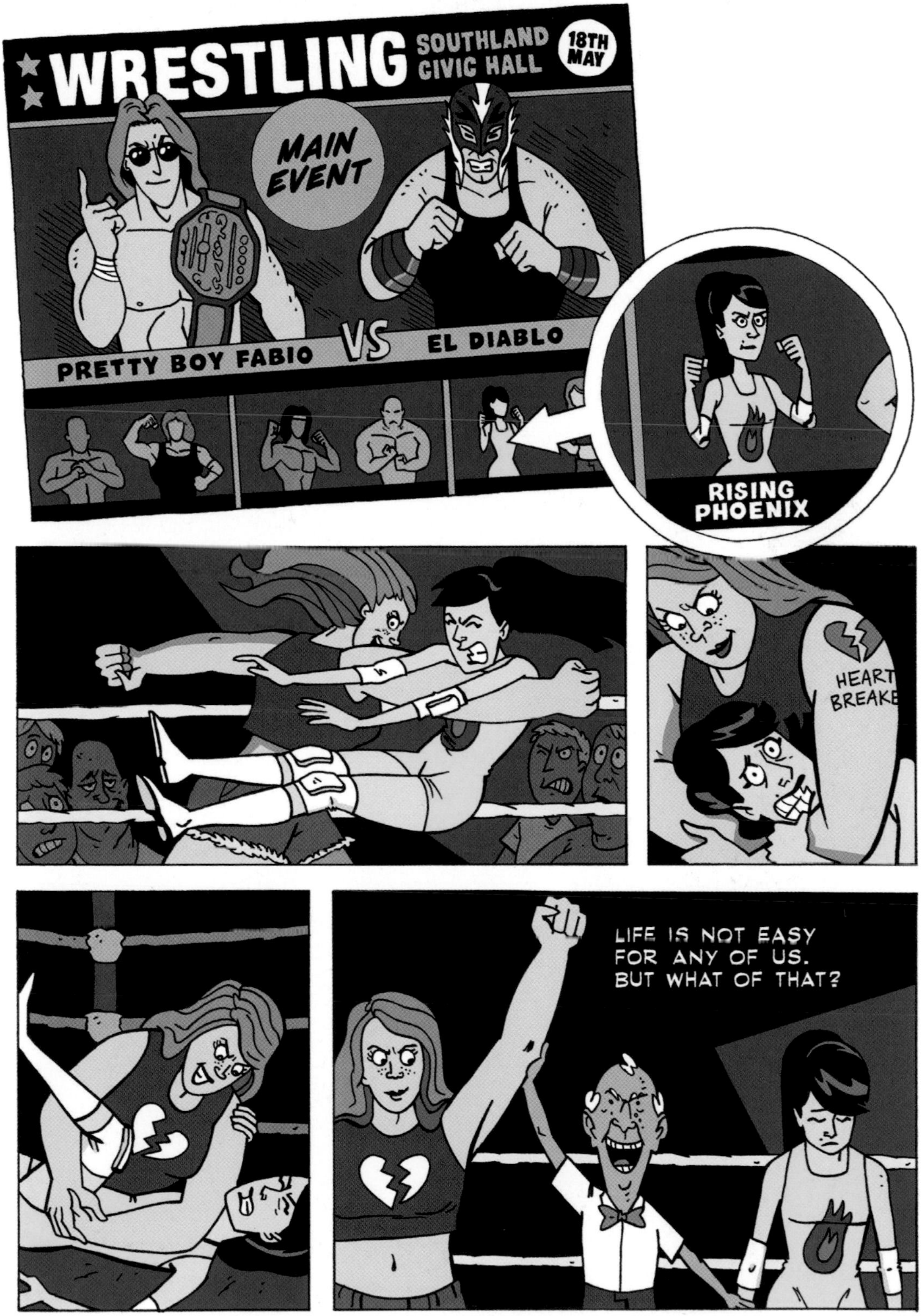
WRESTLING
SOUTHLAND CIVIC HALL
18TH MAY
MAIN EVENT
PRETTY BOY FABIO
VS
EL DIABLO
RISING PHOENIX
HEART BREAKE
LIFE IS NOT EASY FOR ANY OF US. BUT WHAT OF THAT?

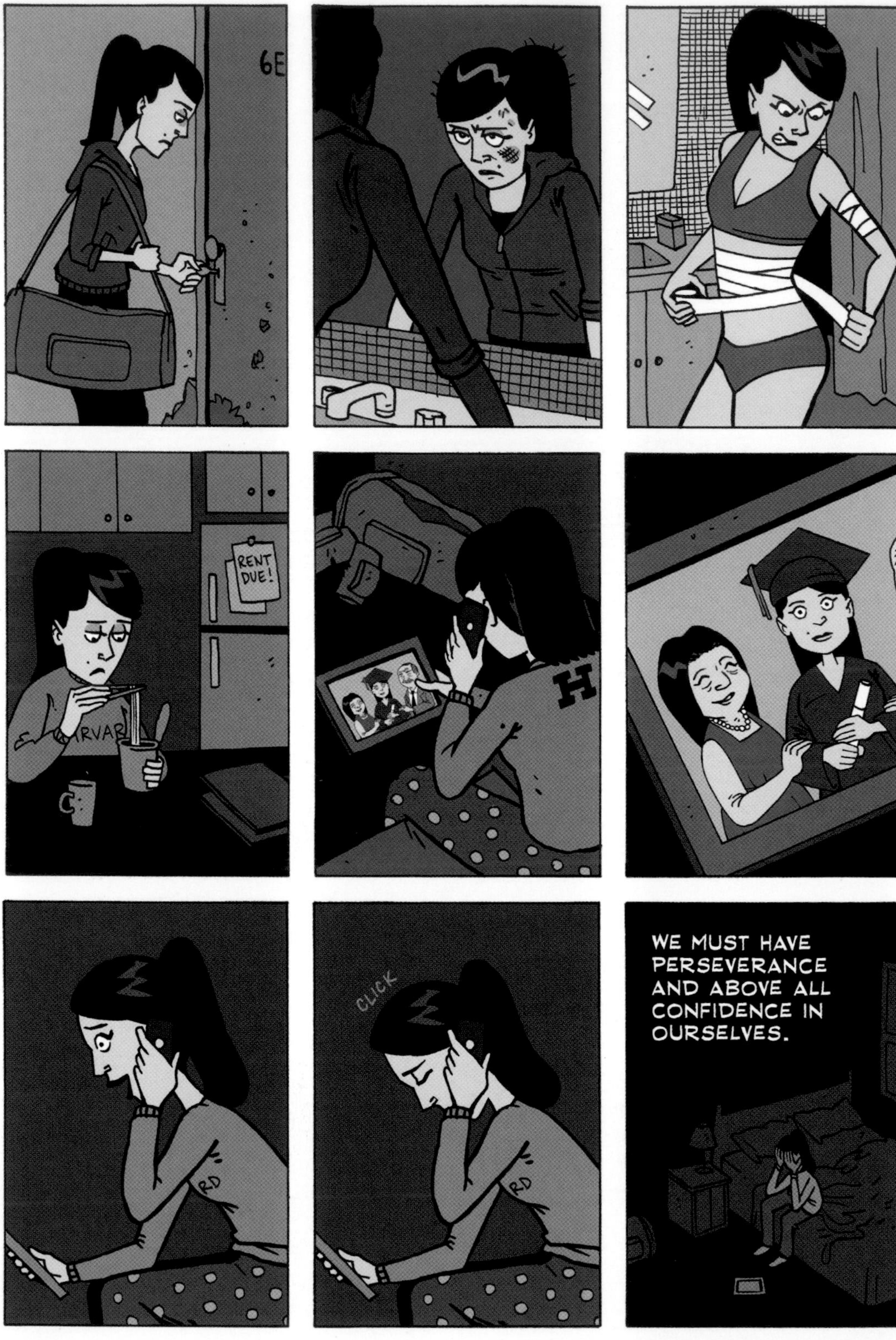
6E
RENT DUE!
CLICK
WE MUST HAVE PERSEVERANCE AND ABOVE ALL CONFIDENCE IN OURSELVES.

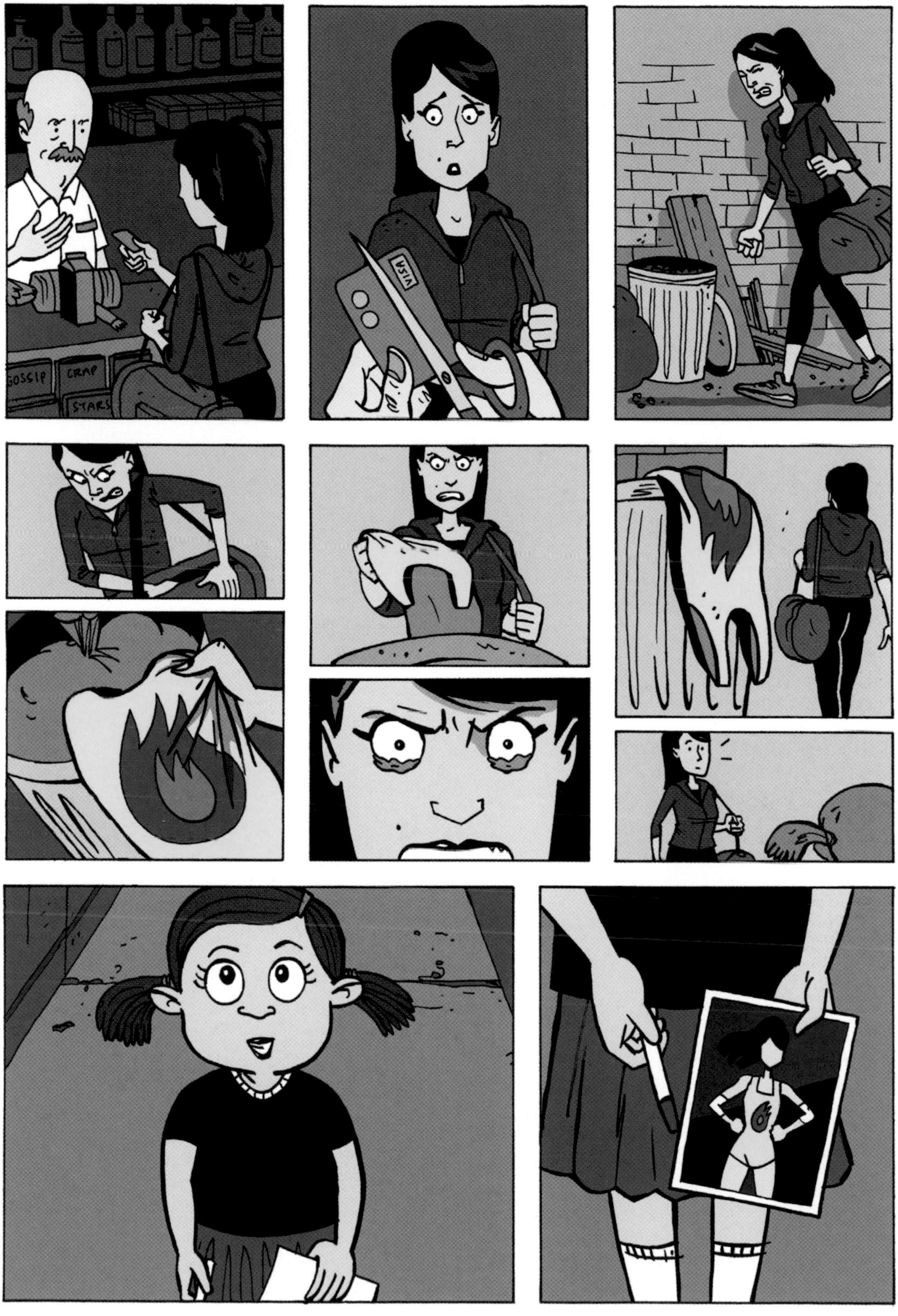
GOSSIP
CRAP
STARS
VISA

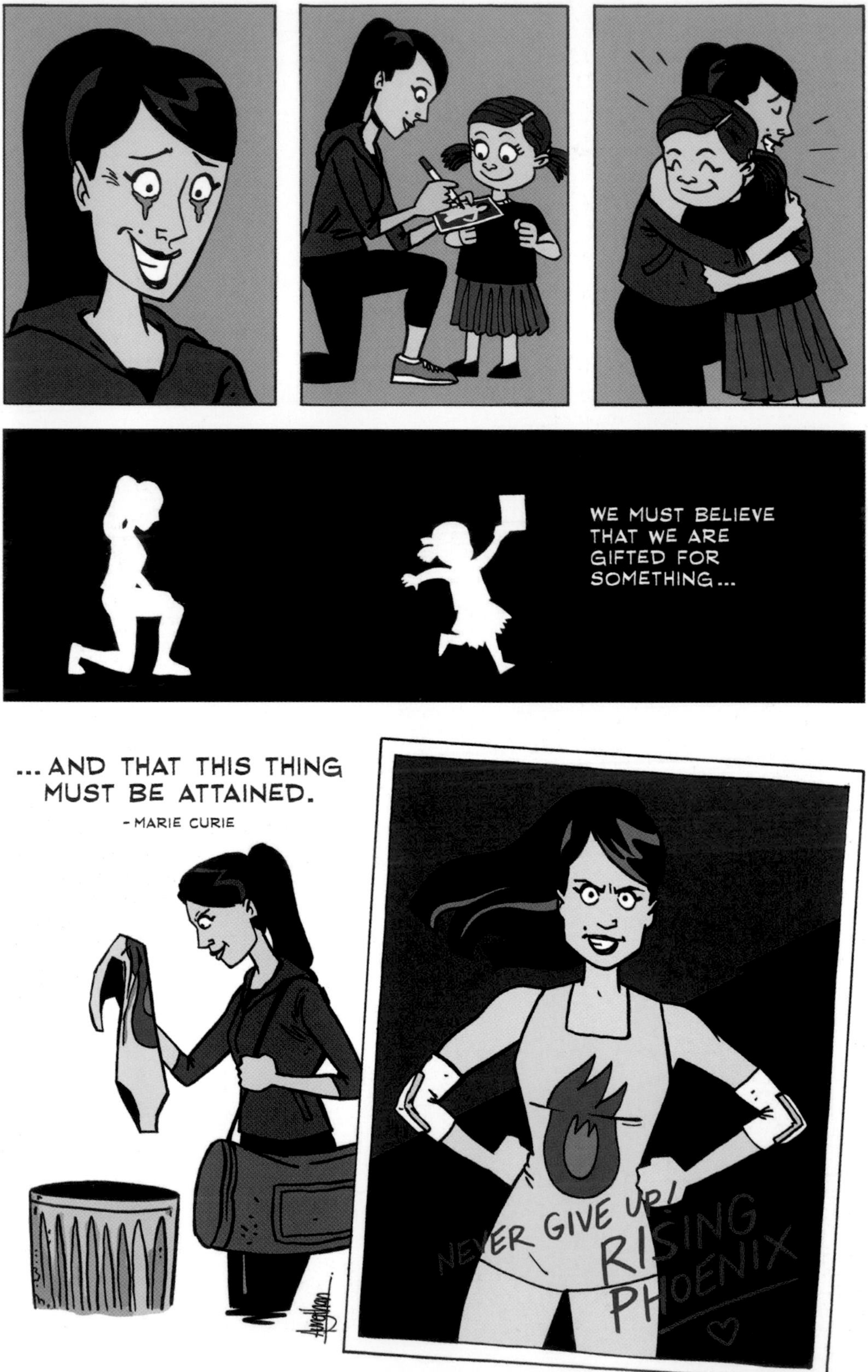
WE MUST BELIEVE THAT WE ARE GIFTED FOR SOMETHING...
...AND THAT THIS THING MUST BE ATTAINED.
-MARIE CURIE
NEVER GIVE UP!
RISING PHOENIX

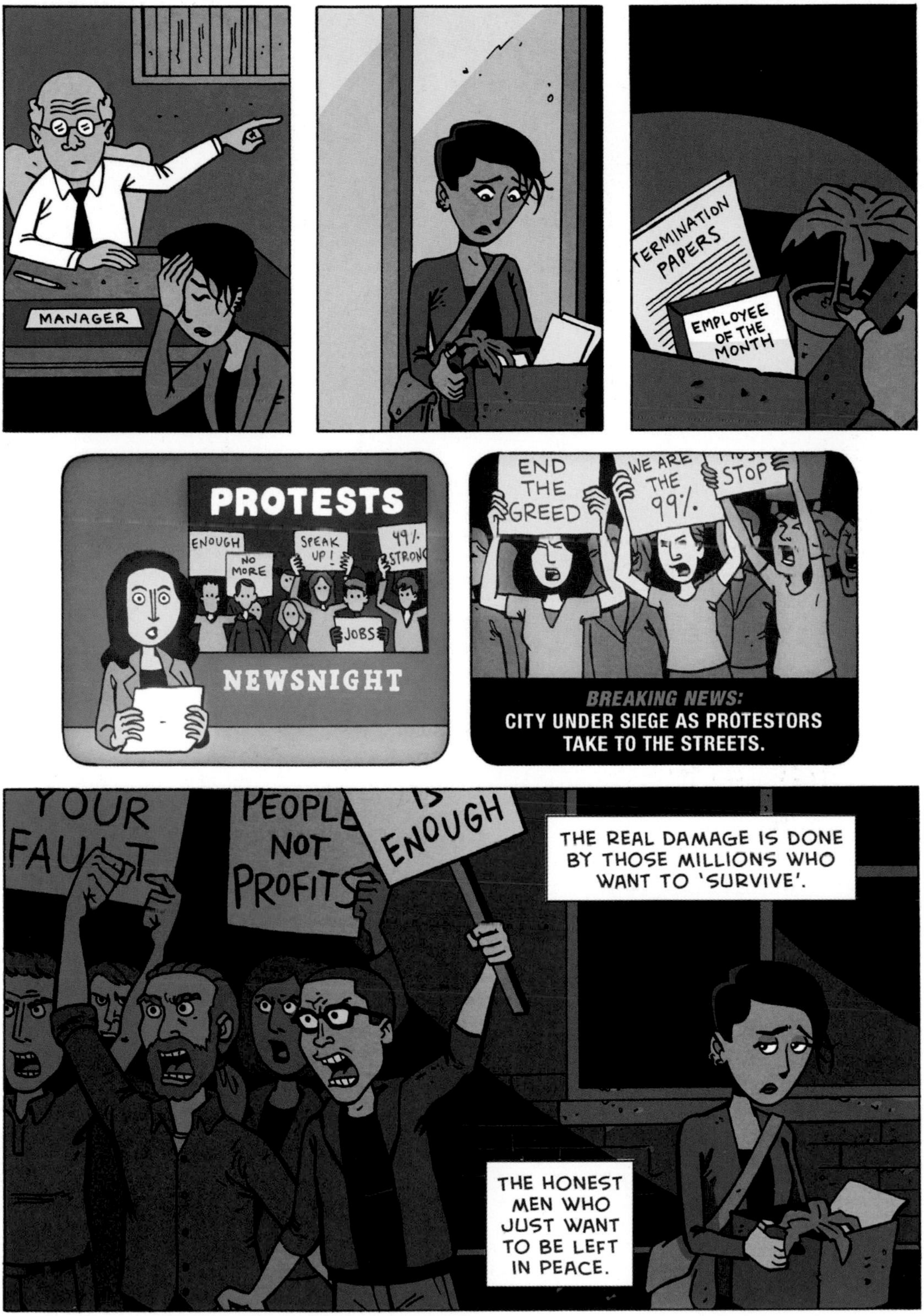
MANAGER
TERMINATION PAPERS
EMPLOYEE OF THE MONTH
PROTESTS
ENOUGH
NO MORE
SPEAK UP!
99% STRONG
JOBS
NEWSNIGHT
END THE GREED
WE ARE THE 99%
STOP
BREAKING NEWS:
CITY UNDER SIEGE AS PROTESTORS TAKE TO THE STREETS.
YOUR FAULT
PEOPLE NOT PROFITS
IS ENOUGH
THE REAL DAMAGE IS DONE BY THOSE MILLIONS WHO WANT TO 'SURVIVE'.
THE HONEST MEN WHO JUST WANT TO BE LEFT IN PEACE.

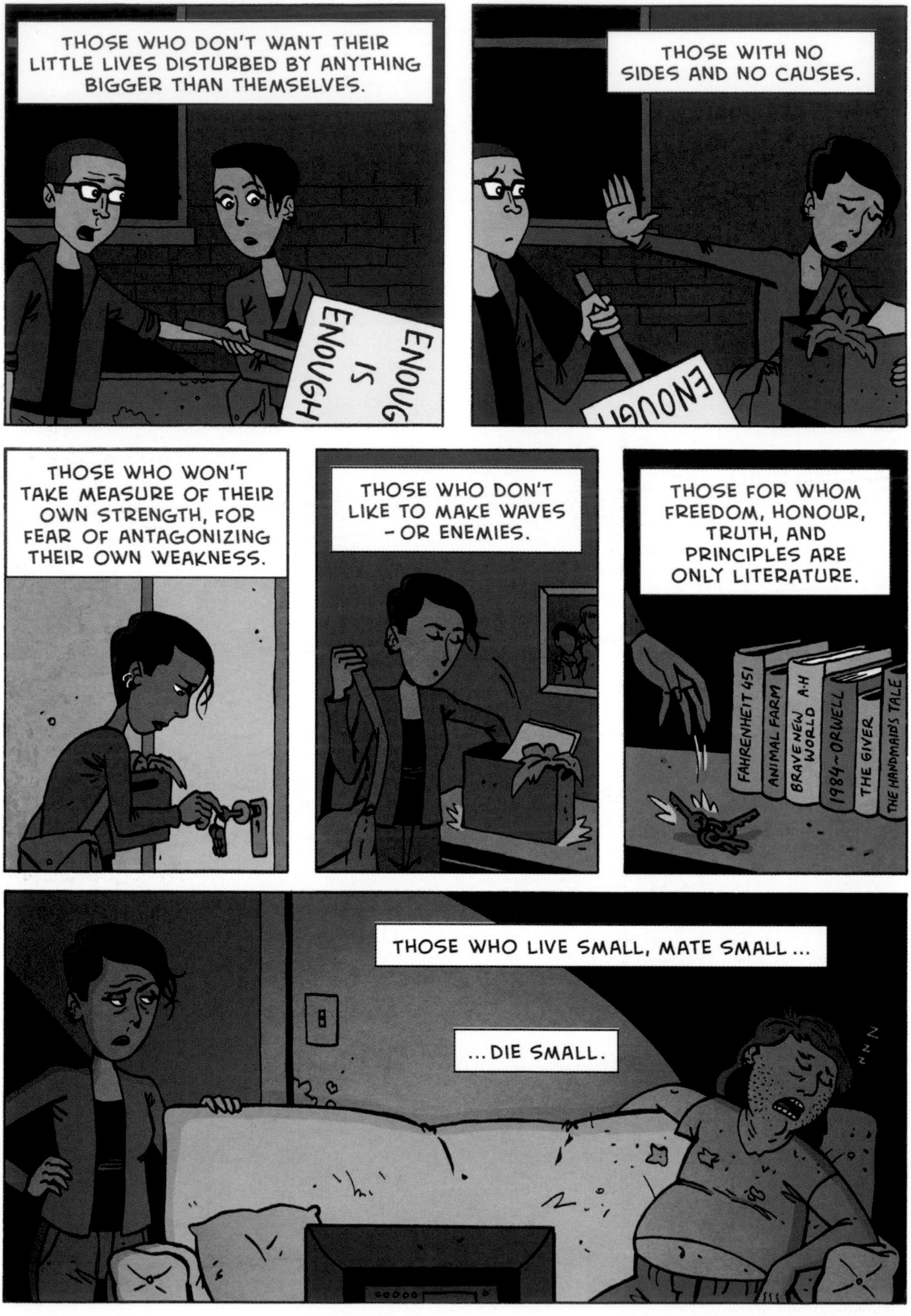
THOSE WHO DON'T WANT THEIR LITTLE LIVES DISTURBED BY ANYTHING BIGGER THAN THEMSELVES.
ENOUGH IS ENOUGH
THOSE WITH NO SIDES AND NO CAUSES.
ENOUGH
THOSE WHO WON'T TAKE MEASURE OF THEIR OWN STRENGTH, FOR FEAR OF ANTAGONIZING THEIR OWN WEAKNESS.
THOSE WHO DON'T LIKE TO MAKE WAVES - OR ENEMIES.
THOSE FOR WHOM FREEDOM, HONOUR, TRUTH, AND PRINCIPLES ARE ONLY LITERATURE.
FAHRENHEIT 451
ANIMAL FARM
BRAVE NEW WORLD A·H
1984~ORWELL
THE GIVER
THE HANDMAID'S TALE
THOSE WHO LIVE SMALL, MATE SMALL ...
... DIE SMALL.
Z Z Z

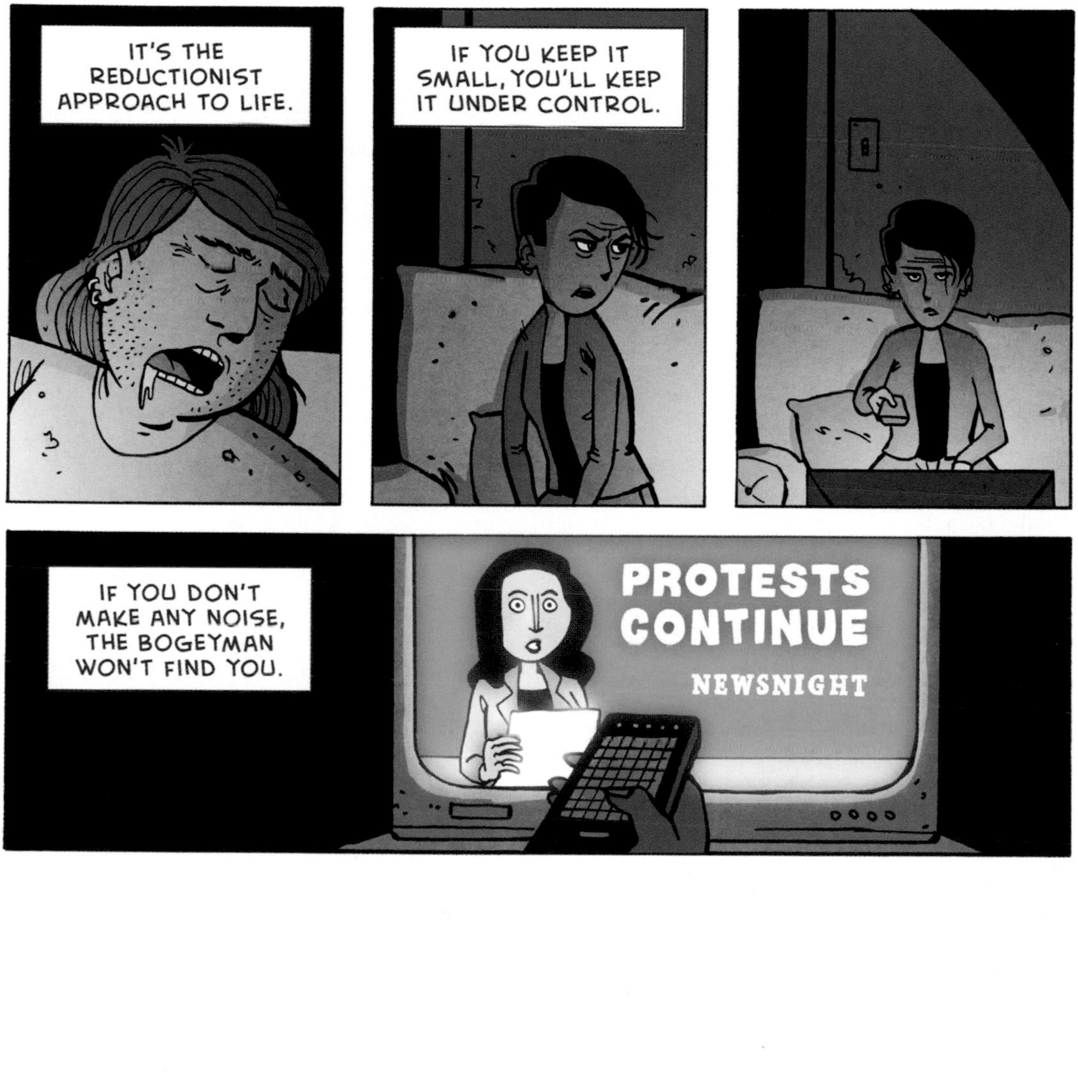
IT'S THE REDUCTIONIST APPROACH TO LIFE.
IF YOU KEEP IT SMALL, YOU'LL KEEP IT UNDER CONTROL.
IF YOU DON'T MAKE ANY NOISE, THE BOGEYMAN WON'T FIND YOU.
PROTESTS CONTINUE
NEWSNIGHT

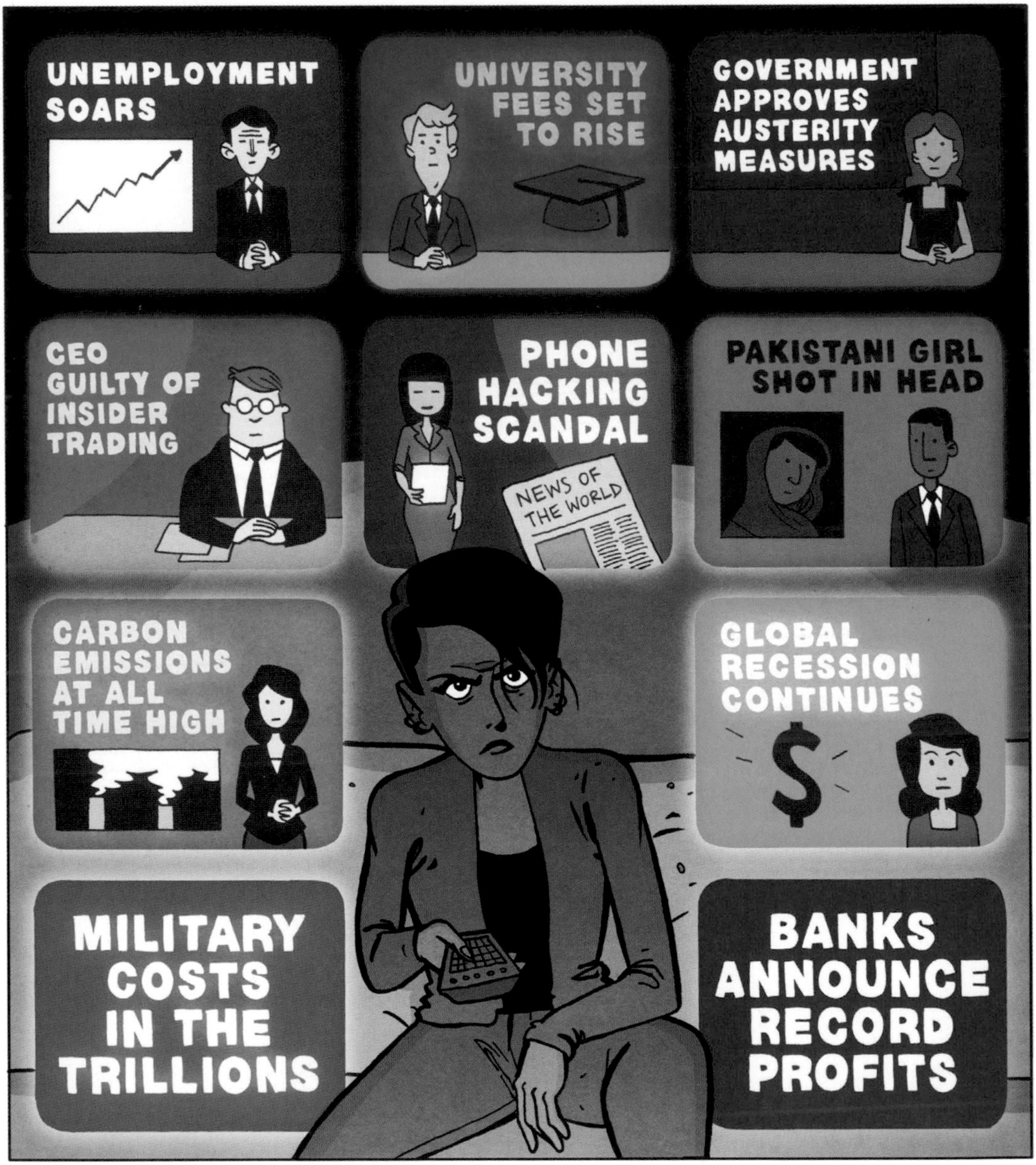
UNEMPLOYMENT SOARS
UNIVERSITY FEES SET TO RISE
GOVERNMENT APPROVES AUSTERITY MEASURES
CEO GUILTY OF INSIDER TRADING
PHONE HACKING SCANDAL
NEWS OF THE WORLD
PAKISTANI GIRL SHOT IN HEAD
CARBON EMISSIONS AT ALL TIME HIGH
GLOBAL RECESSION CONTINUES
$
MILITARY COSTS IN THE TRILLIONS
BANKS ANNOUNCE RECORD PROFITS

BUT IT'S ALL AN ILLUSION, BECAUSE THEY DIE TOO, THOSE PEOPLE WHO ROLL UP THEIR SPIRITS INTO TINY LITTLE BALLS SO AS TO BE SAFE.

SAFE?!

FROM WHAT?

LIFE IS ALWAYS ON THE EDGE OF DEATH.

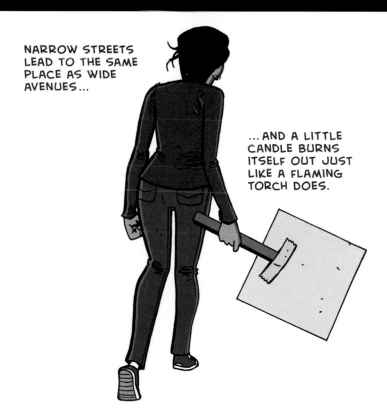

NARROW STREETS LEAD TO THE SAME PLACE AS WIDE AVENUES...

...AND A LITTLE CANDLE BURNS ITSELF OUT JUST LIKE A FLAMING TORCH DOES.

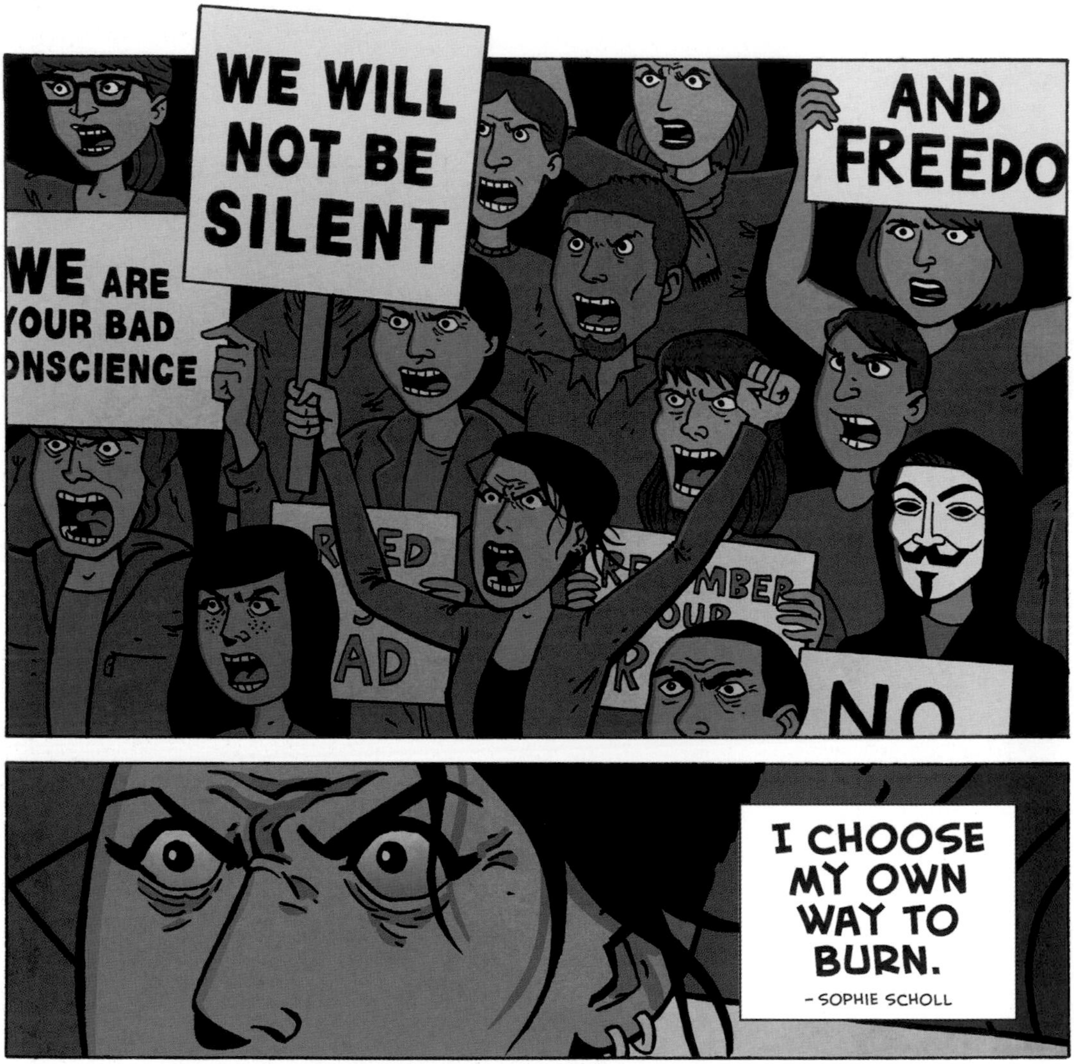
WE WILL NOT BE SILENT
WE ARE YOUR BAD NSCIENCE
AND FREEDO
NO
I CHOOSE MY OWN WAY TO BURN.
– SOPHIE SCHOLL

THROUGHOUT LIFE, FROM CHILDHOOD, FROM SCHOOL UNTIL WE DIE, **WE ARE TAUGHT TO COMPARE OURSELVES WITH ANOTHER.**

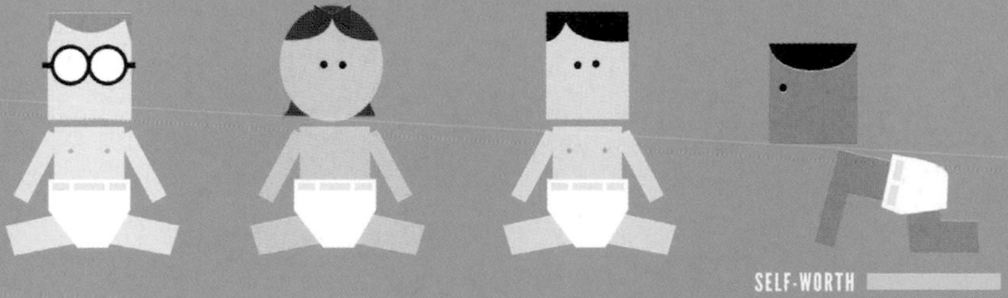
SELF-WORTH

YET WHEN I COMPARE MYSELF WITH ANOTHER **I AM DESTROYING MYSELF.**

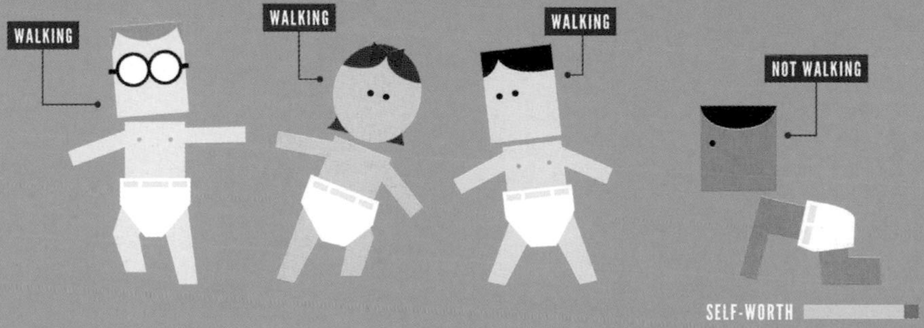
WALKING
WALKING
WALKING
NOT WALKING
SELF-WORTH

IN AN ORDINARY SCHOOL WHERE THERE ARE A LOT OF BOYS, WHEN ONE BOY IS COMPARED WITH ANOTHER WHO IS VERY CLEVER, WHO IS THE HEAD OF THE CLASS, **WHAT IS ACTUALLY TAKING PLACE?**

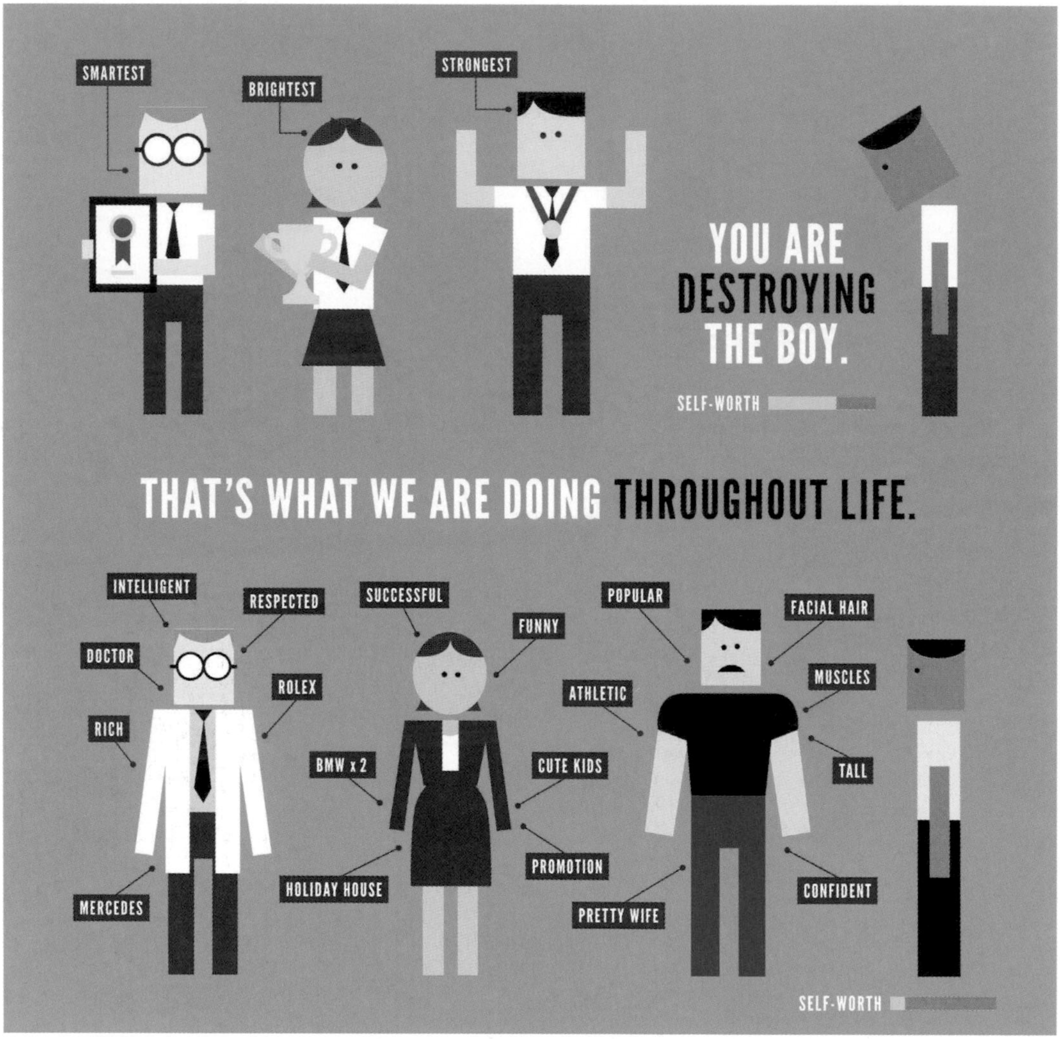
SMARTEST
BRIGHTEST
STRONGEST
YOU ARE DESTROYING THE BOY.
SELF-WORTH
THAT'S WHAT WE ARE DOING THROUGHOUT LIFE.
INTELLIGENT
RESPECTED
DOCTOR
ROLEX
RICH
MERCEDES
SUCCESSFUL
FUNNY
BMW x 2
CUTE KIDS
HOLIDAY HOUSE
PROMOTION
POPULAR
FACIAL HAIR
ATHLETIC
MUSCLES
TALL
CONFIDENT
PRETTY WIFE
SELF-WORTH

NOW, CAN I LIVE WITHOUT COMPARISON WITH ANYBODY? THIS MEANS THERE IS NO HIGH, NO LOW. THERE IS NOT THE ONE WHO IS SUPERIOR AND THE OTHER WHO IS INFERIOR.

INTELLIGENCE
APPEARANCE
HUMOUR
FITNESS
WEALTH
RANKING SUPERIOR
INTELLIGENCE
APPEARANCE
HUMOUR
FITNESS
WEALTH
RANKING INFERIOR

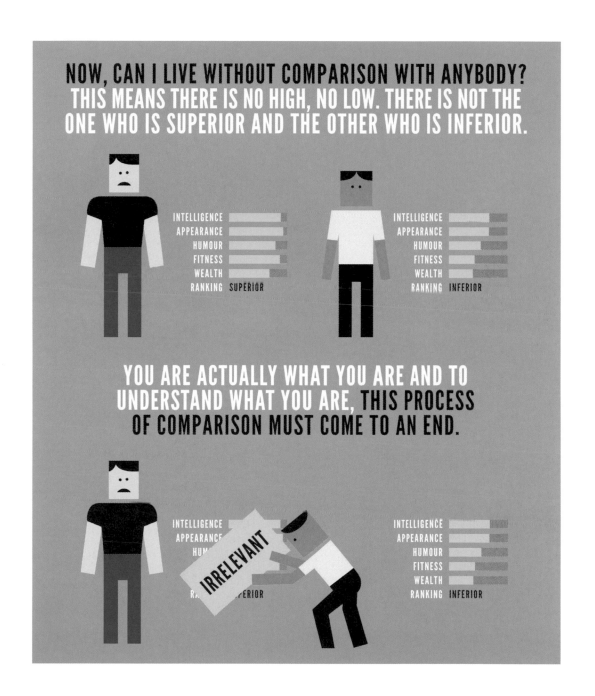

YOU ARE ACTUALLY WHAT YOU ARE AND TO UNDERSTAND WHAT YOU ARE, THIS PROCESS OF COMPARISON MUST COME TO AN END.

INTELLIGENCE
IRRELEVANT
INTELLIGENCE
APPEARANCE
HUMOUR
FITNESS
WEALTH
RANKING INFERIOR

IF I AM ALWAYS COMPARING MYSELF WITH SOME SAINT OR SOME TEACHER, SOME BUSINESSMAN, WRITER, POET, AND ALL THE REST, WHAT HAS HAPPENED TO ME...

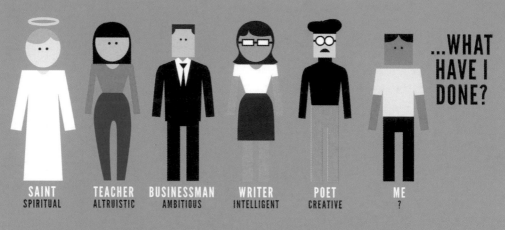

...WHAT HAVE I DONE?

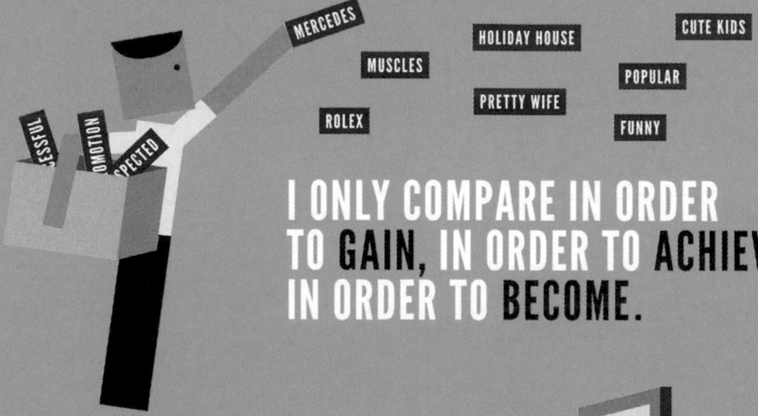

SAINT SPIRITUAL **TEACHER** ALTRUISTIC **BUSINESSMAN** AMBITIOUS **WRITER** INTELLIGENT **POET** CREATIVE **ME** ?

MERCEDES
MUSCLES
ROLEX
HOLIDAY HOUSE
PRETTY WIFE
CUTE KIDS
POPULAR
FUNNY

I ONLY COMPARE IN ORDER TO GAIN, IN ORDER TO ACHIEVE, IN ORDER TO BECOME.

BUT WHEN I DON'T COMPARE I AM BEGINNING TO UNDERSTAND WHAT I AM.

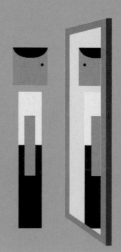

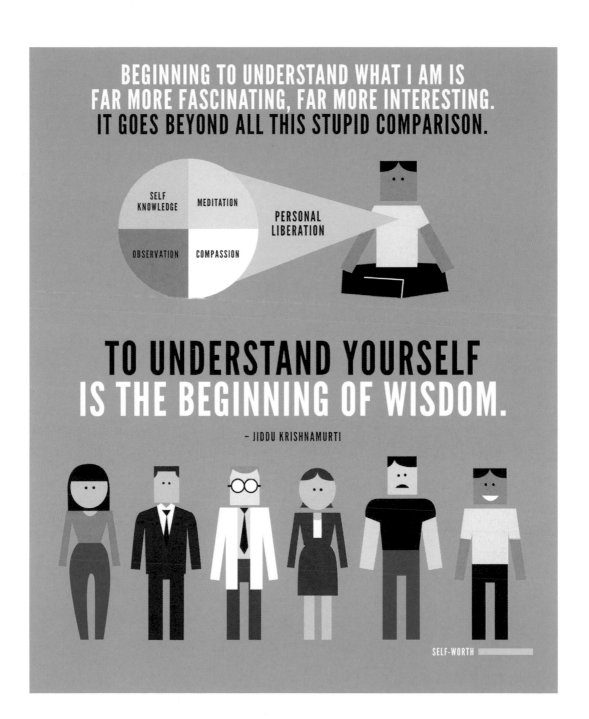

BEGINNING TO UNDERSTAND WHAT I AM IS FAR MORE FASCINATING, FAR MORE INTERESTING. IT GOES BEYOND ALL THIS STUPID COMPARISON.

SELF KNOWLEDGE MEDITATION OBSERVATION COMPASSION

PERSONAL LIBERATION

TO UNDERSTAND YOURSELF IS THE BEGINNING OF WISDOM.

– JIDDU KRISHNAMURTI

SELF-WORTH

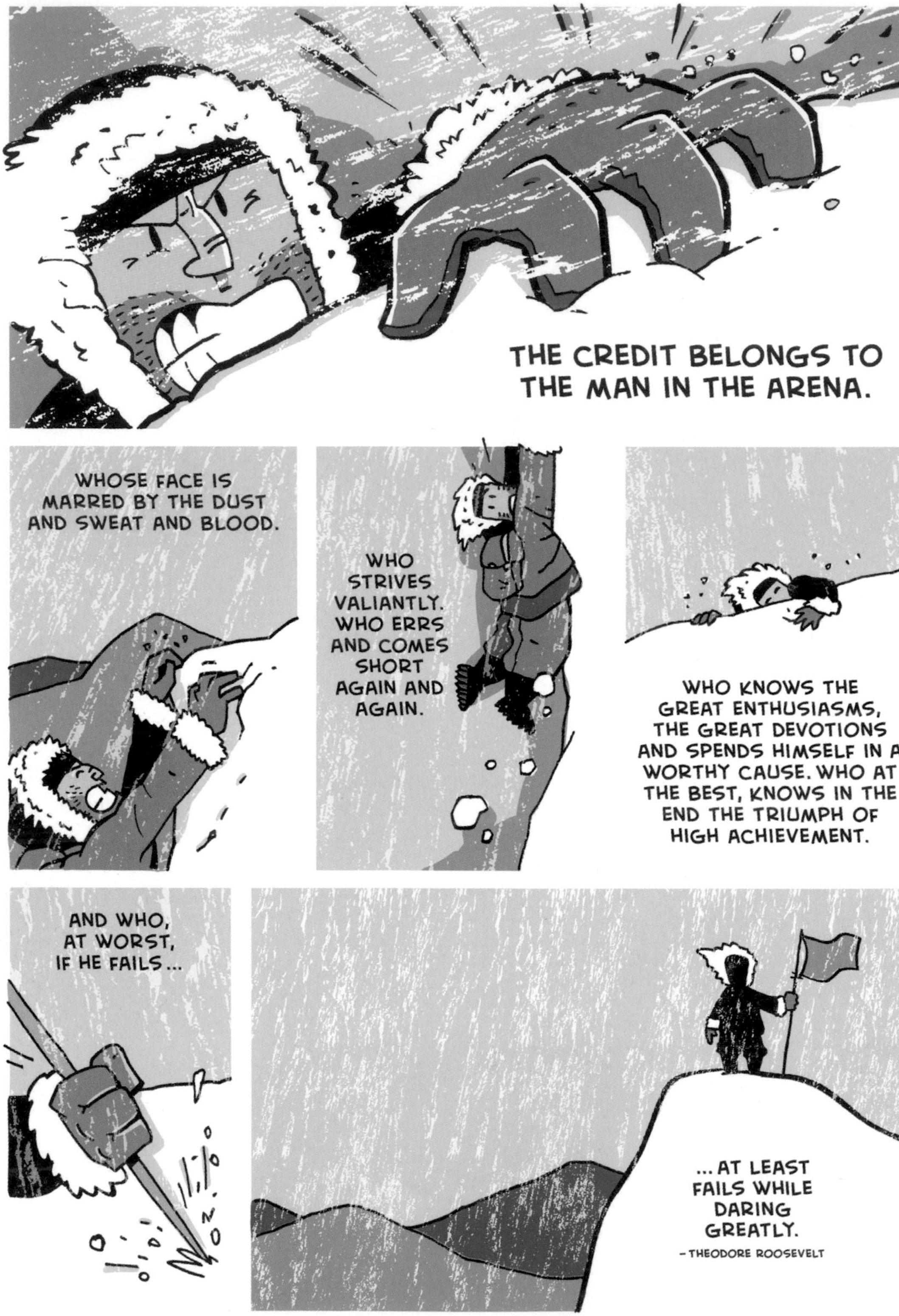
THE CREDIT BELONGS TO
THE MAN IN THE ARENA.
WHOSE FACE IS
MARRED BY THE DUST
AND SWEAT AND BLOOD.
WHO
STRIVES
VALIANTLY.
WHO ERRS
AND COMES
SHORT
AGAIN AND
AGAIN.
WHO KNOWS THE
GREAT ENTHUSIASMS,
THE GREAT DEVOTIONS
AND SPENDS HIMSELF IN A
WORTHY CAUSE. WHO AT
THE BEST, KNOWS IN THE
END THE TRIUMPH OF
HIGH ACHIEVEMENT.
AND WHO,
AT WORST,
IF HE FAILS...
...AT LEAST
FAILS WHILE
DARING
GREATLY.
–THEODORE ROOSEVELT

That's what life is about...

...about daring greatly, about being in the arena.

When you walk up to that arena...

...and you put your hand on the door, and you think...

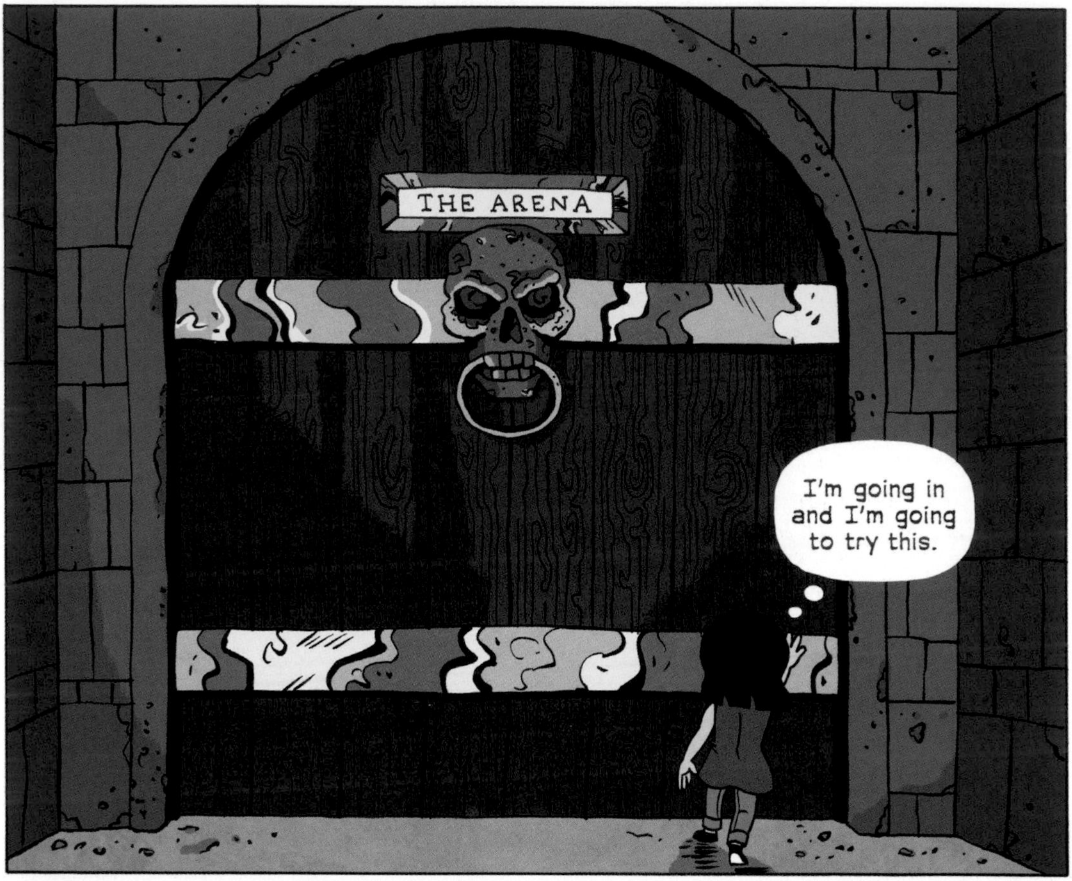
THE ARENA
I'm going in and I'm going to try this.

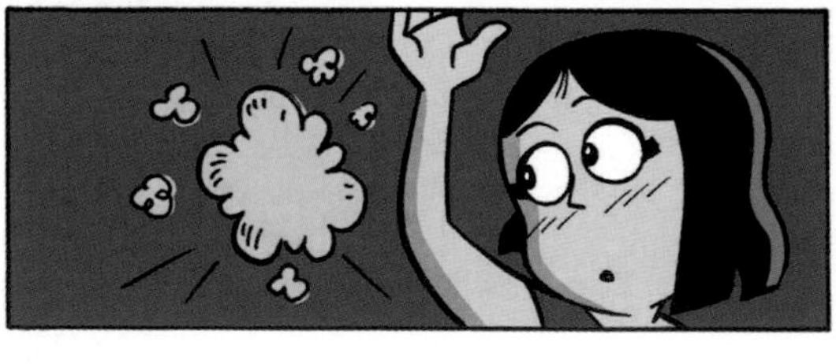

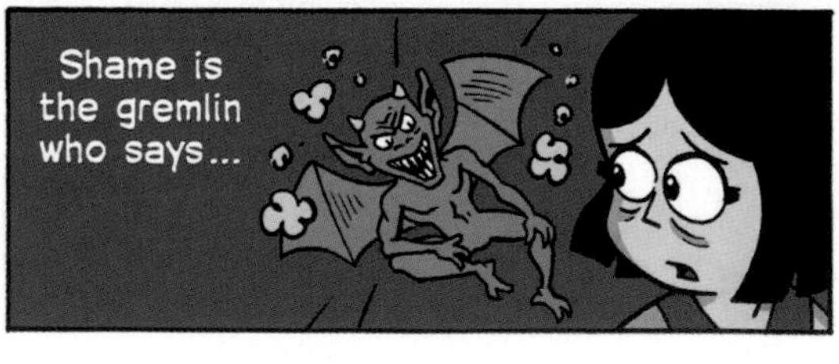
Shame is the gremlin who says...

UH, UH YOU'RE NOT GOOD ENOUGH. YOU NEVER FINISHED THAT MBA Your wife left you. I KNOW YOUR DAD REALLY WASN'T IN LUXEMBOURG, HE WAS IN SING SING. I KNOW THOSE THINGS THAT HAPPENED TO YOU GROWING UP. I KNOW YOU DON'T THINK YOU'RE PRETTY ENOUGH OR SMART ENOUGH OR TALENTED ENOUGH OR POWERFUL ENOUGH. I KNOW YOUR DAD NEVER PAID ATTENTION, EVEN WHEN YOU MADE CFO.

Shame is that thing.

And if we can quiet it down and walk in and say...

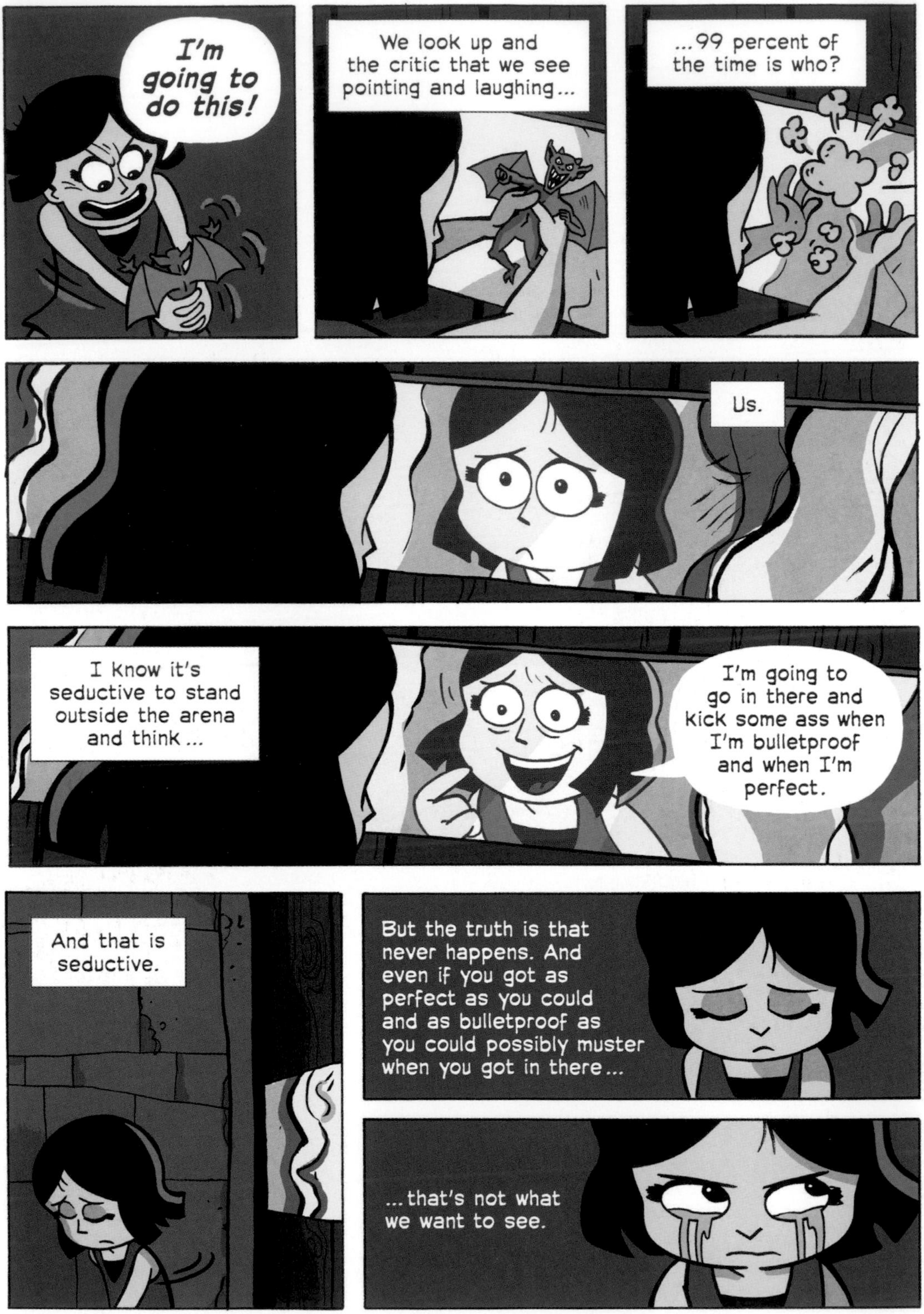
I'm going to do this!
We look up and the critic that we see pointing and laughing...
...99 percent of the time is who?
Us.
I know it's seductive to stand outside the arena and think...
I'm going to go in there and kick some ass when I'm bulletproof and when I'm perfect.
And that is seductive.
But the truth is that never happens. And even if you got as perfect as you could and as bulletproof as you could possibly muster when you got in there...
...that's not what we want to see.

We want
you to go in.

We want to
be with you
and across
from you.

And we
just want, for
ourselves and
the people we
care about and
the people we
work with ...

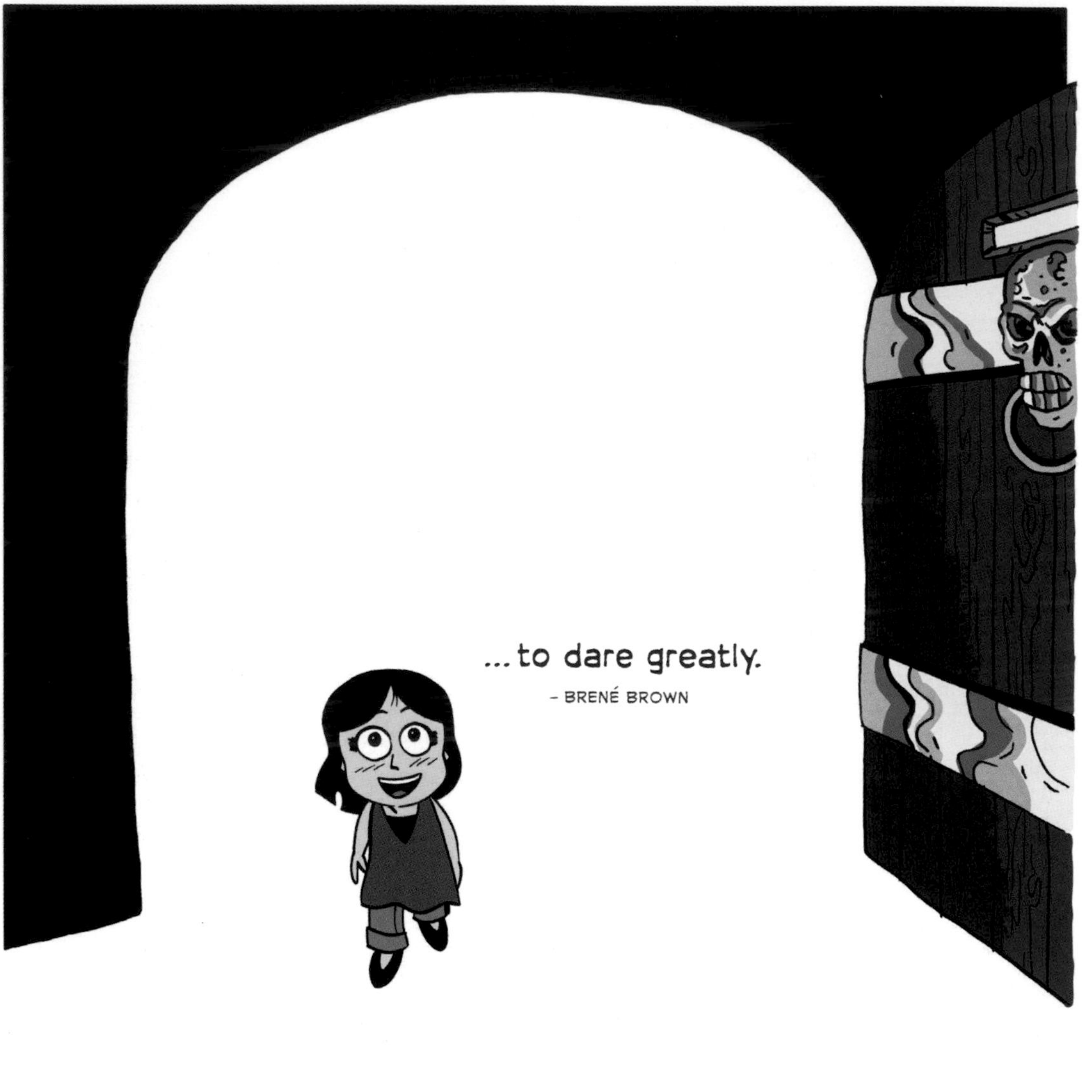
...to dare greatly.
– BRENÉ BROWN

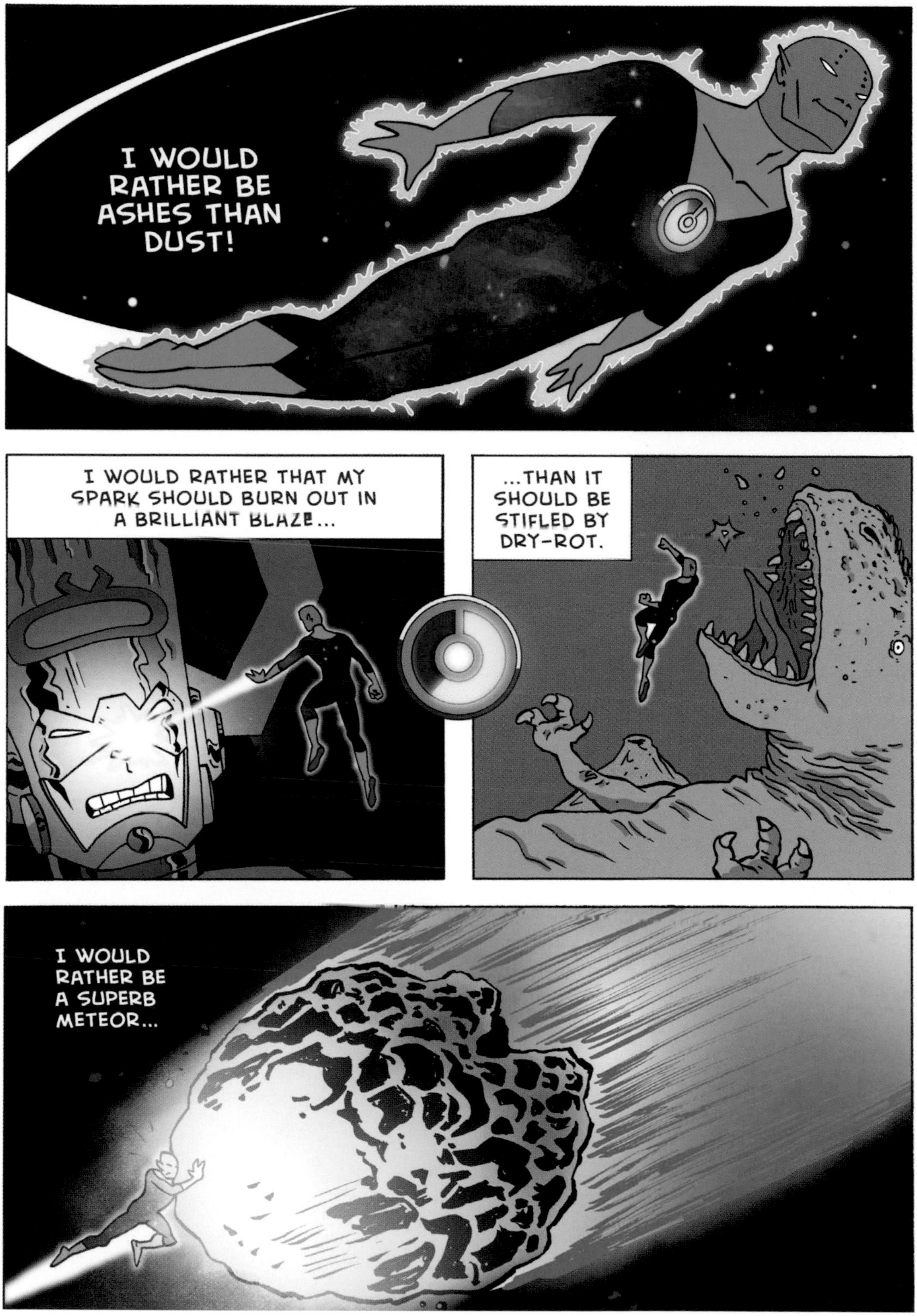
I WOULD RATHER BE ASHES THAN DUST!
I WOULD RATHER THAT MY SPARK SHOULD BURN OUT IN A BRILLIANT BLAZE...
...THAN IT SHOULD BE STIFLED BY DRY-ROT.
I WOULD RATHER BE A SUPERB METEOR...

...EVERY ATOM OF ME IN MAGNIFICENT GLOW...

...THAN A SLEEPY AND PERMANENT PLANET.

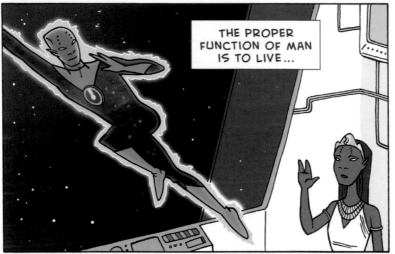

THE PROPER FUNCTION OF MAN IS TO LIVE...

...NOT TO EXIST.

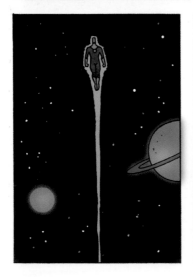

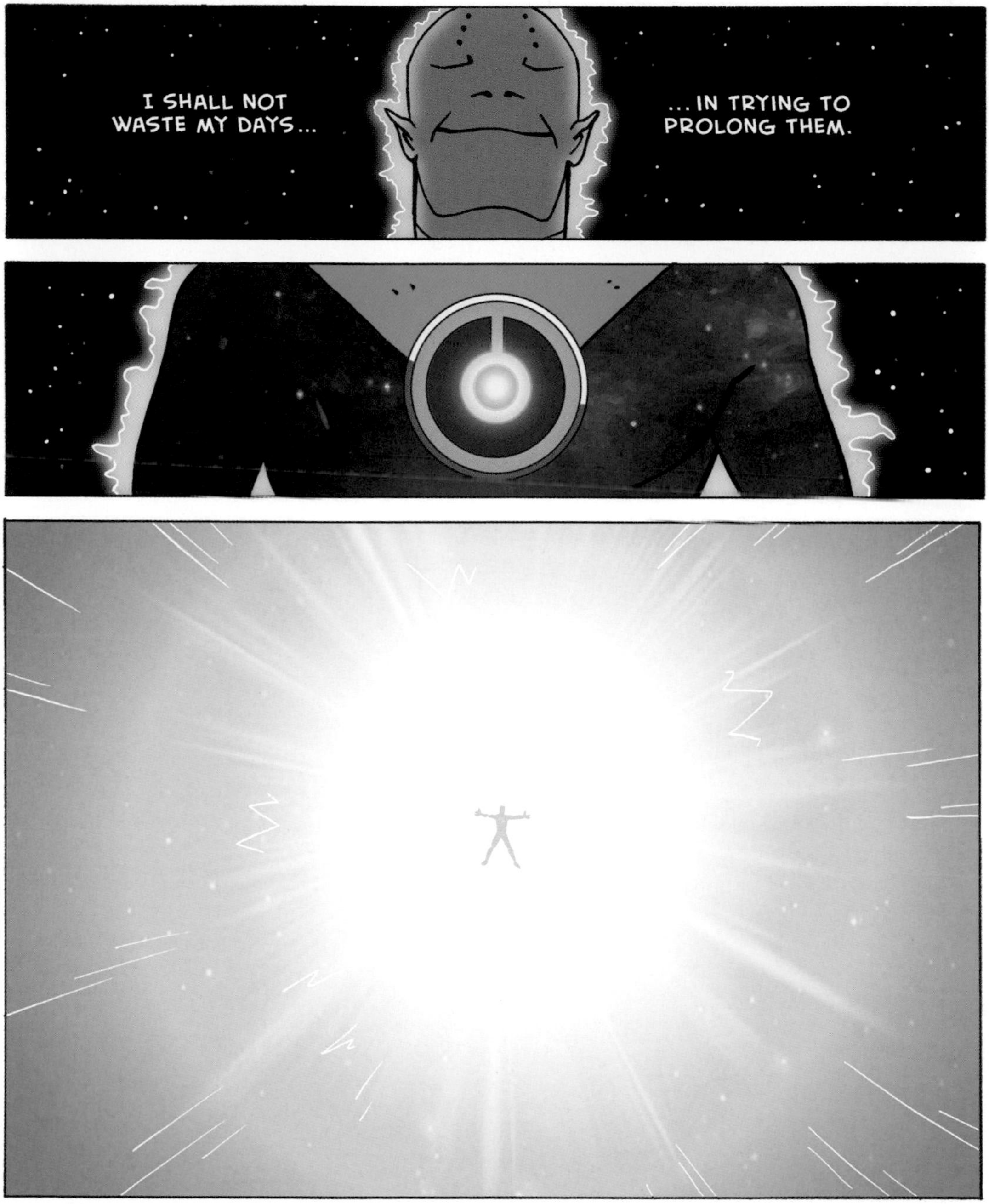
I SHALL NOT WASTE MY DAYS...
...IN TRYING TO PROLONG THEM.

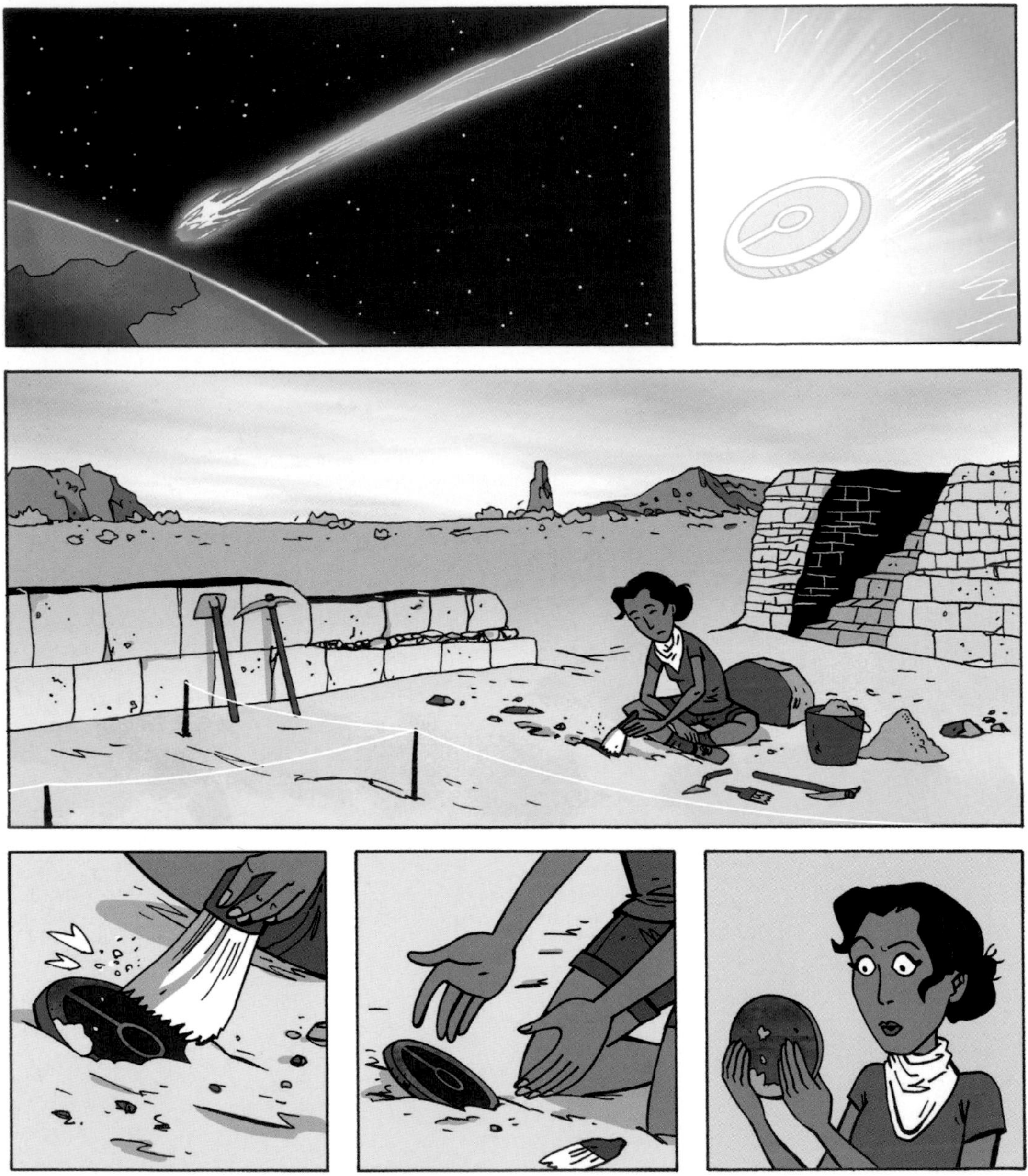

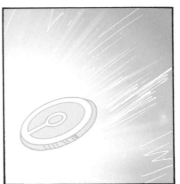

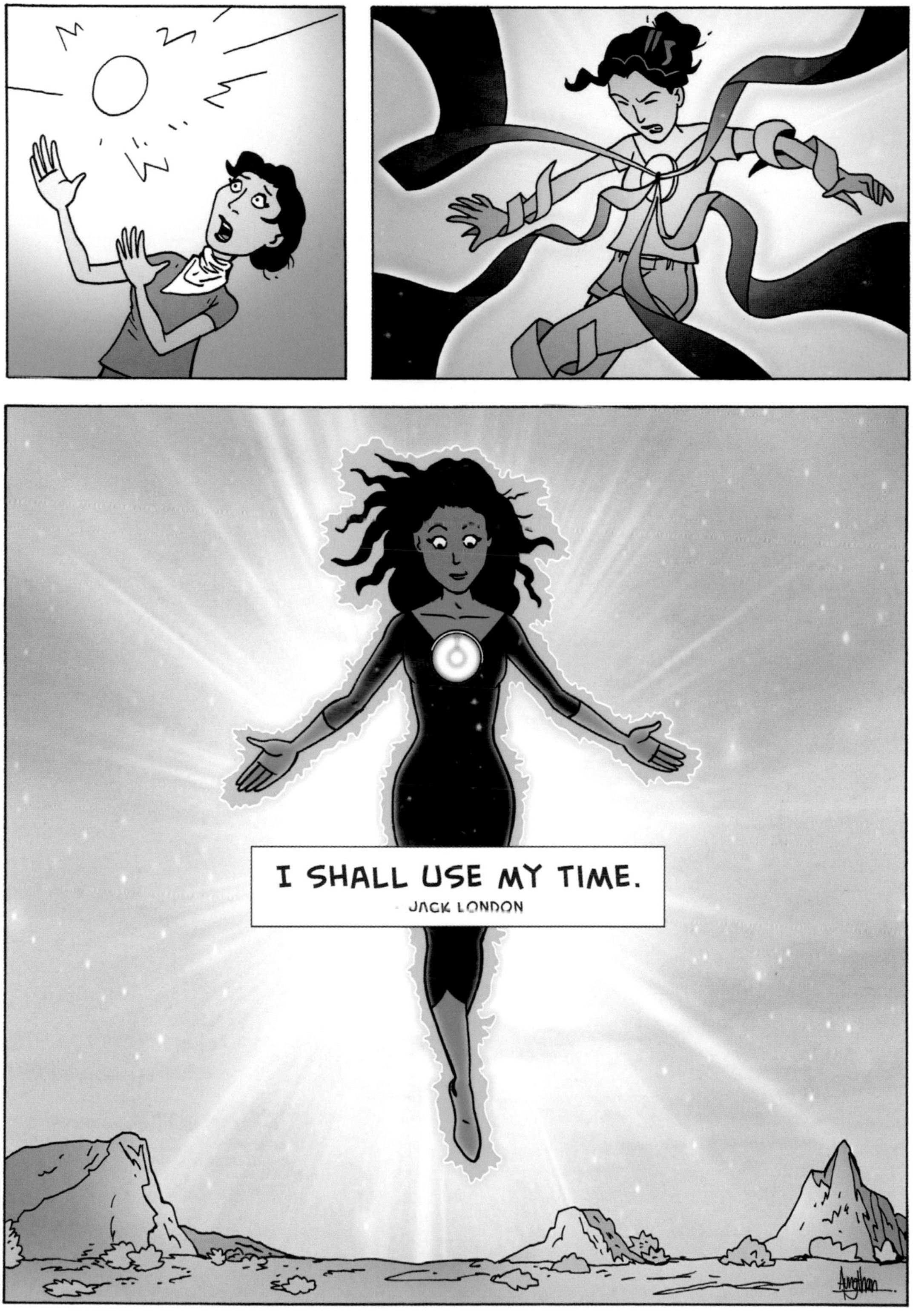
I SHALL USE MY TIME.
- JACK LONDON

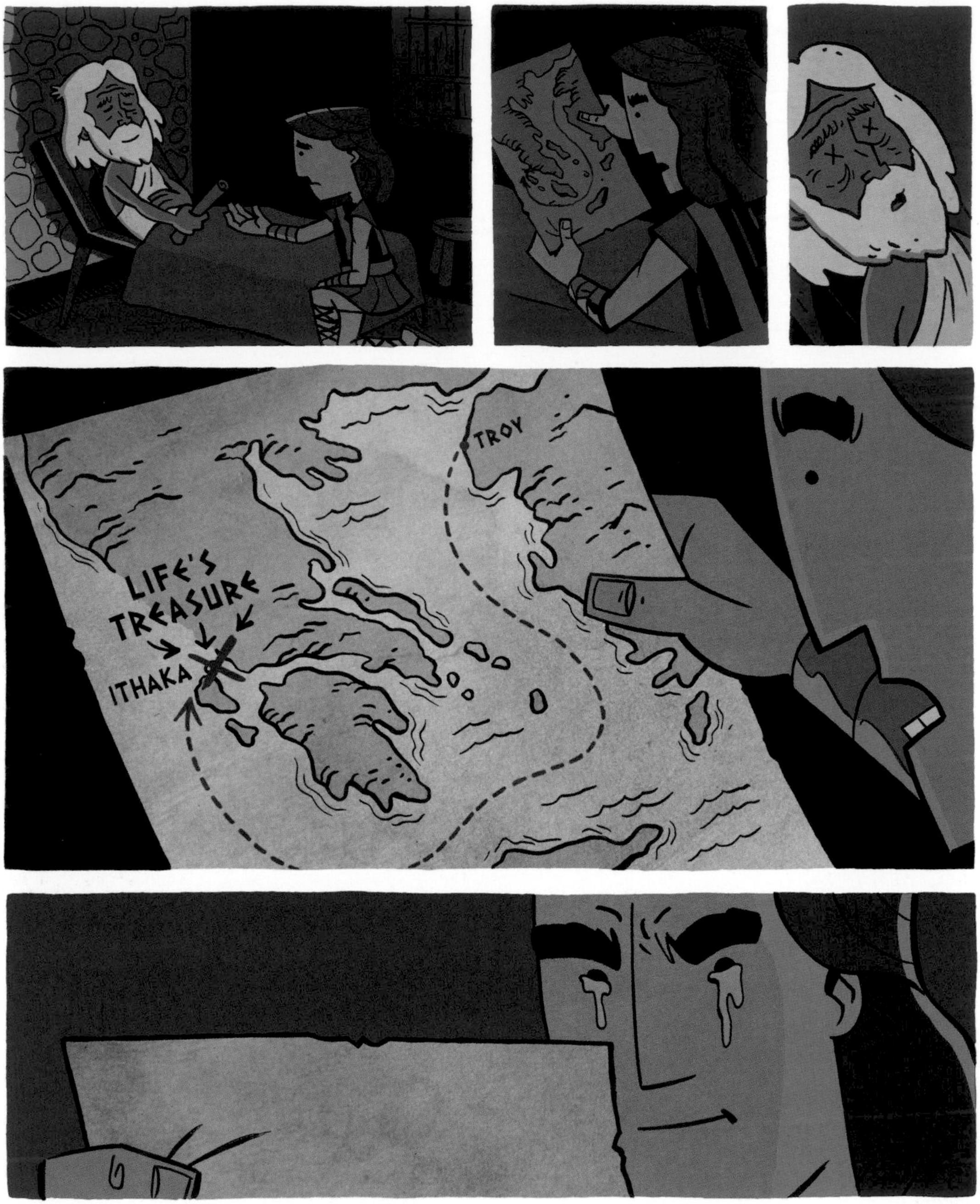
TROY
LIFE'S TREASURE
ITHAKA

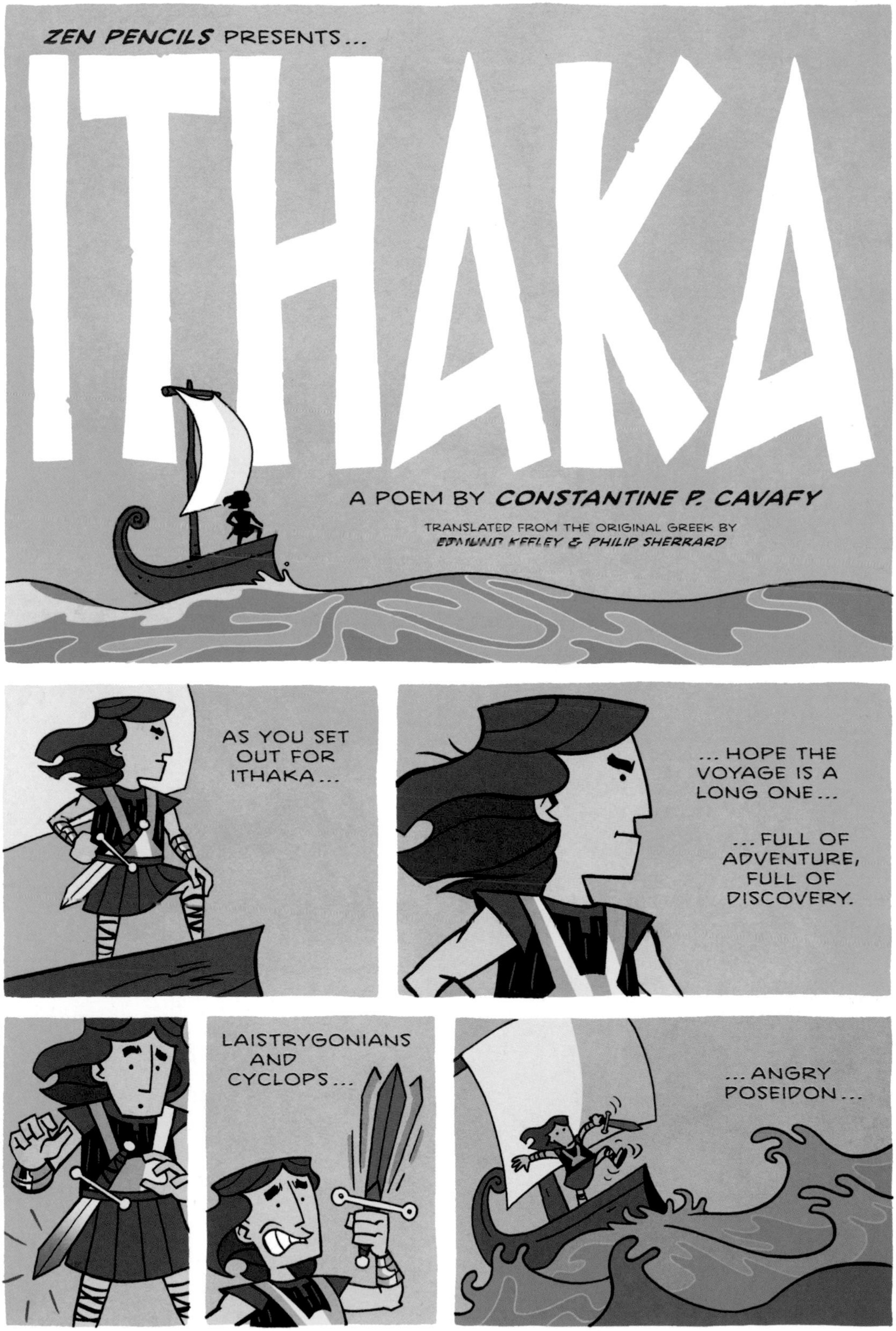
ZEN PENCILS PRESENTS...
ITHAKA
A POEM BY CONSTANTINE P. CAVAFY
TRANSLATED FROM THE ORIGINAL GREEK BY
EDMUND KEELEY & PHILIP SHERRARD
AS YOU SET OUT FOR ITHAKA...
...HOPE THE VOYAGE IS A LONG ONE...
...FULL OF ADVENTURE, FULL OF DISCOVERY.
LAISTRYGONIANS AND CYCLOPS...
...ANGRY POSEIDON...

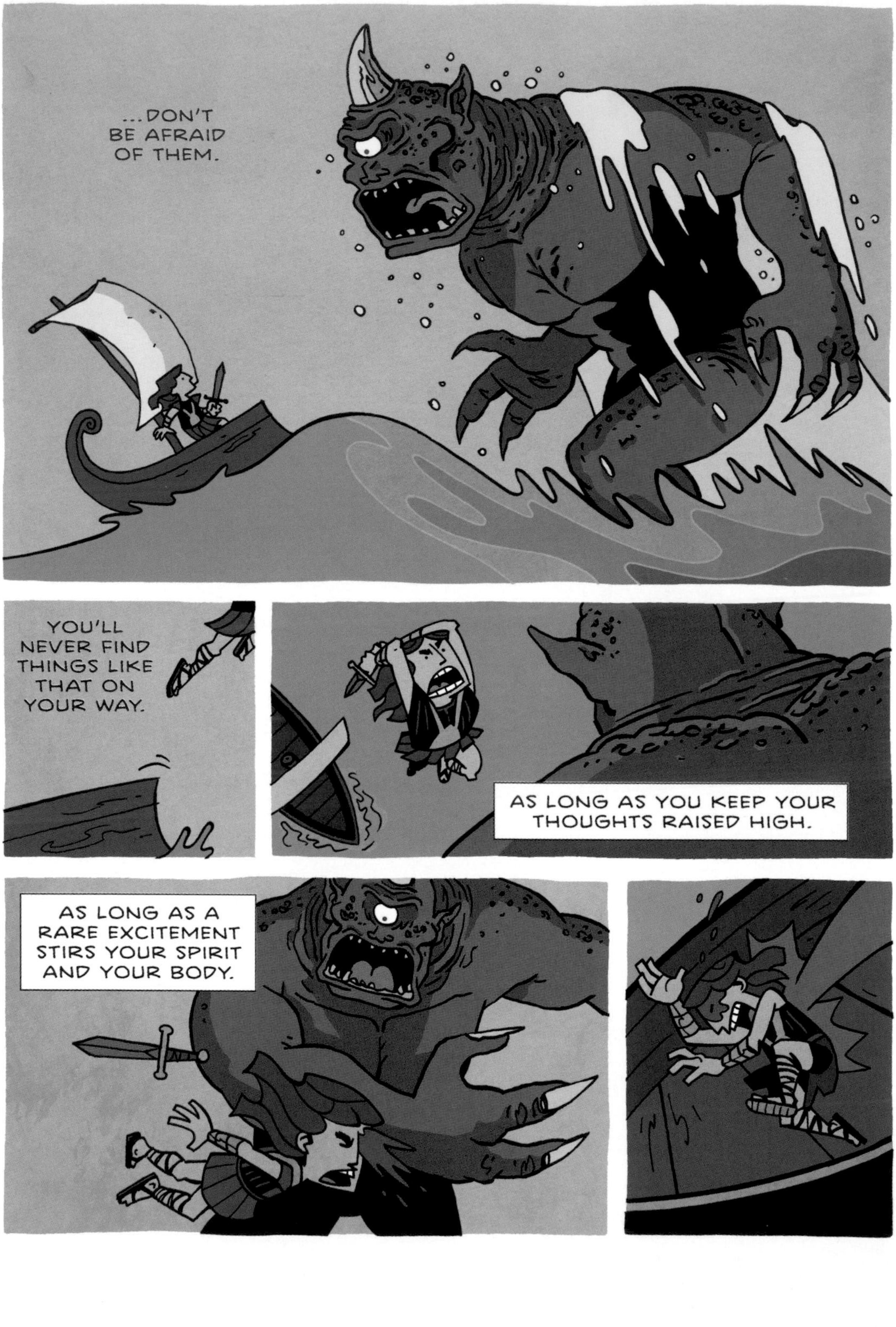
...DON'T BE AFRAID OF THEM.
YOU'LL NEVER FIND THINGS LIKE THAT ON YOUR WAY.
AS LONG AS YOU KEEP YOUR THOUGHTS RAISED HIGH.
AS LONG AS A RARE EXCITEMENT STIRS YOUR SPIRIT AND YOUR BODY.

LAISTRYGONIANS AND CYCLOPS, WILD POSEIDON...

YOU WON'T ENCOUNTER THEM.

UNLESS YOU BRING THEM ALONG INSIDE YOUR SOUL.

UNLESS YOUR SOUL SETS THEM UP IN FRONT OF YOU.

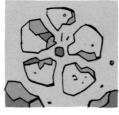

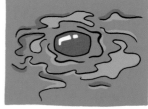

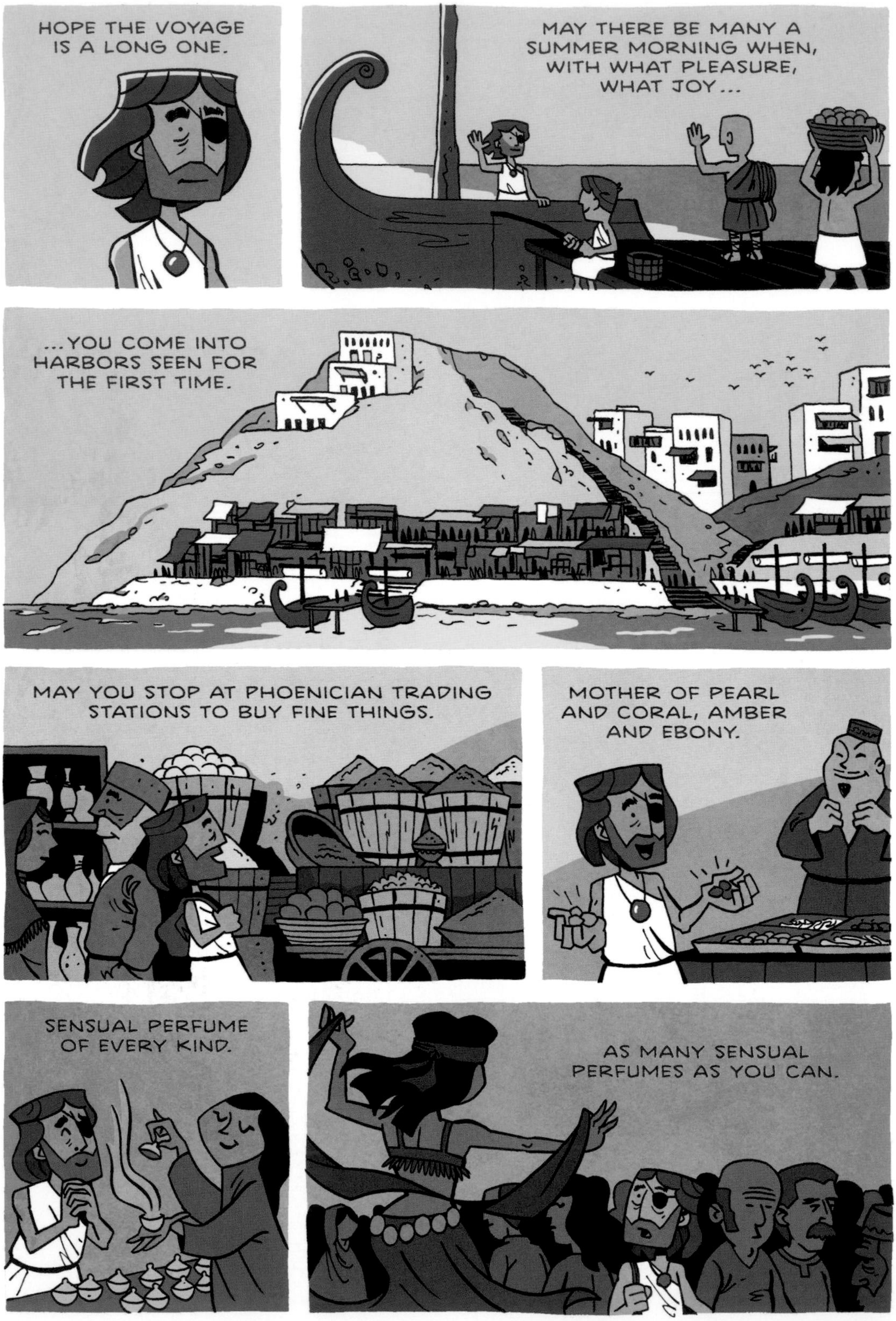
HOPE THE VOYAGE IS A LONG ONE.
MAY THERE BE MANY A SUMMER MORNING WHEN, WITH WHAT PLEASURE, WHAT JOY...
...YOU COME INTO HARBORS SEEN FOR THE FIRST TIME.
MAY YOU STOP AT PHOENICIAN TRADING STATIONS TO BUY FINE THINGS.
MOTHER OF PEARL AND CORAL, AMBER AND EBONY.
SENSUAL PERFUME OF EVERY KIND.
AS MANY SENSUAL PERFUMES AS YOU CAN.

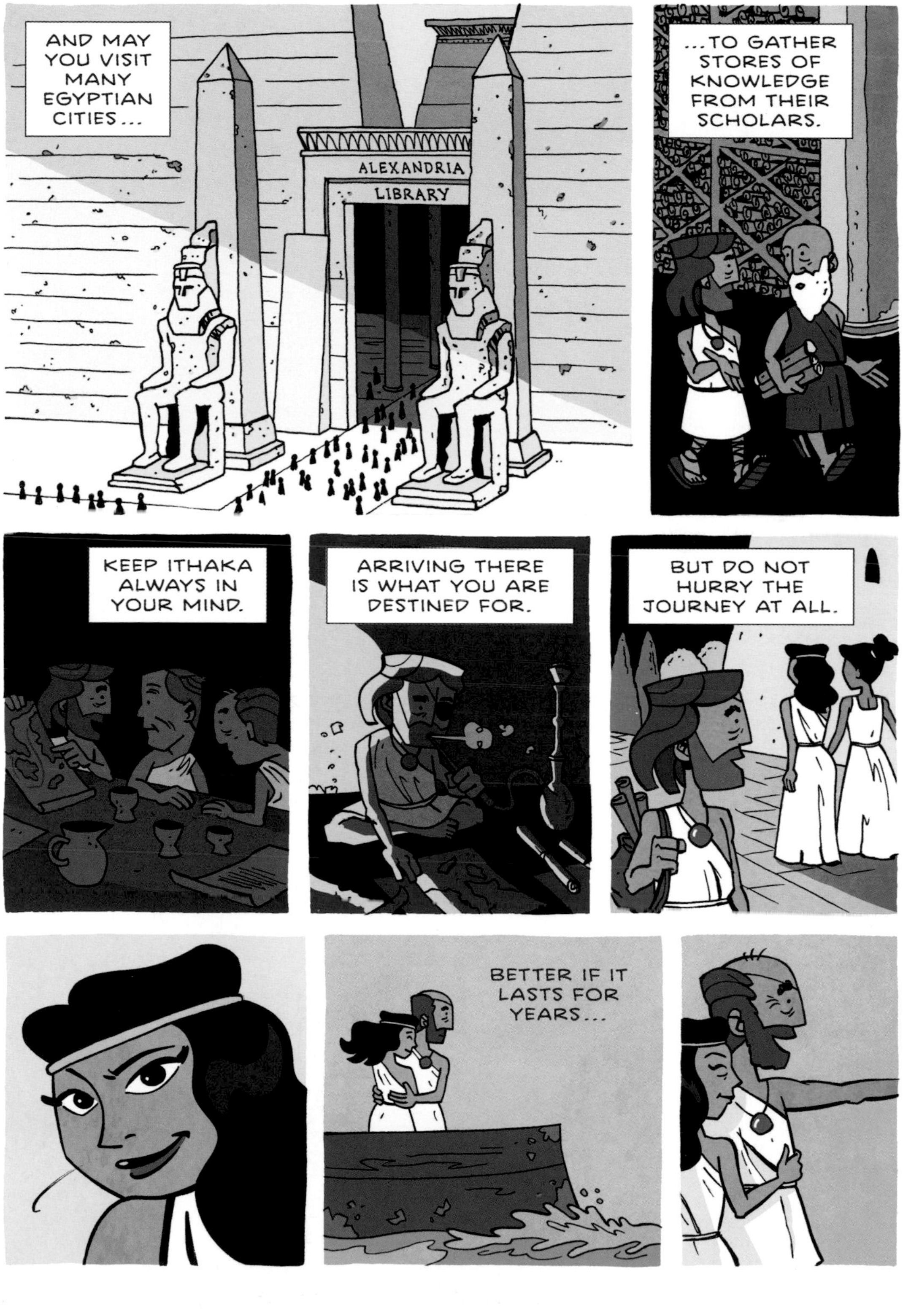
AND MAY YOU VISIT MANY EGYPTIAN CITIES...
ALEXANDRIA
LIBRARY
...TO GATHER STORES OF KNOWLEDGE FROM THEIR SCHOLARS.
KEEP ITHAKA ALWAYS IN YOUR MIND.
ARRIVING THERE IS WHAT YOU ARE DESTINED FOR.
BUT DO NOT HURRY THE JOURNEY AT ALL.
BETTER IF IT LASTS FOR YEARS...

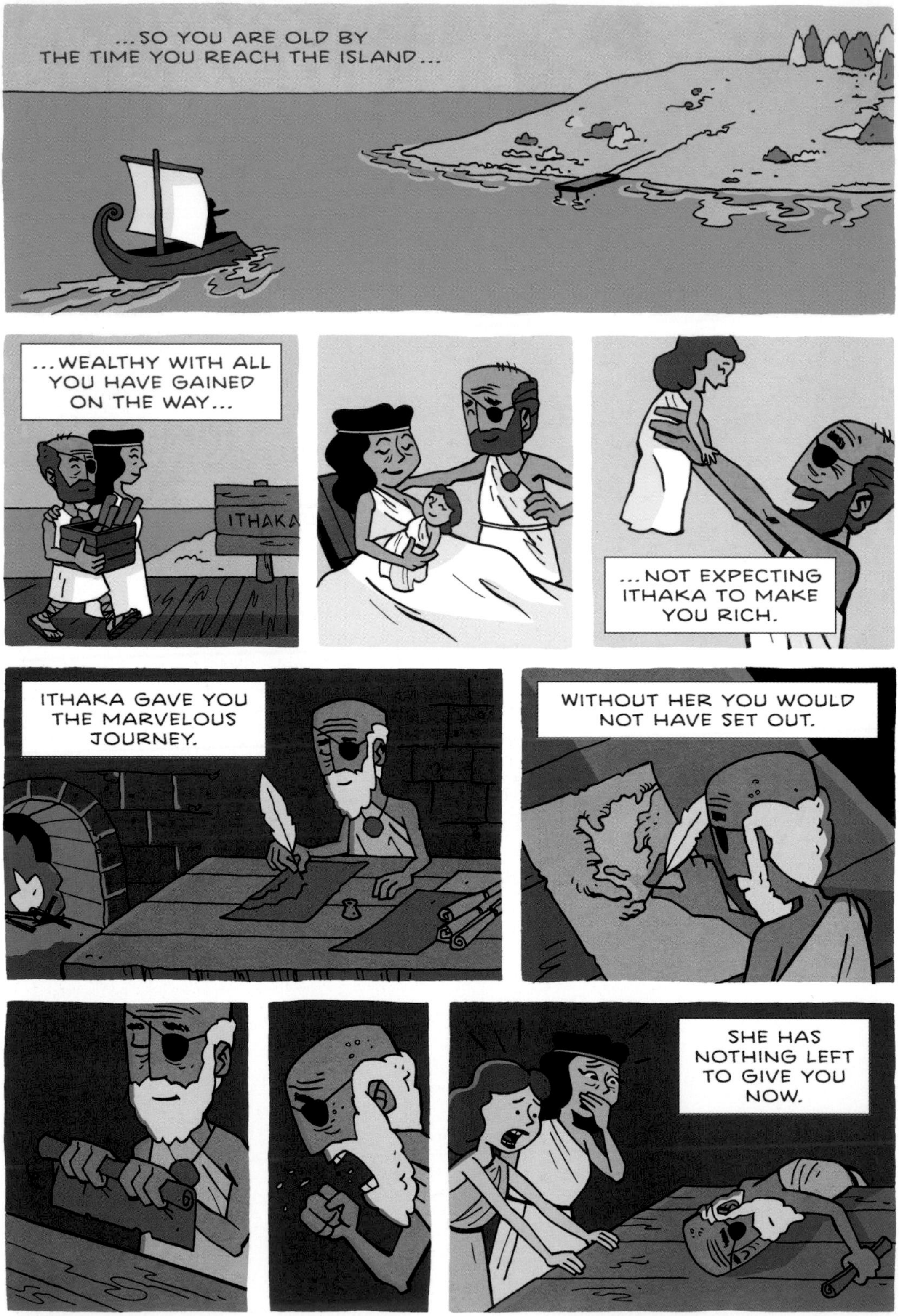
...SO YOU ARE OLD BY THE TIME YOU REACH THE ISLAND...
...WEALTHY WITH ALL YOU HAVE GAINED ON THE WAY...
ITHAKA
...NOT EXPECTING ITHAKA TO MAKE YOU RICH.
ITHAKA GAVE YOU THE MARVELOUS JOURNEY.
WITHOUT HER YOU WOULD NOT HAVE SET OUT.
SHE HAS NOTHING LEFT TO GIVE YOU NOW.

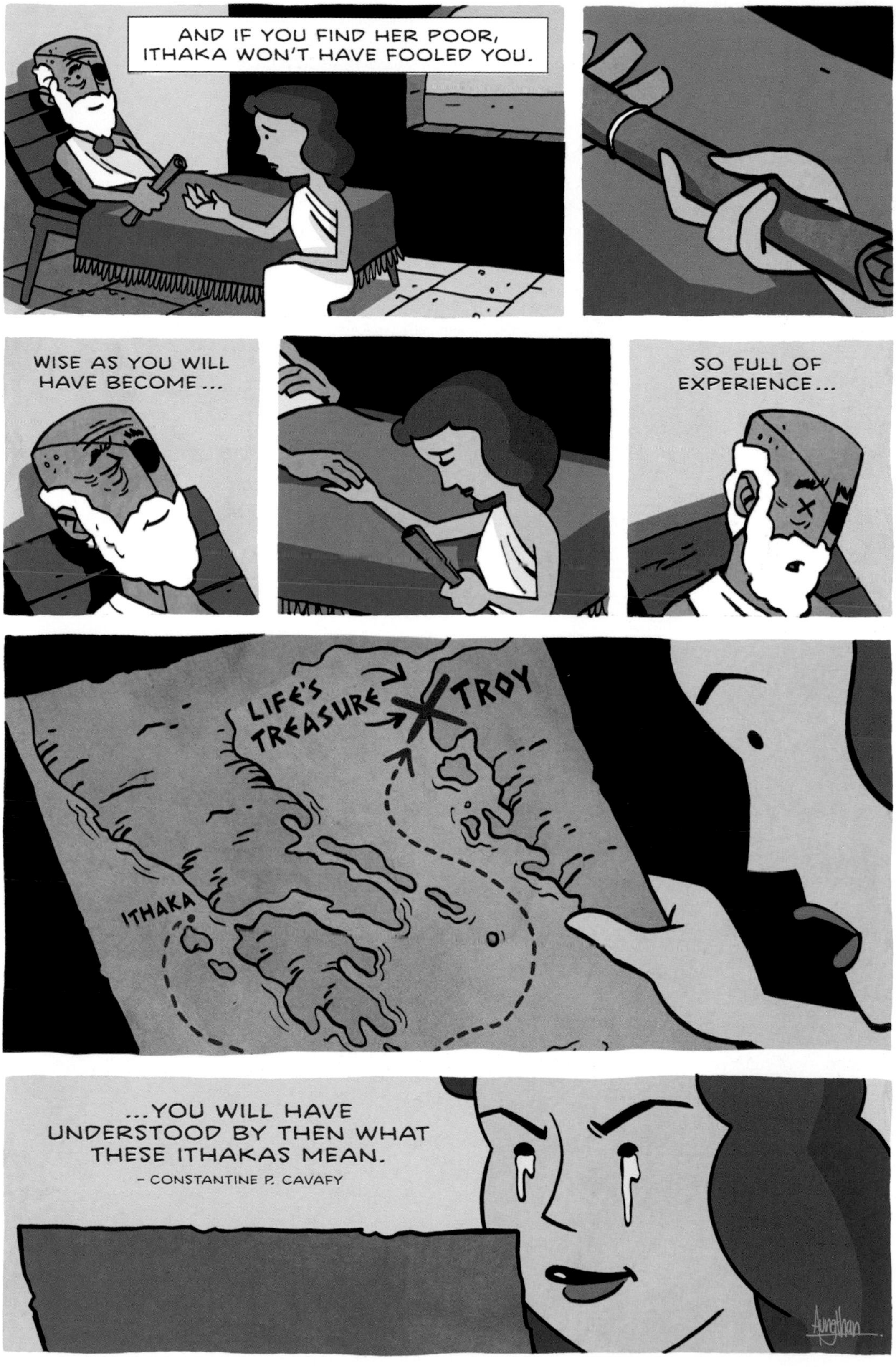
AND IF YOU FIND HER POOR, ITHAKA WON'T HAVE FOOLED YOU.
WISE AS YOU WILL HAVE BECOME...
SO FULL OF EXPERIENCE...
LIFE'S TREASURE
TROY
ITHAKA
...YOU WILL HAVE UNDERSTOOD BY THEN WHAT THESE ITHAKAS MEAN.
– CONSTANTINE P. CAVAFY

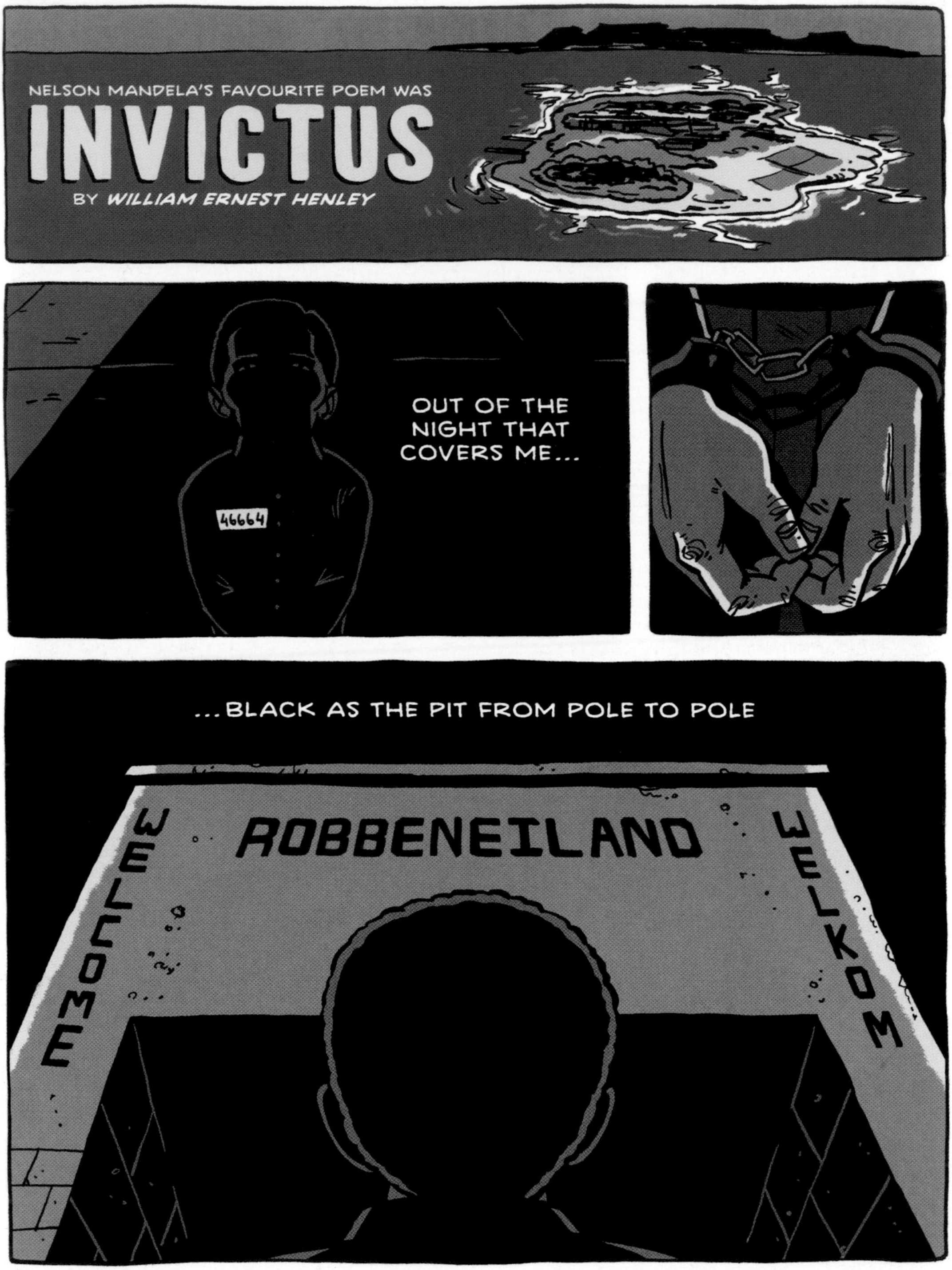
NELSON MANDELA'S FAVOURITE POEM WAS
INVICTUS
BY WILLIAM ERNEST HENLEY
46664
OUT OF THE NIGHT THAT COVERS ME...
...BLACK AS THE PIT FROM POLE TO POLE
WELCOME
ROBBENEILAND
WELKOM

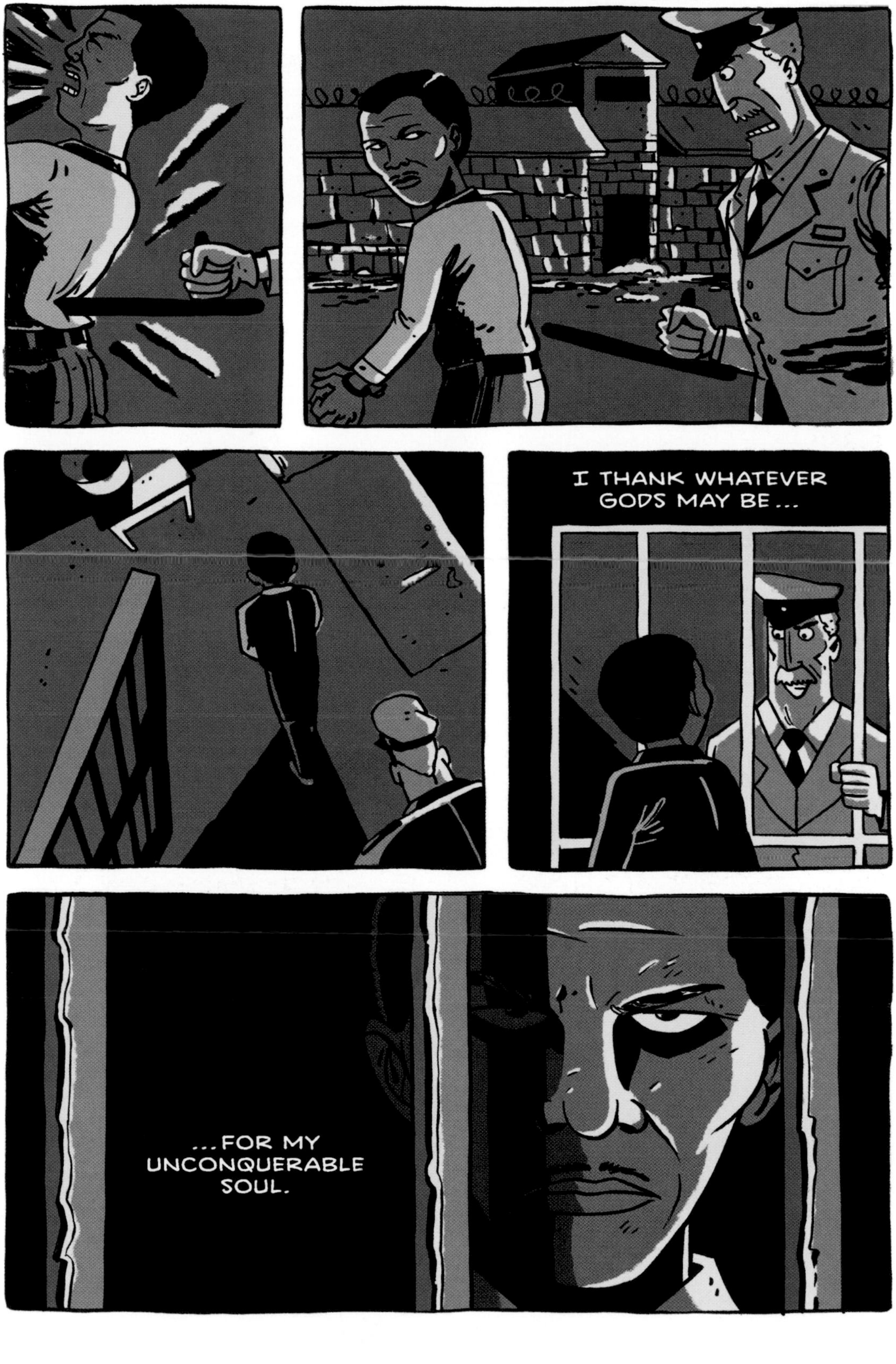
I THANK WHATEVER GODS MAY BE...
...FOR MY UNCONQUERABLE SOUL.

IN THE FELL CLUTCH OF CIRCUMSTANCE...

...I HAVE NOT WINCED NOR CRIED ALOUD.

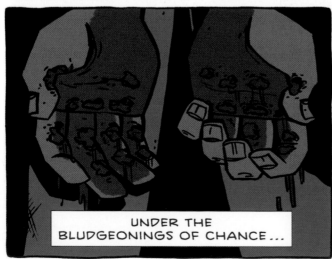

UNDER THE BLUDGEONINGS OF CHANCE...

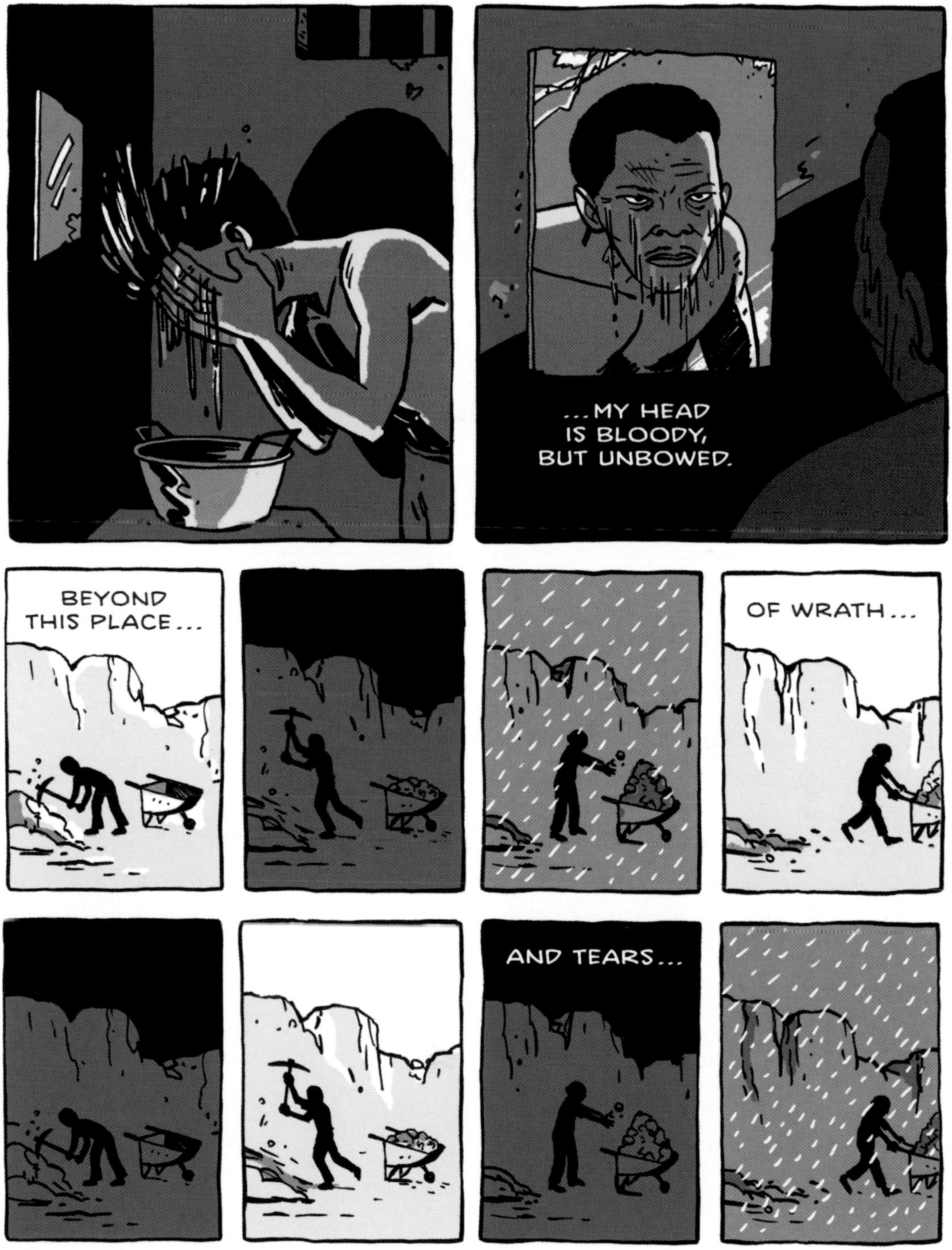
...MY HEAD
IS BLOODY,
BUT UNBOWED.
BEYOND
THIS PLACE...
OF WRATH...
AND TEARS...

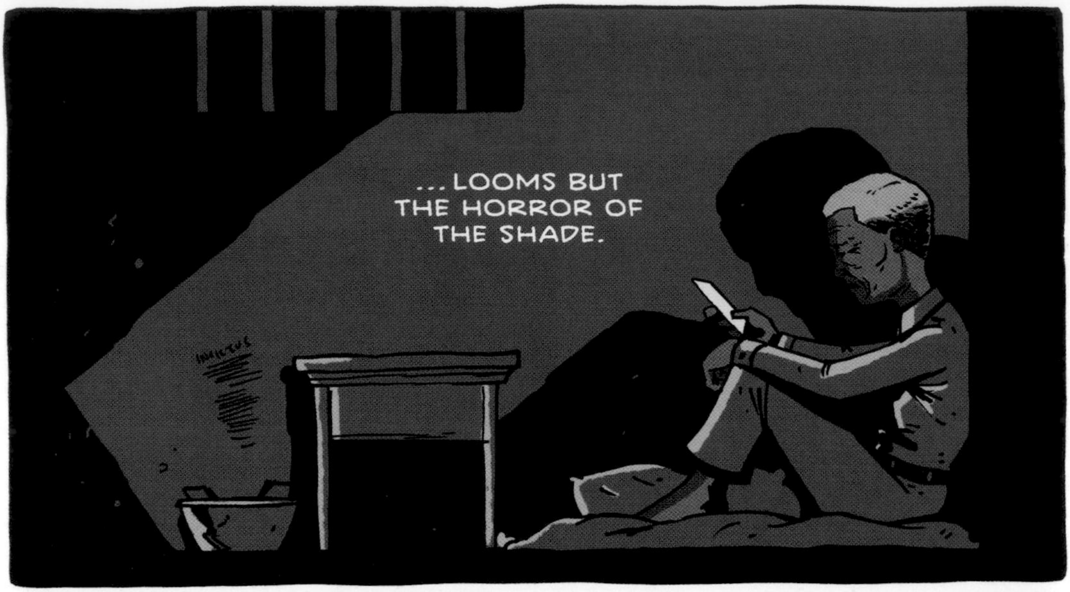
...LOOMS BUT THE HORROR OF THE SHADE.

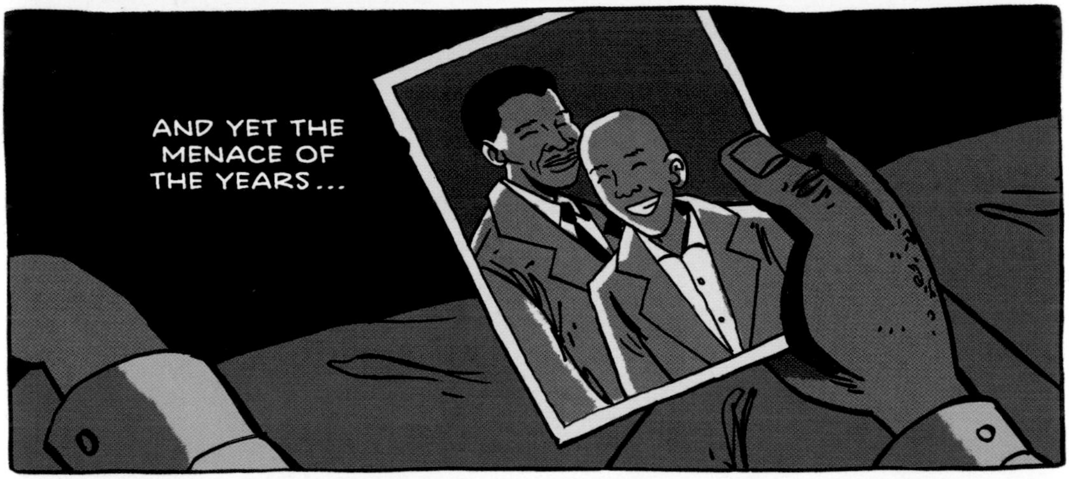
AND YET THE MENACE OF THE YEARS...

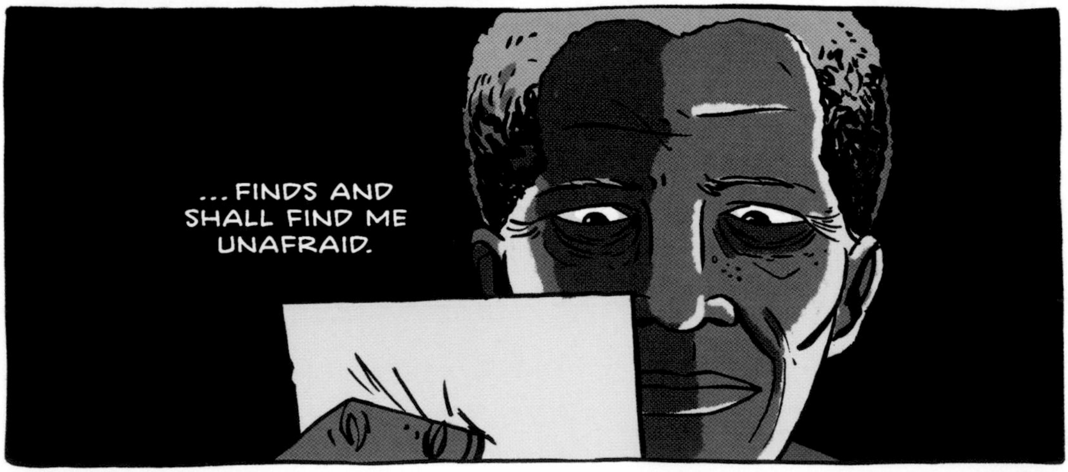
...FINDS AND SHALL FIND ME UNAFRAID.

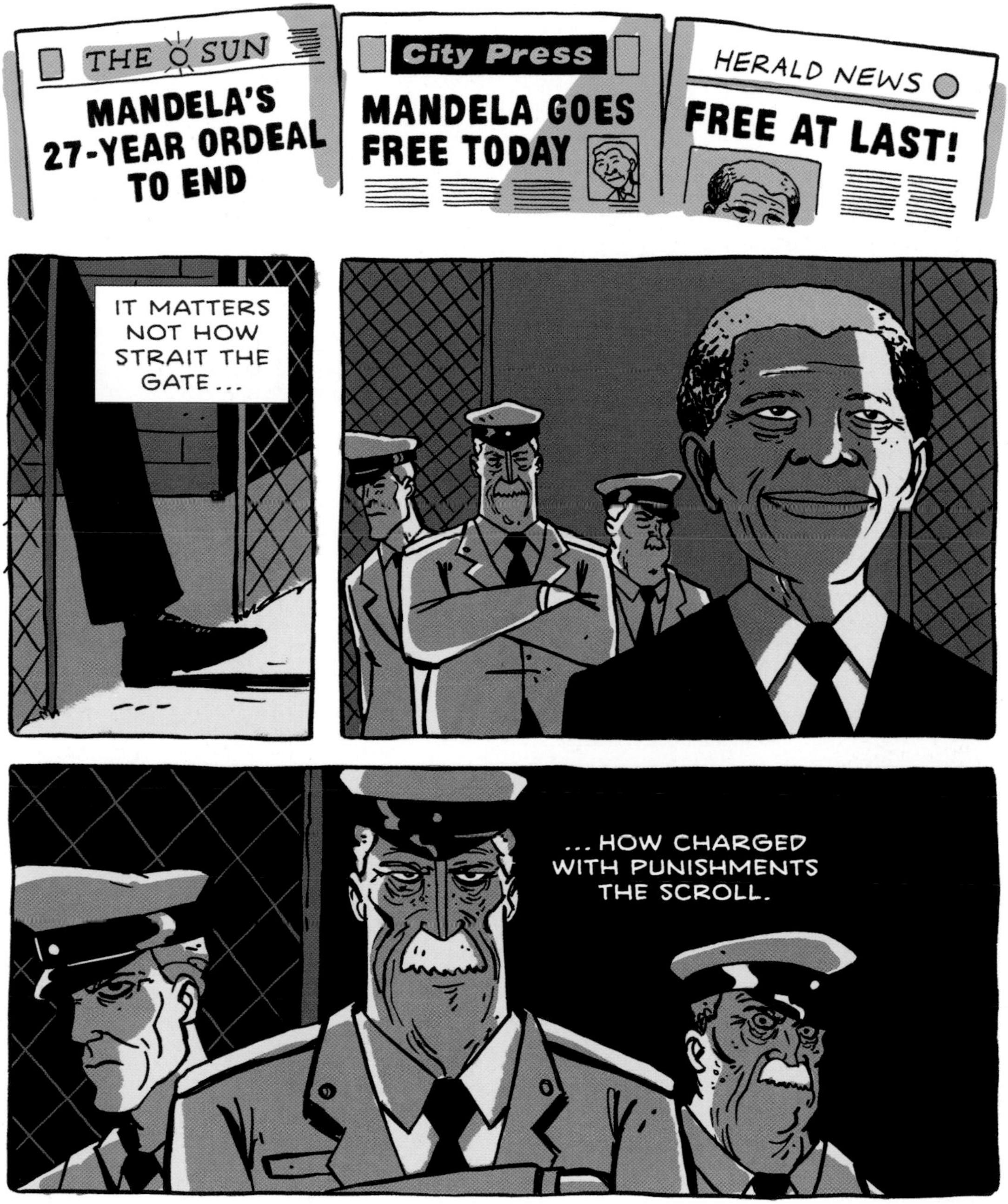
THE SUN
MANDELA'S 27-YEAR ORDEAL TO END
City Press
MANDELA GOES FREE TODAY
HERALD NEWS
FREE AT LAST!
IT MATTERS NOT HOW STRAIT THE GATE...
...HOW CHARGED WITH PUNISHMENTS THE SCROLL.

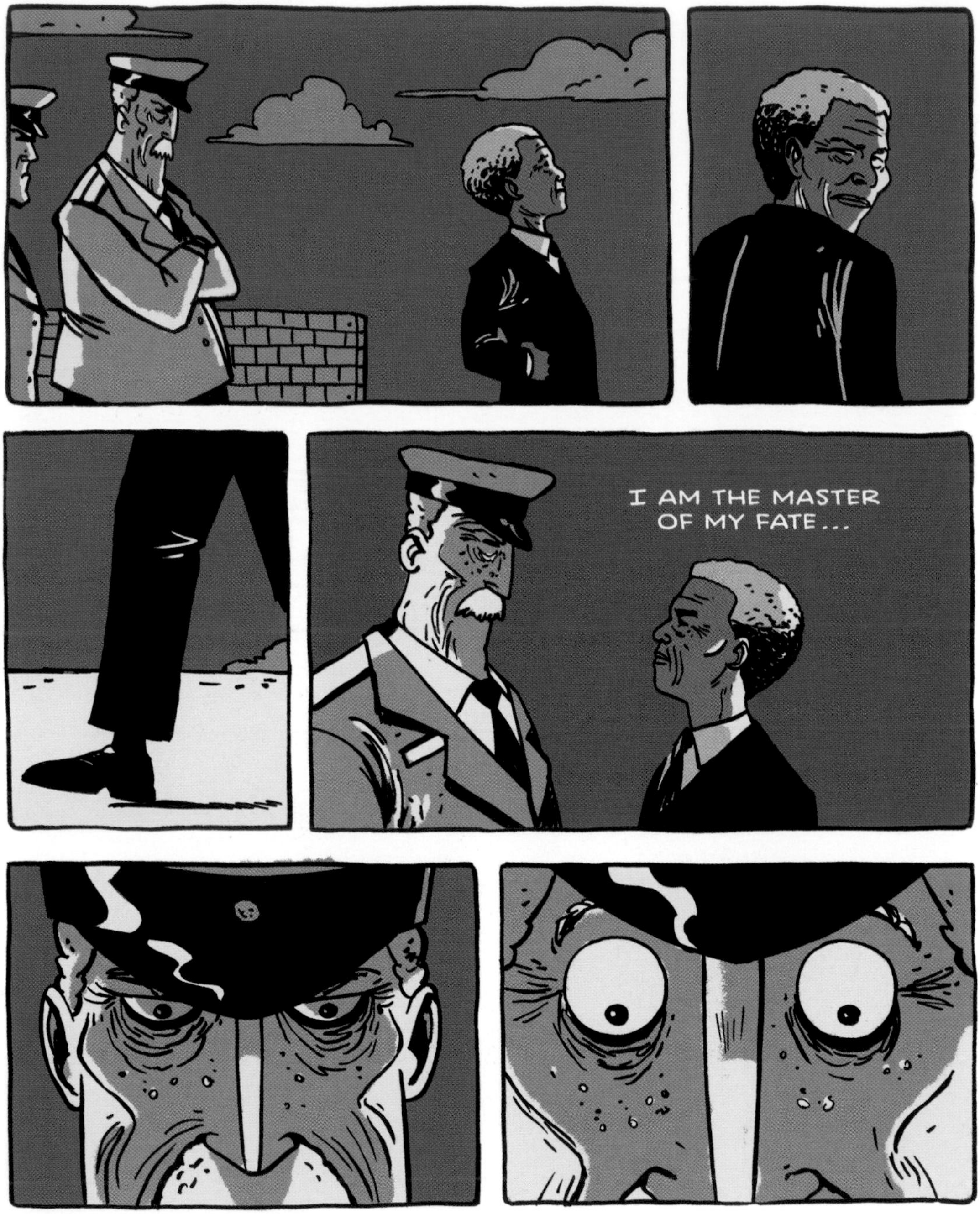
I AM THE MASTER
OF MY FATE...

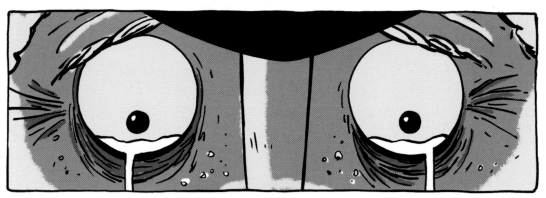

...I AM
THE CAPTAIN
OF MY SOUL.

NELSON MANDELA
1918-2013

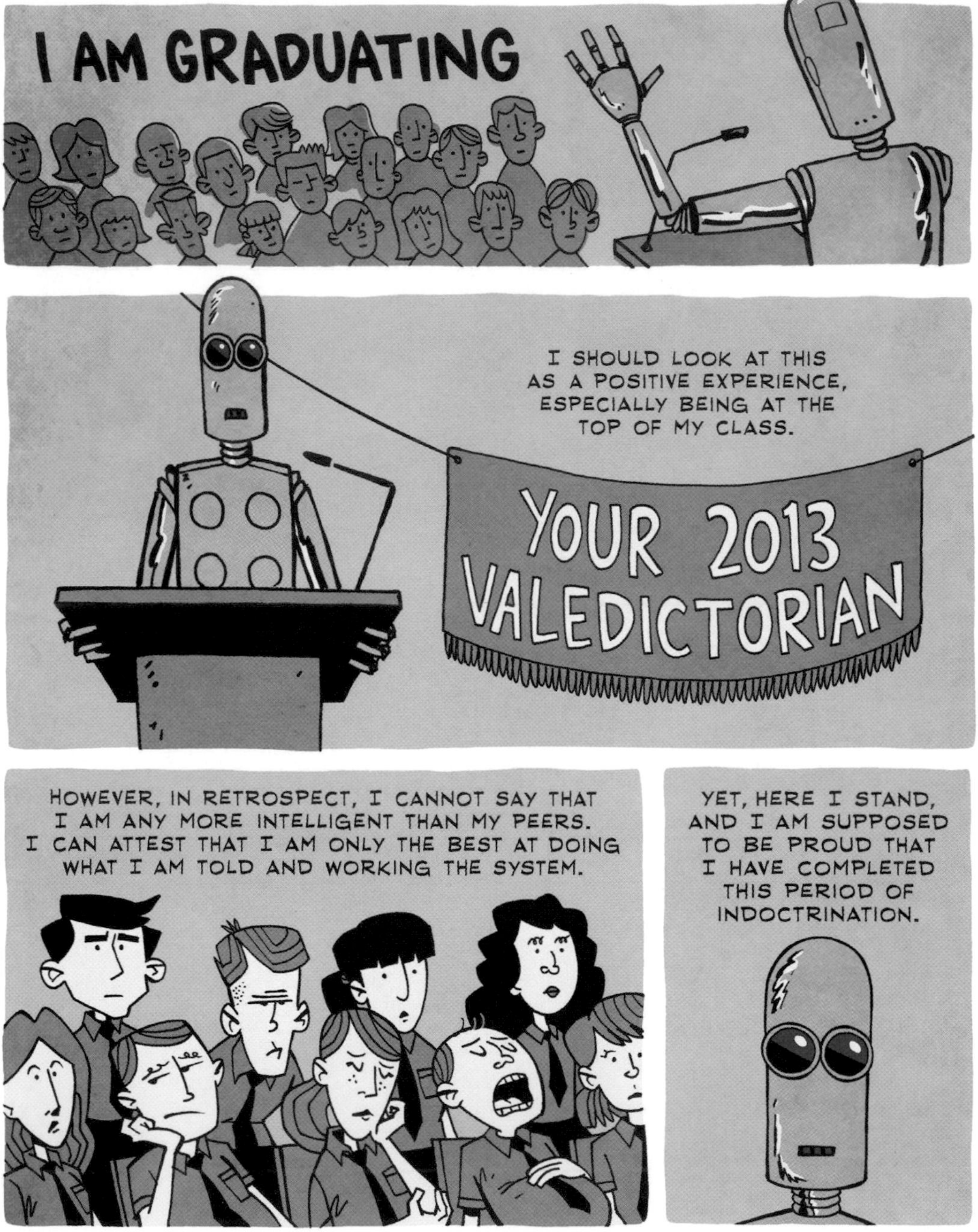
I AM GRADUATING
I SHOULD LOOK AT THIS AS A POSITIVE EXPERIENCE, ESPECIALLY BEING AT THE TOP OF MY CLASS.
YOUR 2013 VALEDICTORIAN
HOWEVER, IN RETROSPECT, I CANNOT SAY THAT I AM ANY MORE INTELLIGENT THAN MY PEERS. I CAN ATTEST THAT I AM ONLY THE BEST AT DOING WHAT I AM TOLD AND WORKING THE SYSTEM.
YET, HERE I STAND, AND I AM SUPPOSED TO BE PROUD THAT I HAVE COMPLETED THIS PERIOD OF INDOCTRINATION.

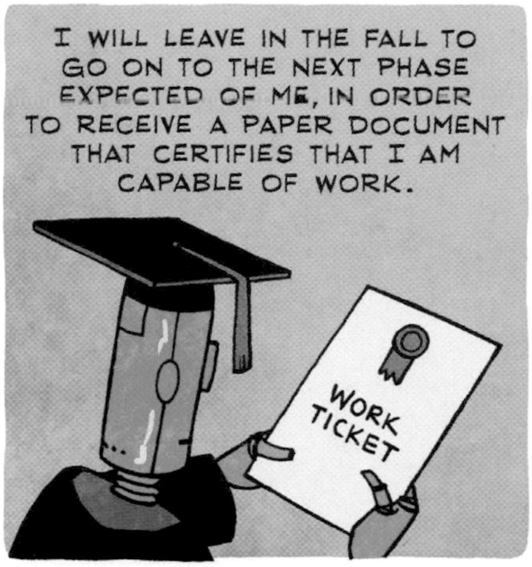
I WILL LEAVE IN THE FALL TO GO ON TO THE NEXT PHASE EXPECTED OF ME, IN ORDER TO RECEIVE A PAPER DOCUMENT THAT CERTIFIES THAT I AM CAPABLE OF WORK.
WORK TICKET
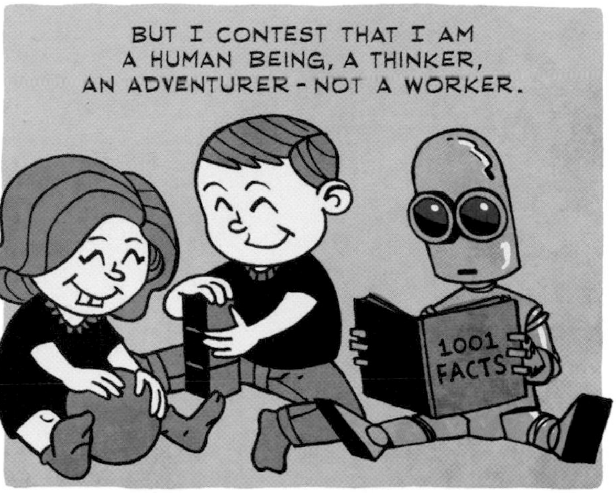
BUT I CONTEST THAT I AM A HUMAN BEING, A THINKER, AN ADVENTURER - NOT A WORKER.
1001 FACTS
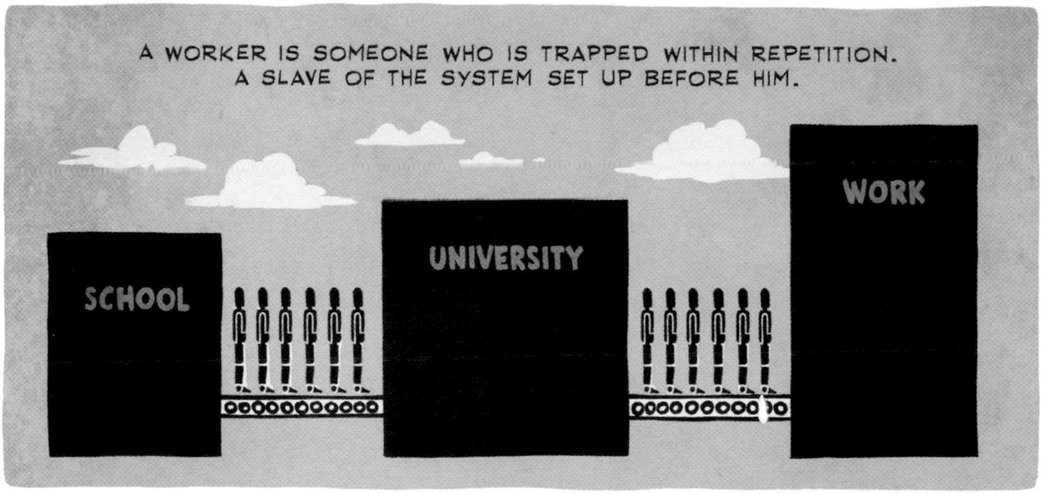
A WORKER IS SOMEONE WHO IS TRAPPED WITHIN REPETITION. A SLAVE OF THE SYSTEM SET UP BEFORE HIM.
SCHOOL
UNIVERSITY
WORK
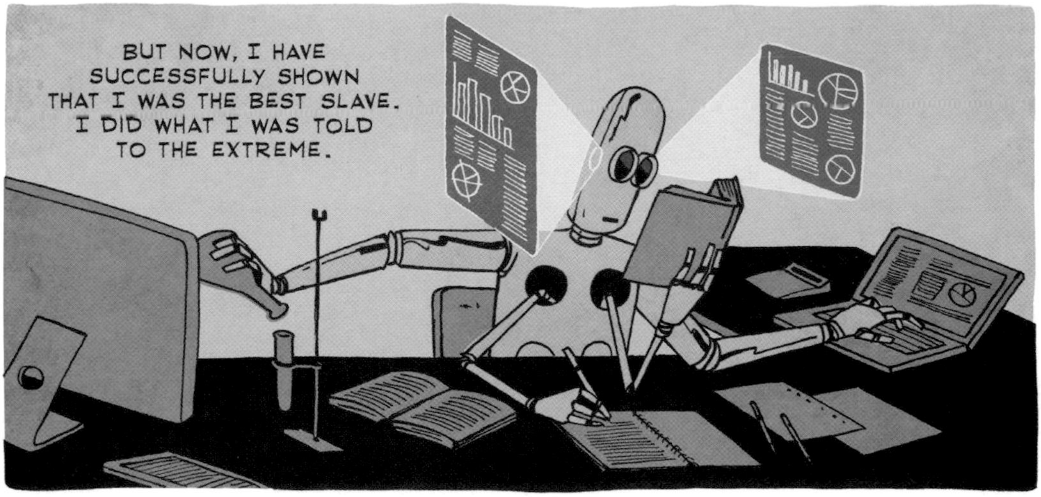
BUT NOW, I HAVE SUCCESSFULLY SHOWN THAT I WAS THE BEST SLAVE. I DID WHAT I WAS TOLD TO THE EXTREME.

WHILE OTHERS SAT IN CLASS AND DOODLED TO LATER BECOME GREAT ARTISTS, I SAT IN CLASS TO TAKE NOTES AND BECOME A GREAT TEST-TAKER.

WHILE OTHERS WOULD COME TO CLASS WITHOUT THEIR HOMEWORK DONE BECAUSE THEY WERE READING ABOUT AN INTEREST OF THEIRS, I NEVER MISSED AN ASSIGNMENT.

WHILE OTHERS WERE CREATING MUSIC AND WRITING LYRICS, I DECIDED TO DO EXTRA CREDIT, EVEN THOUGH I NEVER NEEDED IT.

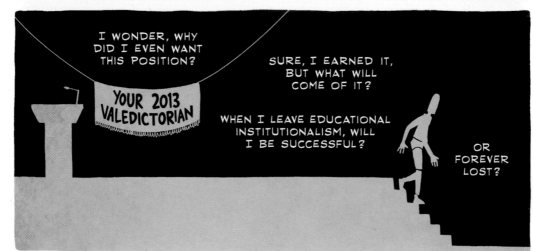

I WONDER, WHY DID I EVEN WANT THIS POSITION?

YOUR 2013 VALEDICTORIAN

SURE, I EARNED IT, BUT WHAT WILL COME OF IT?

WHEN I LEAVE EDUCATIONAL INSTITUTIONALISM, WILL I BE SUCCESSFUL?

OR FOREVER LOST?

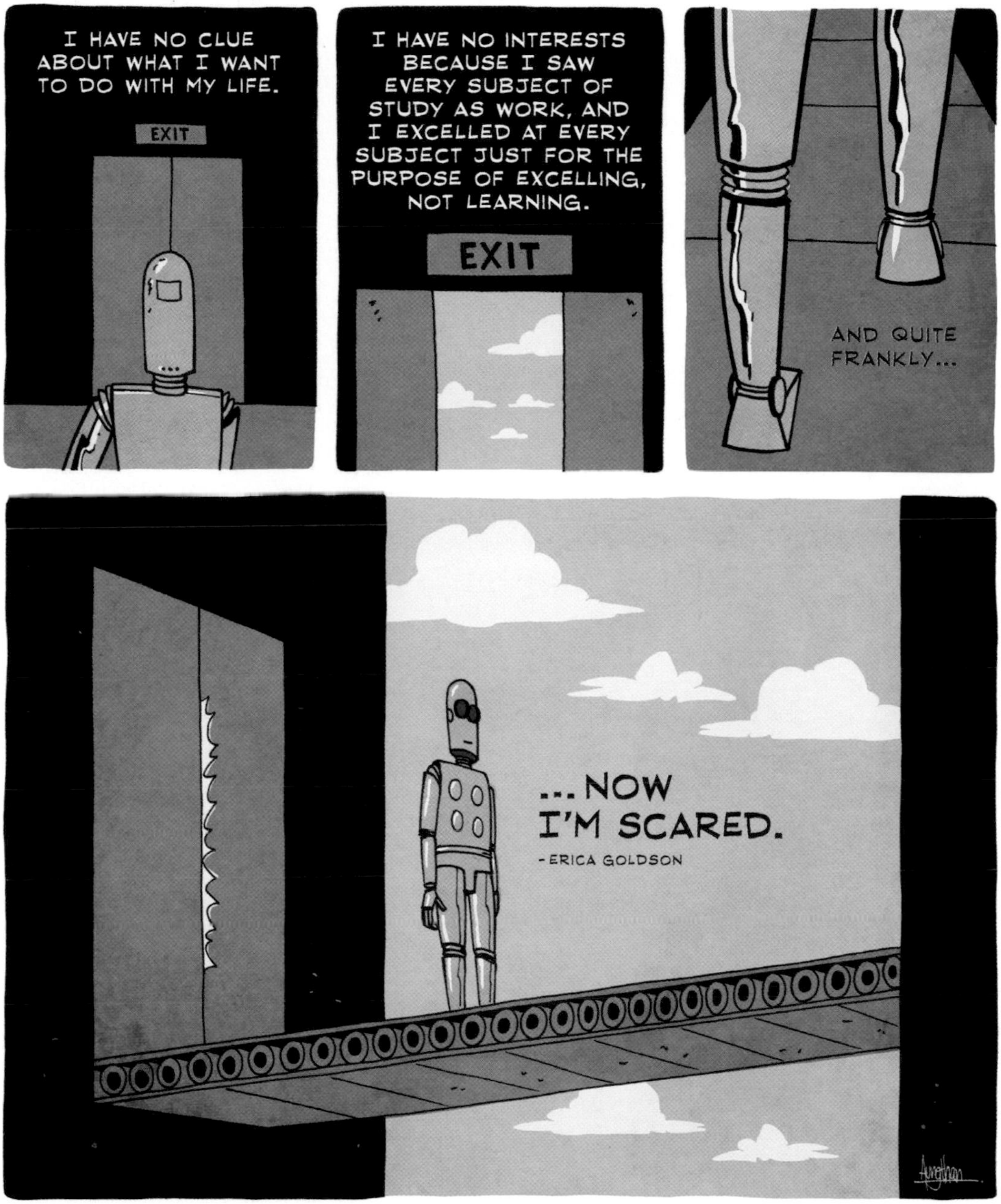
I HAVE NO CLUE ABOUT WHAT I WANT TO DO WITH MY LIFE.
EXIT
I HAVE NO INTERESTS BECAUSE I SAW EVERY SUBJECT OF STUDY AS WORK, AND I EXCELLED AT EVERY SUBJECT JUST FOR THE PURPOSE OF EXCELLING, NOT LEARNING.
EXIT
AND QUITE FRANKLY...
...NOW I'M SCARED.
- ERICA GOLDSON

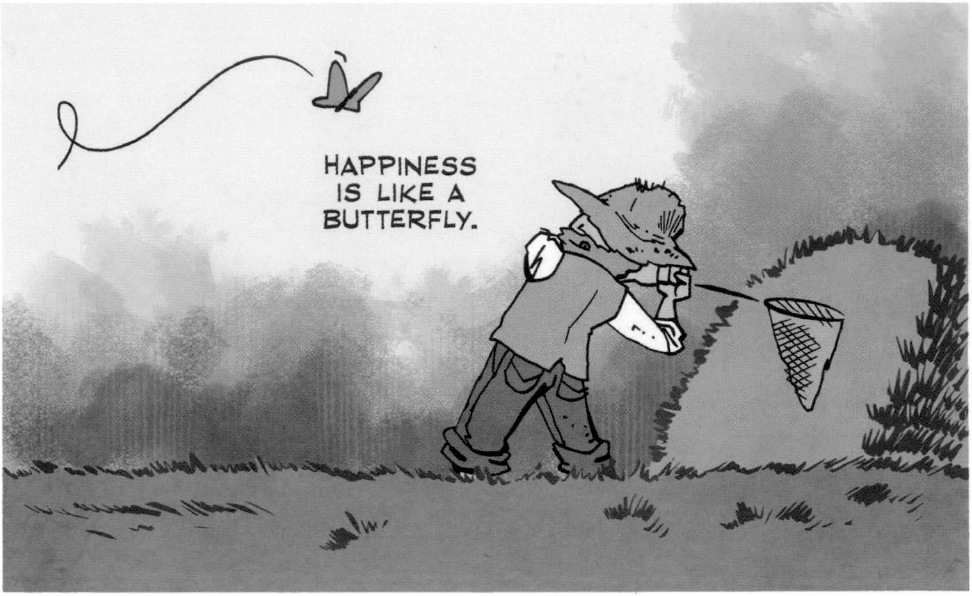
HAPPINESS
IS LIKE A
BUTTERFLY.

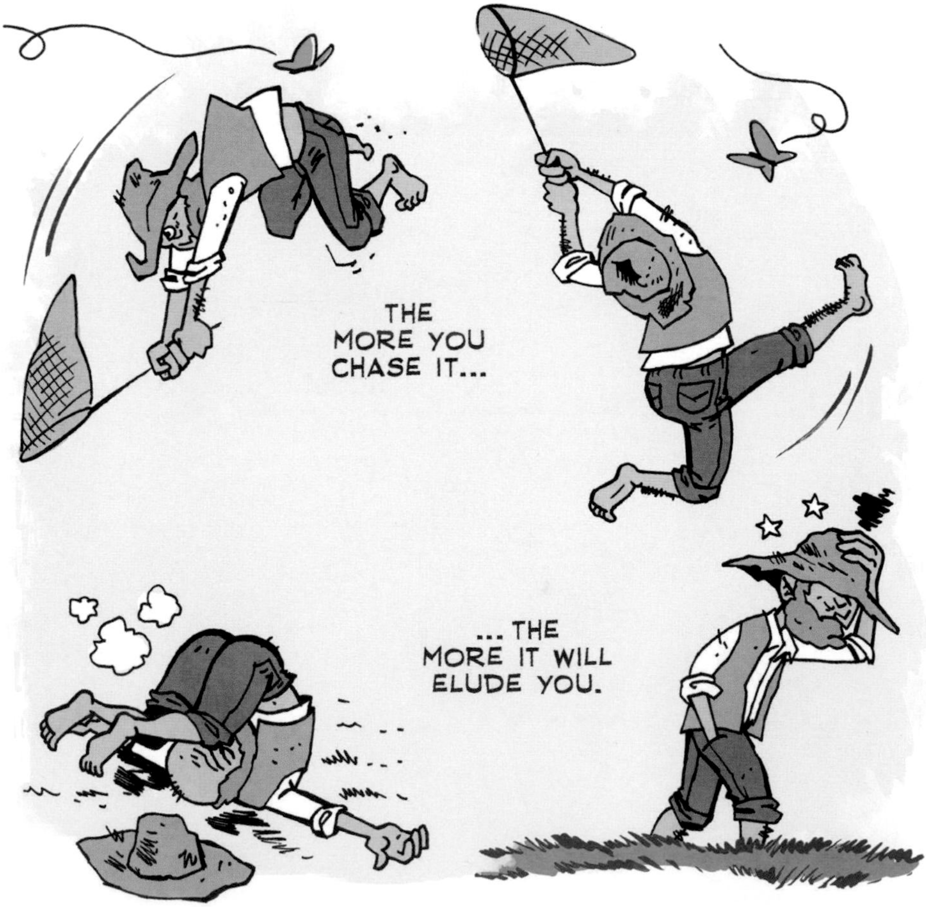
THE
MORE YOU
CHASE IT...
... THE
MORE IT WILL
ELUDE YOU.

BUT IF YOU TURN YOUR
ATTENTION TO OTHER THINGS...

... IT WILL COME
AND SIT SOFTLY ON
YOUR SHOULDER.
– HENRY DAVID THOREAU

Shaolin Monk: There is no definitive origin for the maxim "The more you sweat in training, the less you bleed in battle." It's been claimed as a Chinese proverb, a Roman saying, and a quote by American war hero George Patton. Today, it is a popular motto among the armed forces and martial artists.

Confucius (551 BC-479 BC) was a Chinese philosopher. His work has been formulated into Confucianism, a doctrine of philosophy which teaches that human beings are responsible for their self-fulfillment through moral actions towards others.

Theodore Roosevelt (1858-1919) was not a lazy man. Besides being the twenty-sixth president of the United States for two terms, he was also a naturalist, ornithologist, cowboy, conservationist, ranchman, war hero, writer, and big-game hunter. Roosevelt embraced what he called "the strenuous life" —a philosophy where physical activity, adventure, and action were the keys to a successful life.

H. Jackson Brown, Jr., is the best-selling author of *Life's Little Instruction Book*, which contains 511 reminders on how to live a happy and rewarding life. The quote is taken from Jackson's other bestseller, *P.S. I Love You*, and he actually credits the saying to his mother.

Vincent van Gogh (1853-1890) was a Dutch postimpressionist painter. Although his work was exhibited in his later years, he received no recognition for his work during his life, lived in constant poverty, and died having only sold one of his paintings. Today he is considered one of the most important artists in history.

A Question to the Buddhist: The quote is often attributed to **The Dalai Lama**, and I went ahead and drew him into the comic. After it was posted on my website, it came to my attention that the quote has never been verified as being said by him.

Bruce Lee was (1940-1973) a martial artist, actor, philosopher, and writer. Forty years after his death, he continues to inspire new generations through his writings, films, and cultural importance. The comic is based on an actual event in Lee's life, when he was challenged by an opponent to a duel. Lee was forced to question his martial-arts philosophy after his less-than-impressive victory. brucelee.com

Calvin Coolidge (1872-1933) was the thirtieth president of the United States. A serious and no-nonsense man, Coolidge was unassuming but had a quiet determination that saw him prosper in the White House.

Neil deGrasse Tyson is an astrophysicist and director of the Hayden Planetarium in New York City. He has written numerous popular science books including *Death by Black Hole* and *The Pluto Files*, and is host of the television series *Cosmos: A Space Time Odyssey*. haydenplanetarium.org/tyson

Neil Gaiman is a critically acclaimed and best-selling author. His novels include *American Gods*, *Anansi Boys*, *The Ocean at the End of the Lane*, and the landmark comic series *The Sandman*. The quote was taken from Gaiman's 2013 commencement speech at the University of the Arts in Philadelphia. neilgaiman.com

Phil Plait, better known as The Bad Astronomer, is an astronomer, noted skeptic, and science writer. He currently has a popular science blog on Slate.com called Bad Astronomy. slate.com/blogs/bad_astronomy.html

Henry Rollins is a comedian, entertainer, spoken-word artist, radio DJ, writer, actor, TV-presenter, activist, and former punk-rocker. henryrollins.com

Marianne Williamson is a spiritual activist and best-selling author who has helped millions of people though her books, lectures, workshops, and television appearances. The quote is from Williamson's book, *A Return to Love*. marianne.com

Roger Ebert (1942-2013) was the world's most respected and celebrated film critic. He was the first film critic to win a Pulitzer Prize and to receive a star on the Hollywood Walk of Fame. Much of his huge body of work can be found online at rogerebert.com.

John Green is a best-selling author of young adult novels including *Looking For Alaska, Paper Towns,* and *The Fault in Our Stars,* which was named *Time* magazine's best fiction book of 2012. He is also a hugely successful video-blogger, being one half of the Vlogbrothers and host of the Crash Course History educational series. johngreenbooks.com

Terence McKenna (1946-2000) was a writer, lecturer, and expert on ecology, botany, shamanism, and spiritual transformation. McKenna's books discuss the benefits and mind-altering effects of LSD, psilocybin, and other hallucinogens, and the role they've played in human history and culture.

Howard Thurman (1899-1981) was an author, educator, African-American leader, and was a prominent figure during the American Civil Rights movement. His books on philosophy and theology were a major influence on Martin Luther King, Jr.

Stephen Fry is a modern-day Renaissance man—a comedian, author, actor, playwright, director, documentary-maker, TV host, radio host, journalist, and all-around creative titan. Fry has documented his life in two best-selling memoirs, *Moab Is My Washpot* and *The Fry Chronicles.* stephenfry.com

Ira Glass is a radio broadcaster and host of the award-winning program and podcast *This American Life.* thisamericanlife.org

Chris Guillebeau is an entrepreneur and writer. His website, The Art of Non-Conformity, helps people follow their passion and find a meaningful way to use their talents. Chris is also a travel junkie and has completed a lifelong quest to visit every country in the world. chrisguillebeau.com

Charles Hanson Towne (1877-1949) was an American poet, writer, publisher, and editor.

The Two Wolves fable is often attributed as being an old Native American Cherokee legend (and I've obviously depicted it as such), but its origins are disputed. It most likely evolved from a passage in a book by Billy Graham, a popular American Christian evangelist.

Alan Watts (1915-1973) was an English philosopher and writer who played a large part in popularizing Zen Buddhism in the western world. He gained a wide following after moving to the United States where he published numerous books on Zen and Eastern philosophy.

Taylor Mali is an American slam poet who has been part of four winning teams at the National Poetry Slam competition. *What Teachers Make* is Mali's most well-known poem and was born out of an actual dinner conversation he had. The poem was also the title of a book Mali wrote: *What Teachers Make—In Praise of the Greatest Job in the World.* Mali worked as an English, history, and math teacher for nine years and continues to be an advocate for teachers all over the world. taylormali.com

Timothy Leary (1920-1996) was a psychologist, author, and pioneer of psychedelic drugs. While working as a professor at Harvard, he explored the potential benefits of psilocybin, the active ingredient in magic mushrooms. His later experiments with LSD made him a key figure and hero during the counter-culture movement of the 1960s.

C.S. Lewis (1898-1963) was an Irish author most famous for the *Chronicles of Narnia* series. He was also a noted poet, critic, and served as professor of English Literature at Oxford for twenty-nine years.

Chris Hadfield is a retired Canadian astronaut who became well-known for using social media to share what daily life was like aboard the International Space Station. The quote is taken from a Reddit "Ask Me Anything" session Hadfield took part in while aboard the ISS. Hadfield has written a best-selling memoir, *An Astronaut's Guide to Life on Earth*. colchrishadfield.tumblr.com

Marie Curie (1867-1934) was a Polish scientist (she later became a French citizen) who did pioneering research on radioactivity, discovered two elements (polonium and radium), won two Nobel prizes (the only woman to win in two separate fields—physics and chemistry), and is now an icon of the scientific world.

Sophie Scholl (1921-1943) was a German activist who is famous for speaking out against the Nazi regime. She was a member of The White Rose, a peaceful protest group consisting of students. In February 1943, after the release of the sixth White Rose leaflet, Scholl was arrested and later executed by guillotine. She was twenty-one years old.

Jiddu Krishnamurti (1895-1986) was a philosopher, writer, and lecturer. Krishnamurti was groomed by the Theosophical Society for twenty years to be the "World Teacher," but in a famous speech in 1929, Krishnamurti renounced his position, cut all allegiances with the Theosophical society, and spent the next fifty-plus years traveling the world, writing and lecturing.

Brené Brown is a professor at the University of Houston Graduate College of Social Work who has dedicated her life to social work and the study of vulnerability, courage, worthiness, and shame. Her lectures *The Power of Vulnerability* and *Listening to Shame* are among the most-viewed talks on the TED website. brenebrown.com

Jack London (1876-1916) was an American writer. The quote used was London's life 'credo' as retold by his literary executor in an introduction to one of London's book collections. There are disputes as to whether these are London's own words or embellishment by the executor.

Constantine P. Cavafy (1863-1933) was a Greek poet, although he was born and spent most of his life in Alexandria, Egypt. *Ithaka* is one of Cavafy's most famous poems and is a tribute to the original Greek poet, Homer, and his poem *The Odyssey*.

William Ernest Henley (1849-1903) was an English poet famous for his inspirational poem *Invictus*. The poem was said to be a favorite of former South African president Nelson Mandela (1918-2013), who would often recite it and use it as inspiration during his twenty-seven-year imprisonment.

Erica Goldson was the 2010 Valedictorian of Coxsackie-Athens (New York) High School. At her graduation ceremony, she gave a speech that went viral. Goldson spoke out against the school system that she had excelled in her whole life and urged for more individuality and creative thinking from students. The quote used in the comic is a small extract from the speech.

Henry David Thoreau (1817-1862) was a writer, poet, philosopher, and one of the leading figures of the transcendentalism movement. Besides writing *Civil Disobedience*, which inspired such revolutionaries as Gandhi and Martin Luther King, Jr., Thoreau is most well-known for his book *Walden*, in which he recounts the two years he lived in a small cabin in the woods near Walden Pond in Concord, Massachusetts.

Andrews McMeel Publishing
a division of Andrews McMeel Universal
1130 Walnut Street, Kansas City, Missouri 64106

www.andrewsmcmeel.com

16 17 18 19 20 TEN 10 9 8 7 6 5

ISBN: 978-1-4494-5795-2

Library of Congress Control Number: 2014931930

ATTENTION: SCHOOLS AND BUSINESSES
Andrews McMeel books are available at quantity discounts with bulk purchase for educational, business, or sales promotional use. For information, please e-mail the Andrews McMeel Publishing Special Sales Department: specialsales@amuniversal.com.